THE MUSLIM MATRIMONIAL COURT IN SINGAPORE

LONDON SCHOOL OF ECONOMICS MONOGRAPHS ON SOCIAL ANTHROPOLOGY

The Monographs on Social Anthropology were established in 1940 and aim to publish results of modern anthropological research of primary interest to specialists.

The continuation of the series was made possible by a grant in aid from the Wenner-Gren Foundation for Anthropological Research, and more recently by a further grant from the Governors of the London School of Economics and Political Science. Income from sales is returned to a revolving fund to assist further publications.

The Monographs are under the direction of an Editorial Board associated with the Department of Anthropology of the London School of Economics and Political Science.

THE MUSLIM MATRIMONIAL COURT IN SINGAPORE

JUDITH DJAMOUR

LONDON SCHOOL OF ECONOMICS MONOGRAPHS ON SOCIAL ANTHROPOLOGY

Volume 31

Routledge
Taylor & Francis Group
LONDON AND NEW YORK

First published 1966 by Athlone Press

Published 2004 by Berg Publishes Limited

Published 2021 by Routledge
2 Park Square, Milton Park, Abingdon, Oxon OX14 4RN
605 Third Avenue, New York, NY 10017

Routledge is an imprint of the Taylor & Francis Group, an informa business

ISBN 13: 978-1-85973-879-5 (hbk)

ACKNOWLEDGEMENTS

The fieldwork on which this book is based was financed by a grant from the London Committee of the London-Cornell Project for the Study of Chinese and South-East Asian Societies.

I am profoundly grateful to Inche Ahmad Ibrahim, State Advocate-General, Singapore, for permission to study the files and records of the Shariah Court and of the Registry of Muslim Marriages and Divorces. I had several discussions with him, during which he clarified many aspects of the legislation affecting Muslims. Tuan Haji Mohamed Sanusi, Registrar of Muslim Marriages and President of the Shariah Court, answered my numerous enquiries with unfailing courtesy and patience; he also kindly gave me desk space. Tuan Haji Mohamed Salleh, Acting Chief Kathi, Tuan Haji Ismail, Kathi at the Shariah Court, and all the other officials of the Court and of the Registry helped me in many ways. I also benefited from informal talks with Mrs M. Siraj, Muslim Social Case Worker.

I am grateful to Miss Jean Robertson and Mrs Ann Wee of the Social Studies Department, University of Singapore, to Miss M. Menon of the Women and Girls' Welfare Section of the Department of Social Welfare, to Mr Arul of the Sixth District Court, and to Mr E. H. D'Netto of the Legal Aid Bureau.

My old friends, Mr and Mrs Tan Yeok Seong and Mr and Mrs Teh Cheang Wan, gave me much practical help and offered me frequent hospitality.

Professor J. N. D. Anderson, Professor Raymond Firth, and Dr Paul Stirling read an early draft of this book; Dr Burton Benedict read the final draft. They made comments and suggestions from which I greatly benefited. My husband read the early and final drafts with care and patience and I am deeply indebted to him for his constructive criticisms and for his encouragement.

December 1964 J.D.

CONTENTS

Introduction

I spent two years in Singapore (1949 and 1950) engaged in field work on the structure of Malay kinship and marriage. My interest soon became focused on the instability of marriage: over several decades the Muslim divorce rate had been about fifty per cent. Singapore Muslims are not exclusively Malay; there are Indians and Pakistanis as well as Arabs, but my study was almost wholly concerned with Malays. (I use the term to cover Malays who had been settled in Singapore or the Malay Peninsula for several generations, and more recent immigrants from Indonesia.) Malays are by far the largest single Muslim group in Singapore.

In 1949 and 1950 several Muslim leaders were expressing concern at the high divorce rate, and at public meetings as well as in the English and Malay press several factors were said to be responsible for frequent divorce: forced marriages; the youth and inexperience of many Muslim brides; disparity in the ages of the spouses; ease of repudiation; and lack of an official conciliation machinery. On the other hand, no Muslim seriously advocated that Western practices of courtship be followed, that young girls should be allowed the freedom to go out with the men of their choice, or that they should select their own husbands; reformers only urged that parents exercise greater care in arranging the marriages of their children and that they consider seriously a prospective groom's or bride's objection to a marriage partner.

Several Muslim women's associations were formed with charitable and feminist aims, but most of them were short-lived. Their committee members generally lacked financial resources and administrative skills, and the initial enthusiasm of the majority of their ordinary members quickly waned. Some of these associations had hoped to provide practical help and advice to women abandoned by their husbands. When a Malay woman was divorced she usually retained the custody of the young children of the union and also became in practice responsible for their support. She could sue the father for their maintenance but rarely did so. Her close kin often helped her to care for the children, but if they could not or would not help and if she was unable to earn enough money herself, she might give the children away in adoption as a last resort. The Social Welfare Department of the Colony had provisions for public assistance, but in 1950 few Malays were aware that they could apply for such help.

In my *Malay Kinship and Marriage in Singapore*[1] I noted:

> Phrases such as 'the sanctity of the home', 'the sacred bond of marriage' or the moral and emotional content they carry, have no equivalent in Singapore Malay culture. No such expressions are used, and certainly the bond of marriage is not considered sacred. I saw no evidence of great moral pressure being exercised by *kathi* or by religious teachers to dissuade wives from claiming a divorce or husbands from pronouncing it. In the few cases where a woman had been living for many years with her first husband, her pride in the fact appeared to be due as much to the chastity and equanimity which were implicit in her not having sought other unions, as to the triumph of a woman who had achieved a feat rare in her community. This does not mean that the majority of Malays view the dissolution of marriage with total unconcern, only that they accept the situation with resignation.
>
> Singapore Malays above all value harmony in personal intimate relationships. When a marriage union fails to produce even a small measure of emotional contentment and causes strife and anxiety, they find divorce the most obvious solution to their problem. Material considerations, such as economic security, are usually of secondary importance.

However, it seemed that this attitude might be modified in the future, under pressure from Westernized Muslim leaders both in Singapore and in the Malay Peninsula; the divorce rate among Muslims in the Peninsula was also very high.[2]

In the summer of 1962 I had the opportunity to visit Singapore for a few weeks after an absence of nearly twelve years. I was aware that new legislation affecting Muslims had been enacted in 1957, and that a Court had been established at the end of 1958 for Muslim matrimonial disputes; this Court was known as the Shariah Court (Shariah is Arabic for Muslim law). I attended sittings of the Court and had interviews with several of its

[1] London School of Economics Monographs on Social Anthropology, No. 21, London, 1959, p. 140.

[2] See my *Malay Kinship*, pp. 136–7.

officials. I renewed my friendship with some of the Muslim leaders I had known in 1950, and made the acquaintance of several others.

The Annual Reports of the Registry of Muslim Marriages and Divorces for 1960 and 1961 showed a remarkably sharp decline in the divorce rate, which had been dramatically halved after the establishment of the Shariah Court.[1] I was naturally eager to make a study of the Court in action, and was very fortunate to obtain a grant from the 'London-Cornell Project for the Study of Chinese and South-East Asian Societies' which enabled me to carry out this work in 1963.

I was in Singapore for six months (February to July) and regularly attended hearings at the Shariah Court; I took full notes of the proceedings. When the Court was not sitting I often discussed current matrimonial disputes and hypothetical cases with Court officials, in an attempt to grasp both theoretical and practical applications of the new legislation. I studied files, registers, and documents; I had discussions with kathis, government officials, magistrates, and social workers, and with Muslim men and women of all social strata. The following is a list of the principal records I studied:

I. *Shariah Court and Registry of Muslim Marriages and Divorces*
   (1) Registers of marriages, divorces, and revocations.
   (2) Kathis' personal notebooks.
   (3) Conciliation files.
   (4) Files relating to divorce, recalcitrancy, and annulments.
   (5) Record-books kept by the President of the Court of the evidence heard by him, and of his rulings.
   (6) Maintenance files and record-books of maintenance hearings.

II. *High Court Records*
   (1) Custody of children files.
   (2) Appeals from Shariah Court decisions.

III. *Legal Aid Bureau*
   Files relating to applications by Muslims for legal aid.

IV. *Social Welfare Department*
   Files of Muslim women and girls resident in the Muslim Women's Welfare Home.

[1] See below, p. 143.

Most of the records of the Registry and of the Shariah Court are written in Malay in the Jawi (i.e. Arabic) script in longhand; I found some of them to have been written hurriedly by kathis and therefore extremely difficult to decipher; so did the clerks of the Registry when I sought their help. There were several files and documents which were not readily available, but which I eventually traced after lengthy searches. Some kathis had omitted to fill in entries in the registers of marriages, divorces, and revocations, while others had sometimes been obviously careless about dates; for instance, a comment in a divorce register about the duration of the marriage was contradicted on the same form by the entry referring to the date of the marriage. I was usually able to obtain the details of the missing entries from other sources (e.g. the kathis' notebooks) and to discover the exact dates, but this took a great deal of time. Fortunately, however, as I established by cross-checking, most of the entries in the registers had been carefully and accurately filled in; and after a few weeks I became familiar with the peculiar spelling and handwriting of some of the kathis.

Singapore Muslims are governed in the matter of marriage and divorce by the Muslims Ordinance, 1957, as amended by the 1960 Amendment. The Ordinance also contains sections governing testacy and intestacy (Sections 40–47) and married women's property (Sections 48–57). A Muslim married woman has full control over all the property acquired by her before marriage as well as over earnings 'acquired or gained by her during marriage in any employment, occupation, or trade carried on by her and not by her husband'; and she may dispose of the same without her husband's approval. She may sue in her own name for the recovery of her property and is liable on her own contracts.

According to Malay customary law, a woman is entitled upon divorce to a share of such property as was acquired by the couple during marriage; this property is known as *harta sharikat* or *harta sa-pencharian*. If it was acquired by their joint efforts she is usually entitled to a half-share; if it was acquired largely by her husband's efforts while she kept house for him and generally looked after him, she may be entitled to a third-share. This law is enforced in the Malay States.[1] In Singapore, however, this custom does not have the force of law among the Island's Malays. Nevertheless,

[1] See E. N. Taylor, 'Malay Family Law', *Journal of the Royal Asiatic Society, Malayan Branch*, Vol. xv, Part 1, 1937.

when a husband deserts his wife and subsequently a divorce is registered, he usually allows her to retain possession of the household effects even if they had been acquired solely by his own earnings.[1]

The sections of the 1957 Ordinance which deal with the powers of the Court to make orders in matrimonial disputes (Sections 20–36B) do not specify in any detail the circumstances in which such orders shall be made. (The whole Ordinance covers eighteen pages, which include sections dealing with procedure, appeals, and property.) The Ordinance states that the Court shall make such order or decree 'as is by the law of Islam lawful' (Section 32 (5); also Section 35). Consequently, although in the next chapter it will be necessary to state the broad essentials of the Muslim law of marriage and divorce, there will be no discussion of the conflicting opinions of leading Muslim jurists on specific points. My concern is with the law as it is interpreted in Singapore, and further, with the extent to which the provisions of the 1957 Ordinance are enforced. Therefore, cases illustrating various issues will be reported in some detail; and such comments as the President of the Court makes on points of interpretation are reproduced when they are available from the record-books, or when I heard them in Court. I also report the opinions of the President and of kathis when they explained to me the principles of Muslim law they follow. I had frequent informal discussions with them, and although during the first weeks Court kathis and Registry officials were somewhat guarded, eventually they felt able to speak more freely and critically. I made notes during our conversations and later as an additional check I returned regularly to the points already covered to ensure that I had not misunderstood their statements. I also put to them hypothetical cases and asked how they would be dealt with; and whenever there was a record of a similar case which appeared to have been settled in a different manner, I sought further enlightenment.

Eventually on the basis of these discussions; of the records of one hundred and fifty divorces registered by order of the Court in 1961 and 1962 and of several petitions rejected or postponed *sine die* in these two years; and of my own observation over a period of six months in 1963 of several hearings a week, I was able to arrive at a picture of the broad principles guiding the Court.

The Court is open to the public. As a rule there are no reporters

[1] See my *Malay Kinship*, pp. 124–5.

present unless the case concerns personalities well known in the political scene or in the entertainment world, or unless the case has already been publicised because one or both spouses have been prosecuted in the magistrates' courts for offences connected with the registration of their marriage. I myself saw reporters in Court during the hearings of only two petitions. Thus, apart from rare exceptions, there appeared to be no published or printed records of Shariah Court decided cases; this somewhat handicaps lawyers on the rare occasions on which they are employed by litigating spouses.

I said earlier that I was concerned with the extent to which the provisions of the Ordinance were enforced. I discovered, for instance, that although failure by a couple to register a divorce is an offence (punishable under Section 58 by a fine not exceeding fifty dollars), nevertheless such couples are not always prosecuted.[1] Further, although the Ordinance (as amended in 1960) provides under Section 36A that the Shariah Court shall have power to make orders regarding

(*c*) the custody, maintenance and education of the minor children of the parties; and

(*d*) the disposition or division of property on divorce

in effect the Court did not make such orders up to July 1963. The President of the Court recorded any agreement reached by the parties on these issues (sometimes with guidance from the Court), but if there was an unresolved dispute the spouses were referred to the High Court. Moreover, if a spouse returned to the Shariah Court to complain that the other had contravened the recorded agreement, he or she was similarly referred to the High Court.

I went to Singapore in 1963 with the intention of making a study of divorce among Malays; but since the Shariah Court was concerned with all Muslims, I decided to include non-Malay cases. I had hoped, after my research in the Court, to turn to some fairly intensive field studies to bring up to date the sociological account of Malay marriage and divorce contained in my earlier book. However, in the event a detailed study of the working of the Shariah Court required a much longer period than I had expected. The scope of the present book is therefore limited, and further work needs to be done to link the effect of the new legislation and of the Shariah Court with the institutions of marriage and divorce among Muslims in present-day Singapore.

[1] See below, pp. 130 ff., 163 f.

I

General Background

POPULATION

Singapore was acquired in 1819 by Sir Stamford Raffles on behalf of the East India Company. It is generally believed that the island had then fewer than 200 inhabitants. At the first Census in January 1824, 4,580 Malays and 3,317 Chinese were returned.[1]

In 1826 the British territories of Malacca, Penang and Province Wellesley, and Singapore were united under the title of the 'Straits Settlements', and in 1832 Singapore became their capital. They were governed from India until 1867 when they were placed under the direct control of the colonial office in London, and became a Crown Colony.

In 1946 Singapore became a separate entity, but remained a British Colony until 1957 when it acquired the status of an internally self-governing State within the British Commonwealth. Malaysia had not come into being when I left Singapore, and the Federation of Malaya consisted then of the nine Malay States of Johore, Pahang, Negri Sembilan, Selangor, Perak, Perlis, Kedah, Trengganu, and Kelantan, and the two former Straits Settlements of Penang (and Province Wellesley) and Malacca. There was free movement between the Federation and the State of Singapore.

The last Census of the population of Singapore was taken in 1957, when a total of 1,476,694 persons were returned. If non-locally domiciled Service personnel and their families are excluded, as well as transients by sea, who together numbered 30,765, the resident population totalled 1,445,929. The three main groups are Chinese; Malaysians (i.e. local Malays and immigrant Indonesians); and Indians and Pakistanis; while the residual category of 'Others' includes Eurasians (11,382), Europeans (10,826), Ceylonese (5,426), and Arabs (3,471).

Neither in the 1947 nor in the 1957 Census was there a question about religious affiliation. However, it can be generally assumed

[1] See my *Malay Kinship*, pp. 3–4.

	1957 Census	*End-1962 Estimate*[1]	*End-1963 Estimate*[1]
Chinese	1,090,596	1,319,700	1,351,900
Malaysians	197,059	246,000	253,600
Indians and Pakistanis	124,084	144,900	148,200
Others	34,190	44,500	45,700
	1,445,929	1,755,100	1,799,400

that all Malays[2] and Arabs are Muslims; while one can only hazard a guess at the proportion of Muslims in the total number of Indians and Pakistanis. In 1931, the last Census to give details of religious groups, about a quarter of the total Indian population was Muslim; 13,330 out of 51,019. If we assume the proportion of Muslims to have remained constant, the figure for 1957 would be a quarter of 124,084, or about 31,000. Thus in 1957 there were just over 200,000 Malaysians and Arabs, and perhaps about 31,000 Muslim Indians and Pakistanis. The *Colony of Singapore Annual Report 1956* states:[3]

> A precise enumeration of religions has not been made and, indeed, is scarcely possible. The Malaysians are almost without exception Muslim. . . . Of the Indian community about 70 per cent are Hindu, 20 per cent Muslim, 5 per cent Christian and 2 per cent Sikh.

This comment was also made in the Annual Reports for 1954 (p. 9, Singapore 1955); and for 1955 (p. 21, Singapore 1956). The Annual Reports for the years 1957 to 1962 do not attempt to give an estimate of the religious affiliations of the various sections of the Indian community.

Apart from Malaysians, Arabs, Indians, and Pakistanis, there are some Chinese, Europeans, Eurasians, and others, who became converts to Islam – usually in order to marry Muslims. The Chinese (mainly girls) adopted in infancy by Malaysians are brought up as Malaysians and were returned in the Census as Malaysians. Mr S. C. Chua, Chief Statistician and Superintendent of Census, Singapore, states in his *Report on the Census of Population*

[1] The estimates for 1962 and 1963 are given in the *Monthly Digest of Statistics* (Vol. III, No. 2, February 1964, p. 11) prepared by the Chief Statistician, Singapore.

[2] Malays were peacefully converted to Islam in the fourteenth and fifteenth centuries by missionaries and traders from Sumatra and India.

[3] *Colony of Singapore Annual Report 1956*, Singapore 1958, p. 27.

1957, in his section on 'Notes on the Concepts and Definitions used in the Tables':[1] 'The race of an adopted child is taken as that of his or her foster father even if the natural parents are of a different race.'

In the census category of 'Malaysians' are the descendants of the original Malay inhabitants of Singapore, and of immigrant Malays from the Malay Peninsula and Indonesia. Whereas Singapore Malays do not usually differentiate between the descendants of long-established Singapore residents and Malays from the Peninsula – referring to both groups as *orang Melayu* (Malay persons) – immigrants from the Indonesian Islands and their children (and sometimes also, their grandchildren) are often specifically labelled *orang Jawa*, *orang Sumatra*, *orang Bugis*, or *orang Bawean*. It is also common for the Indonesian immigrants themselves to state, e.g., that they are *orang Melayu Bawean*, or simply *orang Bawean* ('Malay persons from Bawean', or 'persons from Bawean').

Malays from the Indonesian Islands and 'local Malays', however, form one broad unit when differentiating themselves from Indians.[2] Among the Indians are persons of one or more generation's settlement in Singapore or in the Malay Peninsula, recent immigrants from India, Pakistan, and other parts of South-East Asia, and children of such immigrants. They can usually be differentiated on account of their physical characteristics, their form of dress, and their names.

The Arabs are the descendants mainly of nineteenth-century settlers from the Hadramaut, but there have also been some immigrants from various other parts of Arabia in the last few decades. Many of Singapore's Arabs are descended from unions between Arab men and Malay or Indian women.[3]

As far as the present study is concerned, however, perhaps the most important difference between Indians, on the one hand, and Malays and Arabs on the other, is that generally the Indians are followers of the Hanafi School of Islam while Malays and Arabs

[1] Paragraph 13. The Report on the Census had not been published when I left Singapore in July 1963. I am greatly indebted to Dr Goh Keng Swee, Finance Minister for Singapore, for allowing me to see a draft of the Report. This draft is not paginated.

[2] Unless I specify otherwise, I shall use the term 'Indian' henceforth to cover both Indians and Pakistanis. This accords with general Malay usage in Singapore.

[3] See my *Malay Kinship*, p. 13.

generally follow the Shafi'i School. Both Shafi'i and Hanafi Muslims belong to the orthodox, or Sunni, sect of Islam.[1] The bulk of Singapore Muslims are not familiar with the terms 'Shafi'i' and 'Hanafi'. It is generally assumed, however, that all Malays and Arabs are Shafi'i unless they make a deliberate affirmation to the contrary; as for the Indians, the parallel assumption is that they are Hanafi unless they assert that they are not.[2] Some of the children of Indian fathers and Malay (or Arab) mothers consider themselves to be Shafi'i, because there is a tendency for such children to mix socially with Malays (or Arabs), to become assimilated to their mother's ethnic group, and to pray in mosques or gatherings of Shafi'is. They may not always be aware that their mosque is a Shafi'i mosque, but they will say, 'I pray in a Malay mosque', or 'I pray in a mosque where the *imam*[3] is a Malay'; or again, 'I go to the mosque where my mother's brothers and her kinsmen go'.[4]

Some Indians of long settlement in Singapore or Malaya, even when they have not intermarried with Malays, dress like Malays, speak Malay, and declare themselves to be Malays when asked to state their *bangsa* ('race'). They tend, however, to retain specifically Indian names.

In none of the petitions I heard in Court,[5] and in none of the records I studied of the proceedings of the one hundred and fifty divorces registered in 1961 and 1962 by order of the Shariah Court, did the President allude to the School of Law followed by the petitioners. A Muslim kathi or judge may apply the law of his own personal school, even if the petitioners before him belong to

[1] The other two schools of the Sunnis are the Hanbali and the Maliki. There are also unorthodox schools of Islam such as the various Shiah Schools. A few Singapore Muslims, mainly immigrants of Indian and Persian descent, are Shiah.

[2] Ahmad Ibrahim states that many South Indians are Shafi'i. See Ahmad Ibrahim, 'Muslim Marriage and Divorce in Singapore', *Malayan Law Journal*, vol. XXVIII, February 1962.

[3] The religious official in charge of a mosque; some Malays also refer to a kathi (in Singapore, the official empowered to register marriages, divorces, and revocations of divorce) as an *imam*. Some kathis, in fact, are also mosque *imam*, whence the confusion perhaps.

[4] An Indian witness, the President of a Welfare Organization, stated at a meeting of the Select Committee on the Muslims (Amendment) Bill, in the course of his evidence: 'I am a Hanafi. . . . My wife is a *Shafei*. My children are *Shafei*.' State of Singapore, *Report of the Select Committee on the Muslims* (*Amendment*) *Bill*, L.A. 14 of 1960, Singapore 1960, paragraphs 244–6.

[5] With one exception cited below, p. 175.

another school. (Vesey-Fitzgerald in his *Muhammadan Law*[1] states: 'The Qadi will ordinarily administer the school of law to which he personally belongs.') However, in Singapore there appears to be no deliberate attempt to ignore the personal allegiance of the individual. Indeed, the opposite is true: special provision is made in the 1957 Ordinance to allow adult Hanafi girls to dispense with the consent of a *wali* or guardian for marriage. Section 7 of the Ordinance contains five subsections, the first three of which deal with the rights of the *wali*; subsection (5) reads:

(5) The provisions of this section shall not apply where the woman to be wedded belongs to a school of law under which she can be married without the consent of her guardian.

Moreover, as long ago as 1878 in Singapore in the case of *Salmah* v. *Soolong* (Kyshe, Civil 1. 421) it was held that a Shafi'i adult girl may lawfully change her School of Law and become a Hanafi to enable her to give herself in marriage. This judgment followed Indian cases. Ameer Ali in *The Personal Law of the Mahommedans* (*According to All the Schools*) cites[2] the case of *Muhammad Ibrahim* v. *Gulam Ahmed* (B.H.C. 236) which was heard by the Bombay High Court; the Court held that a Muslim female who belonged to any of the four Sunni (i.e. Orthodox) schools 'can, after attaining puberty, elect to belong to whichever of the other three sects she pleases. . . '. Ameer Ali praises the judges of this case for their 'exhaustive and well-considered judgment', and he cites a comment they made in the course of their judgment:

There is not any ceremonial required to indicate the change of sect; the only outward difference between a follower of Shâfeī and a follower of Abû Hanîfa consists in the former at the conclusion of prayer in a mosque saying *Ámîn* in a loud tone, whilst the latter pronounces it softly, and also that in praying, a Shâfeī extends his arms, whilst a Hanafî keeps them down.

Vesey-Fitzgerald[3] states:

Change of doctrine may be partial, to escape an inconvenient rule of law of one's own school. Thus Shafii women who desire to defeat the

[1] S. Vesey-Fitzgerald, *Muhammadan Law, An Abridgement According to its Various Schools*, London, 1931.

[2] London, 1880, pp. 186–7.

[3] *Op. cit.*, p. 18.

rights of their marriage guardians do so by professing their conviction of the correctness of Hanafi doctrine in this respect – a practice which has been recognized as valid in the Dutch East Indies, in the Straits Settlements, in Bombay, and in Southern Arabia. . . . But a *Qadi* acting judicially must always follow the same school; and a private litigant cannot mix the law of two schools in a single transaction.

Earlier, Vesey-Fitzgerald had said[1] that with one exception, 'Shafii doctrines are definitely less favourable to women than either the Hanafi or the Maliki.' The exception is that only in Shafi'i law is inability to maintain a wife a ground for the judicial decree of divorce known as *fasah*. N. B. E. Baillie, in *A Digest of Moohammadan Law*, the first volume of which deals with 'The Doctrines of the Hanifeea Code of Jurisprudence' states:[2]

A man is not to be separated from his wife for inability to maintain her. But the judge may direct her to raise her maintenance by borrowing on his credit. And if a judge should decree a separation, the decree would not be valid; nor even though allowed by another judge would it become operative, because it is not within the power of a judge to pass such a decree, for the reason already given, that inability to maintain a wife is not a sufficient reason for separating the parties.

Baillie uses the word separation in this context to mean divorce; for in his Introduction he said (p. xxviii): 'With regard to the dissolution of marriage during the lives of the parties, this is termed *firkut*, or separation . . .'

The President of the Shariah Court in Singapore has ordered the registration of a decree of *fasah* on the ground of a husband's failure to maintain his wife in cases where the couple appeared to be Hanafis. There was no explicit mention of their allegiance during the hearing of their petition or in the papers they filed, but I noted that a Hanafi kathi had officiated at their marriage.

In the one case before the Shariah Court where the School of Law of the parties was mentioned, it was the lawyers acting for the petitioner and the respondent (both of whom were Hanafis) who appear to have introduced the matter. The President, when he delivered his judgment, applied Hanafi law.[3]

Singapore has no *mufti*, but Section 38 of the 1957 Ordinance provides for the appointment of a *mufti*:

[1] *Op. cit.*, p. 16.
[2] Vol. 1, second edition, London 1875, p. 447.
[3] See below, p. 175.

38. The Governor may appoint a *Kathi* or some other male Muslim to be a *Mufti* and to assist the Registrar, the Court and the Appeal Board with advice in all matters connected with the law of Islam.

A *mufti* in Muslim countries is usually an eminent theologian and jurist, and those countries which boast several such learned men appoint one of them to be Chief *Mufti* to give authoritative rulings or *fatwa* in specific cases.[1] Malay States do have *mufti*, and on occasion the Chief Kathi of Singapore has sought the guidance of the *Mufti* of the near-by State of Johore.

Singapore Muslims are subject to some of the broad principles of Muslim law only in the fields of marriage, divorce, and inheritance. The law of contract and tort and criminal law closely follow English law and apply to all residents of the State, whatever their religion.

Brief mention has been made of Chinese children adopted in infancy,[2] and of adult Chinese converts. There are also in Singapore a handful of Chinese Muslim immigrants from China, i.e. Chinese who have been Muslims in China for many generations. Indeed, when representatives of the Young Women Muslim Association gave evidence before the Select Committee on the Muslims (Amendment) Bill, on 31 March 1960, one of the three lady representatives was a Chinese Muslim from China, resident in Singapore. The adopted Chinese children follow the school of law of their adoptive parents, as a general rule; and the converts that of the spouse they intend to marry. Since 1961 it has been compulsory for a groom and the prospective bride's *wali* (guardian for marriage) to fill in an official stamped application form, which includes a statement regarding the bride's 'race' and the 'School of Muslim Law' which she follows. I have seen an application form by a Chinese female convert (whose conversion was stated to be only of a few weeks' standing) who wished to marry an Indian, in which she declared that she was a follower of the Ḥanafi school.[3]

Occasionally a Chinese girl adopted in infancy attracts a non-Muslim Chinese man, who becomes a Muslim in order to marry her. There was at least one such marriage in 1961.

[1] See below, pp. 78, 179.
[2] See also my *Malay Kinship*, pp. 98–100.
[3] A Hanafi woman need not have a *wali*, and may sign the form herself. See below, p. 16.

MARRIAGE

According to Muslim law a Muslim man may marry, apart from a Muslim woman, a Jewess or a Christian; he may not marry an idolatress. He may be married simultaneously to no more than four women. On the other hand, a Muslim woman may marry only a Muslim and may have only one husband at a time.

A man may not marry his mother, grandmother, daughter, granddaughter, sister, parent's or grandparent's sister, sibling's daughter or granddaughter. He may not marry the former wife of his father, grandfather, son, or grandson. Also prohibited are the mother, grandmother, daughter, granddaughter, sister, and sibling's daughter of his wife;[1] he may, however, marry the sister or the sibling's daughter of his divorced or deceased wife. He may also marry the widow or divorced wife of his brother. A woman related to him through fosterage ('milk kinship') in any of the degrees cited above is also prohibited; or, as Ahmad Ibrahim states:[2]

> A man is prohibited from marrying any woman connected with him through some act of suckling as, if it had been instead an act of procreation, would have brought her within the prohibited degrees of consanguinity or affinity.

A polygynous Muslim is required to treat his wives with equal consideration, and to show no discrimination in respect of material welfare or conjugal affection.

The Koran, in the opening sentences of the Chapter on Women, states:[3]

> . . . take in marriage of such other women as please you, two or three, or four, and not more. But if ye fear ye shall not act with equity towards so many, marry only one . . .

One of the most important differences between Hanafis and Shafi'is in the realm of marriage concerns legal guardianship of a woman. A Hanafi woman who has reached puberty may give herself in marriage. A Shafi'i woman may not; she must have a guardian, or *wali*, to give her away, whatever her age, and whether or not she has been married before. Section 2 of the 1957 Ordinance states: '"Wali" means the lawful guardian according to the

[1] 'Wife' includes any woman with whom he has had sexual intercourse.
[2] In his 'Muslim Marriage . . .', op. cit.
[3] G. Sale, trans., *The Koran, translated from the Original Arabic*, London, n.d.

law of Islam for purposes of marriage of a woman to be wedded.' A Shafi'i girl who has not attained puberty may be given away in marriage only by her father or (in his absence) by her paternal grandfather. They alone also have the right to give her away in marriage, against her declared wishes, after she has reached puberty and provided she is a virgin. It is not unknown for this right of compulsion (*jabr* in Arabic) to be exercised in present-day Singapore.[1] A Shafi'i woman who has been previously married or who, though a spinster, is not a virgin, cannot be given away in marriage without her consent.

When, as in the majority of Singapore Muslim marriages, there is no compulsion in this legal sense, a Shafi'i woman who has reached puberty may be given away, in the absence of her father or of her father's father, by another male agnate.[2] Certainly, her father's brother or her own full brother or half brother on the father's side may act as her *wali*. Winstedt errs when he says that a Malay bride's *wali* 'must be an ascending agnate, father or grandfather, never an uncle or brother'.[3] This is true only of brides who have not reached puberty, as Wilkinson correctly noted in his pioneer study.[4] I have witnessed several marriage contracts of Malay brides where the *wali* has been a collateral agnate, and there are records of many such contracts in the registers.

Among Hanafis a father or father's father also has the right of compulsion, but this right can be exercised only if the bride has not attained puberty.[5] Moreover, a bride who has been thus married off against her wishes may (whether she is a Shafi'i or a Hanafi) repudiate the marriage before consummation by pleading that her father acted from motives of hostility, or that her bridegroom is inferior to her in status. As we know, a Hanafi woman who has reached puberty may give herself in marriage. However, if she contracts herself to a man whom her *wali* considers unequal

[1] See below, pp. 153 ff.

[2] See Nawawi, *Minhaj et Talibin*, translated by E. C. Howard from the French edition of L. W. C. Van den Bergh, London, 1914, p. 285. Nawawi's manual is considered one of the most authoritative texts of Shafi'i law; it was written in the thirteenth century.

[3] Richard Winstedt, *The Malays, A Cultural History*, revised edition, London, 1950, p. 47.

[4] See R. J. Wilkinson, *Law, Part I, An Introductory Sketch*, in *Papers on Malay Subjects*, Kuala Lumpur, 1908, p. 52. Also, Ahmad Ibrahim, 'Muslim Marriage and Divorce in Singapore'.

[5] See Vesey-Fitzgerald, op. cit., pp. 56–9.

to her in social status, the *wali* has a right to apply for the marriage to be rescinded. One such application was allowed in Singapore by the Shariah Court in July 1963.[1] Moreover, the *wali* of a Shafi'i or of a Hanafi woman cannot, without her consent, give her away in marriage to a man who is her social inferior.

If a Shafi'i woman has no *wali* living, or if her *wali* lives a considerable distance away, or if he withholds his consent on grounds which the Muslim authorities (in Singapore, the Chief Kathi) consider unreasonable, the civil authority (in Singapore, the Chief Kathi) becomes such a woman's *wali* in order to give her away in marriage, and is then known as her *wali hakim* or *wali tahkim*. Some Singapore Muslims colloquially refer to the *wali hakim* as *wali king*, 'king' being the English word. The Pahang *Administration of the Law of the Religion of Islam Enactment, 1956* uses (Section 120) the term *wali raja*. (Pahang is one of the Malay States.)

The fact that a Hanafi woman who has attained the age of puberty may give herself away in marriage does not mean that such a woman has no *wali*, but only that she may (if she chooses) dispense with his presence or consent if the marriage into which she enters is unobjectionable in Islam. The registers of marriages show that, in fact, the overwhelming majority of Hanafi women are given away by their *wali*, or when no *wali* is present, by the kathi solemnizing the union acting as *wali hakim*.[2]

A Muslim marriage is essentially a contract. A valid marriage requires an offer and an acceptance in the presence of two male Muslim witnesses.[3] It is also usual for the amount or nature of the marriage payment (*mahr*) which a Muslim groom must pay to his bride to be specified at the time of the contract. This payment is known among Malays as the *mas kahwin* (or *emas kahwin*), the 'marriage gold'. It has remained fixed at $22.50 in the overwhelming majority of marriages in the last few decades. (The Malayan dollar is worth 2s. 4d.) There are cases on record, however, of the payment being $10, and even as little as $2.50; moreover, I saw a handful of entries in the marriage registers of the

[1] See below, p. 175.

[2] Until the provisions of the 1957 Ordinance came into force, any kathi in Singapore could act as *wali hakim*.

[3] Hanafis do not insist on both being males, and indeed generally accept the evidence of two female witnesses as equivalent to that of one male witness. It is unheard of in Singapore for a woman to be a witness at a marriage contract between Hanafis.

1950's where a bride who was a widow or a divorcee was paid one solitary dollar as *mas kahwin*. At the other extreme, there is the odd bridegroom who pays as much as one thousand dollars *mas kahwin*, in addition to gifts of jewelry or clothing, and to a sum of money as marriage expenses (*belanja kahwin*).[1]

The *mas kahwin* may be, and in some cases in Singapore has been, one or more items of jewelry—frequently a gold chain or a ring; the value of the jewelry in dollars is usually noted in the marriage register – '*mas kahwin:* one gold chain, worth $40'. Indian bridegrooms exhibit a tendency to give jewelry as *mas kahwin* while Malays and Arabs usually give cash. The *mas kahwin* may be paid on the day the marriage contract (*nikah*) is effected, or payment may be deferred; whichever course is followed, the kathi registering the marriage is careful to make a note in the register. A woman divorced after consummation of the marriage, however guilty a wife she may have been, has an absolute right to the payment of *mas kahwin*, and the Shariah Court has power to make such an order against a defaulting husband.

Although it is customary for Muslim grooms to make a payment to the bride or her guardians towards the expenses of the wedding ceremonies, if a marriage has been hastily arranged as a result of an elopement or of the couple having been caught in a compromising situation, the groom may refuse to pay, arguing that he has no money and can raise none. If the bride or her parents decide that the marriage must be contracted at once, that they cannot wait until the man has saved a reasonable amount of money, the entry in the marriage register against 'Wedding Expenses' reads: 'None'. Some kathis go further and note *Suka sama suka*, i.e. a union at the wish of the bride and groom without deliberate prior arrangements such as an engagement ceremony and provision for wedding expenses. The wedding expenses, like the *mas kahwin*, are not returnable if the marriage has been consummated.

It has been customary in Singapore since the last century for a special condition or *ta'alik* to be included in the marriage contract to enable a woman whose husband has failed to maintain her over a specified period to petition for a divorce.[2]

The registration of Muslim marriages and divorces has been

[1] For details of marriage payments in 1949 and 1950, see my *Malay Kinship*, pp. 81–2.

[2] See below, Chapter 2.

compulsory since 1909, but registration by itself does not constitute proof of validity. Conversely, a marriage, divorce, or revocation of divorce which has not been registered is not necessarily invalid in the eyes of the law.

In 1963 there were ten kathis in Singapore who acted as Deputy-Registrars of Muslim Marriages and Divorces; the Registrar was the President of the Shariah Court. Of the ten kathis, two (the Acting Chief Kathi – to whom I shall refer henceforth as the Chief Kathi, for he was not deputizing for any other appointed kathi – and one other kathi) were known as Court kathis; they had offices in the building of the Shariah Court, which also houses the Registry. These two kathis are Government servants, and are paid a monthly salary by Government. The other eight kathis are known as 'outside kathis'; they are appointed by the Head of State but draw no salary: they retain the fees they are authorized to charge for registering marriages, divorces, and revocations. The fee for registering a marriage or a divorce is $15; in addition, the couple must pay $4 for a stamped application form. The fee for registering a revocation is $10, and no application form is necessary. Some popular kathis register changes in marital status in large numbers, and in addition to the fixed fee receive gifts of money or goods for their services; it is said that their income exceeds that of the Chief Kathi, and even that of the President of the Shariah Court.

In 1961 there were 1,560 Muslim marriages; the Registry of Muslim Marriages has classified them according to 'race':

Malaysians	1,256
Inter-racial	170
Indians and Pakistanis	117
Arabs	16
Others	1
Total	1,560

The inter-racial category is one where the spouses belong to different 'races'; the category 'Others' applies to couples both of whom are other than Malaysian, Indian, Pakistani, or Arab. In 1961, the one couple who fell into this category were both Chinese;[1] but the category also covers couples who are both either Europeans or Eurasians.

[1] See above, p. 13.

In 1962, there were 1,483 marriages registered, the comparative figures being:

Malaysians	1,211
Inter-racial	178
Indians and Pakistanis	73
Arabs	20
Others	1
Total	1,483

There are no comparative details available for the years preceding 1961, the year in which application forms were introduced; in these forms the spouses must state their 'race'.

DIVORCE

Four types of divorce are differentiated in the registers: *talak* (or *cherai biasa*, lit. ordinary divorce), *ta'alik*, *fasah*, and *khula*. *Talak* means repudiation in Arabic, and in Singapore this is the term used to describe a divorce effected by a man uttering an unconditional form of repudiation. A *talak* divorce is further qualified by the description of the number of times a husband has repudiated his wife. Thus *talak satu* is one *talak*; *talak dua*, two *talak*; and *talak tiga*, three *talak* (*satu*, *dua* and *tiga* are Malay words). The Malay word for dissolution or divorce is *cherai*.[1] It is also the word sometimes used to describe the dissolution of a union by death. This can lead to unfortunate ambiguities, for unless the marital status of the spouse is further specified, it is not possible to discover whether the person is divorced or widowed. Most of the kathis who fill in the marriage registers, however, do specify *cherai hidup* or *cherai mati* (*hidup* = alive, i.e. the spouse is divorced; while *mati* = dead, i.e. the spouse is widowed).

A Muslim who wishes to repudiate his wife may say to her, 'You are repudiated with one *talak*' (or with two, or with three *talak*). If he does not specifically state the number of *talak*, it is assumed that the repudiation is by one *talak*; she ceases at once to be his wife, in so far as his right of access to her person is concerned, but he is liable to maintain her for about three months

[1] *Cherai* is a term also used to mean 'separation'. An elderly Malay woman once told me that of all her children, one daughter was most attached to her, and had never left her side, but lived with her own husband and children in the old lady's house. She commented with pride, '*Dia tidak boleh cherai same saya!*', 'she cannot be parted from me!'

from the day of repudiation. This period is known as the *iddah* period, and consists strictly of three periods of purity or of an interval in the course of which the woman has had three menstrual flows. Its chief function is to ascertain whether the woman is pregnant. In Singapore the general rule is that three calendar months, or one hundred days according to many Muslims, is the proper *iddah* period.[1] Section 2 of the 1957 Ordinance states:

'*Eddah*' means the period within which a divorced woman or widow is forbidden by the law of Islam to remarry.

The husband, during the period of his wife's *iddah*, may revoke the divorce and take her back in marriage. Since the 1960 Amendment to the 1957 Ordinance, such a revocation may not be registered without the wife's consent. If the couple wish to resume lawful cohabitation after the expiry of the *iddah* period, they may do so by entering into a fresh marriage contract.

After either revoking the divorce or entering into a second marriage contract, a husband may repudiate his wife a second time, again with one *talak*. Such a repudiation, however, must be recorded as a second *talak*, or to be more precise, as a one-*talak* repudiation added to a former one-*talak* repudiation, which therefore ranks as a second *talak*. The couple may come together once more (again, either by the divorce being revoked, or by a remarriage after the expiry of the *iddah* period). However, if the husband should a third time utter a formula of repudiation, it will rank as the maximum amount permissible to him in respect of this same wife, i.e. as a third repudiation. (The same is true of a repudiation effected at once by three *talak*, or successive repudiations once of one *talak* and once of two *talak*.) A woman repudiated by three cumulative *talak*, or by three *talak* uttered on a single occasion, is forbidden as a wife to the man who has thus repudiated her. He cannot revoke such a repudiation, nor can he enter into another marriage with her, except on the condition that she lawfully be wedded to another Muslim, and that such an intervening marriage be consummated, and then dissolved. The intervening husband is known as *muhallil* in Arabic, and popularly by Malays as a *China buta*.[2] A widow must observe an *iddah* period of

[1] See below, p. 138.

[2] *China buta* literally means 'blind Chinese'. The origin of the Malay expression is obscure, cf. my *Malay Kinship*, pp. 113–14 *fn*. Russell Jones in his review of my *Malay Kinship* in *Oceania*, Vol. XXXIII, No. 4, June 1963, comments: 'Perhaps the

four months and ten days; if she is pregnant her *iddah* lasts until delivery. If a divorcee is pregnant, her *iddah* likewise lasts until delivery.

A Singapore woman divorced by three *talak* is not entitled to maintenance during her *iddah* period, but she is entitled to be housed.[1] A divorced wife who is pregnant is entitled to maintenance until her delivery, unless it can be satisfactorily proven that her pregnancy is the result of her adultery.

Khula (also *khul'*, *kholo*) is divorce by redemption. A wife may persuade her husband, who is otherwise unwilling to repudiate her, to agree to a dissolution of their union on condition that she pay him a sum of money fixed by mutual agreement, or in exchange for some other consideration. *Fasah* (also *faskh*, *pasah*) is a judicial dissolution of marriage. The most common grounds are lack of maintenance, impotence, and insanity. A *ta'alik* divorce is a divorce resulting from either spouse breaking a condition or stipulation made by the husband either at the time of the marriage contract or subsequently. The most usual *ta'alik* in Singapore is that which a bridegroom utters, and which is duly recorded in the marriage certificate:

> If I should fail to maintain my wife . . . *binte*[2] . . . over a period of three months or longer, or should beat her so as to cause her injury, and she cannot endure it and states her case to the Shariah Court, and her case is found proven, a one-*talak* divorce will befall her.

Such a 'suspended repudiation' or 'conditional repudiation',

most satisfactory comment on this mystifying term is to be found in J. Gonda, *Sanskrit in Indonesia*, Nagpur, 1952, p. 177. Examining the Sanskrit word *cihna*, 'mark, spot, characteristic', Professor Gonda writes (p. 177): 'In Javanese *cihna* was used for "token showing something, document in support, corpus delicti",, and the longer expression was *cihna bukti* or *cihna bekti*, "corpus delicti". With these words the Malay term *cina buta* must be connected: it denotes, as a popular name, the intermediate husband engaged to allow a divorcee to remarry her former husband and must, I think, by way of popular etymology, represent the phrase under discussion, the intermediate husband being the "token or document".' But E. W. Lane in *Modern Egyptians*, London ,1890, says (p. 165) of the intermediate husband: 'A poor man (generally a very ugly person, and often one who is blind) is usually chosen to perform this office.'

[1] See below, p. 140.

[2] *Binte* means 'daughter of' in Arabic. Malays use the Muslim form of naming; a man has a first, personal, name followed by the word *bin* (i.e., 'son of') and the personal name of his father; thus, Ahmad *bin* Ali, Ahmad son of Ali, or Puteh *binte* Ali, Puteh daughter of Ali. There are no surnames. Islam, however does not forbid the additional use of surnames or tribal names: Singapore Arabs generally use surnames.

once it is proven that the man who uttered it has indeed broken a specific stipulation, becomes effective and may be registered as a *ta'alik* divorce. However, the repudiation is revocable within the wife's *iddah* period, whereas neither a *fasah* nor a *khula* divorce is revocable. A couple divorced by *khula* or *fasah* may nevertheless enter into a fresh contract of marriage – provided, of course, that the wife had not been repudiated by three *talak* by the husband in question.

Since 24 November 1958 (the date on which the Shariah Court was constituted), only the Shariah Court may order the registration of divorces which are other than by mutual consent of the spouses. A kathi, even the Chief Kathi, is empowered to register a divorce only if both husband and wife appear before him, declare that they are agreed on the conditions of their divorce, and sign a stamped application form for divorce to this effect. Thus, once the above formalities have been observed, any Singapore kathi may register an ordinary *talak* divorce or a *khula* divorce.

On the other hand, a *ta'alik* or *fasah* divorce may be registered only after a petition to the Shariah Court, and after at least one Court hearing. Similarly, a husband who is unable to obtain his wife's consent to a repudiation he has uttered, or is eager to utter, must petition the Court for the registration of his divorce. The parties may be legally represented during proceedings, but in fact this is rare.

Before a summons is issued, the petitioning spouse is first interviewed by one of the Court kathis,[1] who attempts a reconciliation. If he fails, his next step is to persuade the spouses to agree to a divorce by mutual consent. Only if he again fails is the matter referred to a summons clerk for the fixing of a Court hearing.

If the respondent's address is known, the process-server serves the summons personally; if the address is not known, the Court grants permission for the summons to be served by way of an insertion in a Malay-language newspaper. The petitioning spouse bears the expense of initiating the proceedings. If the respondent

[1] From September 1960 to October 1962, there was a Muslim Woman Social Worker who played a very active role in the conciliation machinery; a petitioning spouse was frequently referred to her, and only if she failed to effect a reconciliation did she refer the person to a Court kathi, who in turn attempted to persuade the couple to settle the divorce amicably, without recourse to a Court hearing. The Social Worker had an office in the Court building.

is served with the summons at the first attempt, the cost (including transport of the process-server and of the petitioner or his agent who usually accompanies the process-server in order to identify the respondent) may be as little as $10. If several attempts are necessary, the transport expenses will, of course, increase this figure. The total cost of the summons alone is $6. If the address is not known, the petitioner pays for the cost of the newspaper notice, and of the Court messenger's transport to the newspaper office; this usually amounts to about $8.

Apart from this initial expense, the petitioner has to pay his or her own transport expenses to the Shariah Court for the hearing, and that of any witnesses who may have to be called. It is also common usage for the witnesses to be compensated for loss of earnings and for the inconvenience caused.

If the respondent spouse does not enter an appearance, and the Court orders the registration of the divorce, the petitioner pays for the cost of the registration – $20 – and $2 for a copy of the divorce certificate. If both spouses are present at the hearing, the President has power to make an order as to the cost of the registration. There are no other Court costs.

As we have seen, a divorce registered by mutual consent by a kathi costs $19: $4 for the stamped application form and $15 for the kathi's fee.[1] When one of the Court kathis registers a divorce (or a marriage) the fees are paid to the Registry.

Section 35 of the Muslims Ordinance, 1957, empowers the President of the Shariah Court to consider an application by a husband for an order of *nushuz* (recalcitrancy) against his wife. Such an order deprives a woman of her right to maintenance until such time as she makes obeisance (*ta'at*).[2] However, as soon as she signifies that she is willing to do so, her husband is bound to maintain her from that day. Only the President of the Shariah Court may make a *nushuz* order, and he rarely grants a husband such an application. There were no *nushuz* orders in 1962, but two were made in 1961.

[1] I asked several kathis and Registry officials whether some kathis offered to remit their fee, or to take a lesser amount, when the spouses were impoverished. My question was invariably greeted with a mixture of amazement and hilarity, for apparently such a situation was unknown. Comments were, 'A kathi wants even more than $15, not less!', or 'If a kathi accepted a lower fee, the other kathis would round on him for undercutting'.

[2] See my *Malay Kinship*, p. 84.

LEGISLATION SINCE 1880

In 1880 the first *Mahomedan Marriage Ordinance, 1880*, was enacted:

> WHEREAS it is expedient to provide for the voluntary registration of marriages and divorces, for the recognition of kalis, and for the improvement of the law relating to property as affected by marriage among Mahomedans.
>
> It is hereby enacted by the Governor of the Straits Settlements, with the advice and consent of the Legislative Council thereof, as follows . . .

There followed four parts: Part I, dealing with Registration; Part II with Kalis; Part III with the Effect of Marriage on Property; and Part IV was 'General'. The Ordinance provided for the appointment of Registrars; 'kalis' (an early spelling of 'kathis') were not then, as they were later to become, ex officio Deputy-Registrars. Their jurisdiction was very strictly limited in 1880; Part II, Section 24, read:

> I. If it shall be made to appear to the Governor that any person has been chosen by a number of Mahomedan inhabitants at any of the Settlements to act as Kali for any district or place, or for any nationality, in the Settlement, the Governor may, if he thinks fit, recognize such person as Kali, in all matters relating to the law of marriage and divorce; and may give to him a certificate of recognition, . . .
>
> II. No Kali recognized under this section shall be held to have any judicial authority other than is necessary to decide upon questions relating to the existence, or non-existence, of the status of marriage or divorce, between persons voluntarily appearing before him, and no such Kali shall have any authority to impose fines, nor to adjudicate in matters of property, unless the parties affected voluntarily agree to accept such Kali's adjudication after the adjudication has been made.

Provision was also made for the registration of Muslim marriages and divorces which had taken place before 1880. Roland Braddell stated in *The Laws of the Straits Settlements. A Commentary*:[1]

> Marriages and divorces according to Mohammedan Law were always held to be valid in the Colony. As Maxwell R. said in *Hawah* v. *Daoud*, 1865, 'But still, that the Mohammedan marriage was a good marriage in the eye of our law seemed incontestable; at all events it could not be contested here, without bastardizing the mass of the population.' . . .

[1] 2 vols., Singapore, 1931; Vol. 1, p. 89.

The 1880 Ordinance was amended in 1908; the Amendment, among other things, made the registration of Muslim marriages and divorces compulsory after 1 July 1909. Nevertheless, every Ordinance dealing with Muslim marriages and divorces has continued to embody the clause which first appeared in the 1880 Ordinance:

> Nothing in this Ordinance contained shall be construed—to render valid or invalid, merely by reason of its having been, or not having been, registered, any Mahomedan marriage or divorce, which would otherwise be invalid or valid . . .

Minor variations have been introduced in this clause, such as the substitution of the word 'Muslim' for 'Mahomedan', and the addition of the words 'revocation of divorce'. Thus in the 1957 Ordinance the clause (Section 19) reads:

> Nothing in this Ordinance shall be construed to render valid or invalid merely by reason of its having been or not having been registered any Muslim marriage, divorce or revocation of divorce which otherwise is invalid or valid.

The effect of making registration compulsory is that a Muslim may be prosecuted for the offence of not registering a change in his or her marital status. Although it is extremely rare that a Singapore Muslim marriage goes unregistered, there is ample documentary evidence to show that many divorces have been unregistered. Nevertheless, Muslims guilty of the offence do not appear to have been prosecuted,[1] and when they appear before a kathi to request the revocation of an *unregistered* divorce, many kathis do so without first insisting upon their registering the divorce, and paying the appropriate fee.[2]

The 1908 Amendment gave wider powers to kathis. A kathi could now consider an application by a Muslim woman resident for at least four months in the district within which he had jurisdiction, for the divorces known as *fasah* and *ta'alik*, and could grant such a decree. Kathis were further given jurisdiction to decide upon claims for 'dowry' (*mas kahwin*, or *mahr*) up to the amount of $101, and for maintenance up to $10 per month.

[1] According to Government officials whom I interviewed; I certainly never saw a case reported in the Press in 1949 or 1950, or in 1963.

[2] See below, pp. 130 ff.

There were further Amendments in 1909, 1917, 1923, 1934, 1936, and 1952.[1]

In the 1950's there were serious proposals by some Singapore Muslims to introduce new legislation in order to reduce the very high rate of Muslim divorce in the Island.[2] For many decades the rate had been about fifty per cent, i.e., in every year about fifty divorces were registered for every one hundred marriages registered in the same year.[3] In 1951 the Muslim Advisory Board (whose members were then appointed by the Governor, and are now appointed by the Head of State, to advise on matters relating to Muslim religion and law) formed a sub-committee which was to suggest a draft to amend existing legislation.

In July 1954 the subject of the draft Bill was raised in the Legislative Council. Dissatisfaction with the procedure employed by some Singapore kathis, who granted Muslim women *ta'alik* decrees without full inquiry, was mounting. One such case, in which a woman resident in Johore had obtained a *ta'alik* divorce from the Singapore Chief Kathi, was highly publicized; her husband was dissatisfied with the procedure of the divorce, and the Muslim Advisory Board appointed a sub-committee to look into the matter. Government finally agreed to introduce new legislation, and a bill, the Muslims Bill, was introduced in the Legislative Assembly in November 1955. It was referred to a Select Committee, but before the Committee could submit its report, the Assembly was prorogued and the Bill lapsed. It was re-introduced in October 1956.

The *Muslims Ordinance, 1957* provided *inter alia* for the establishment of a Shariah Court which alone would have jurisdiction to register divorces not arrived at by mutual consent. Henceforth, Singapore kathis would have no authority to register a divorce unless both spouses appeared together and signed the register

[1] Nos. 5 of 1880; 25 of 1908; 17 of 1909; 4 of 1917; 26 of 1923; 35 of 1934; 41 of 1936; and 37 of 1952. Further, Ordinance 32 of 1952 changed 'Mohammedan' to 'Muslim'; and the expressions 'Mohammedan religion' to 'religion of Islam', and 'Mohammedan law' to 'law of Islam'. In the 1955 Edition of *The Laws o the Colony of Singapore* (in 8 vols., prepared by E. J. Davies, C. H. Butterfield, and A. H. Simpson, Singapore, 1955), Chapter 46 of Vol. 1 stated: 'This Ordinance may be cited as the Muslims Ordinance'.

[2] See my *Malay Kinship*, p. 147, and M. Siraj, 'The Shariah Court in Singapore and its Control of the Divorce Rate' in *Malaya Law Review*, Vol. v, No. 1, July 1963.

[3] See my *Malay Kinship*, p. 117.

voluntarily. All applications made by a woman to have a *ta'alik* or *fasah* divorce registered would be referred to the Shariah Court. Similarly, a Muslim man could no longer come alone to a kathi and ask for the registration of a repudiation he wished to utter, or had already uttered: he was to bring his wife, and only if the kathi was satisfied that she freely consented to the divorce would the dissolution of the marriage be registered. Otherwise, the husband was to institute proceedings in the Shariah Court.

The Shariah Court, however, was not constituted until 24 November 1958, and Singapore kathis continued until then to register divorces as in the past. I examined the 1958 divorce registers and found that as late as 26 November 1958 (i.e. two days after the Court had been constituted), a woman was granted the registration of a *ta'alik* decree by a Singapore kathi (not the then Chief Kathi). The first divorce registered by order of the Shariah Court was on 7 January 1959; in that year the Court ordered the registration of 139 divorces.

One of the major effects of the new Ordinance, then, was a severe limitation on the jurisdiction of Singapore kathis. Until the Shariah Court was constituted, any Singapore Muslim woman could go from kathi to kathi (in 1957 there were twelve kathis and one Chief Kathi) in an effort to secure a *ta'alik* or *fasah* decree, until she found one who would agree to grant her petition. Allegations that some kathis were notoriously corrupt were very frequent when I was in Singapore in 1949–50, and there is no doubt – as an examination of divorce registers for the years up to 1958 shows – that some kathis registered a very high proportion of *ta'alik* and *fasah* divorces, and failed to make a detailed report of their preliminary enquiries. I examined every divorce entry for 1957, paying special attention to those made by a kathi (now dead) who was famous for his indulgence to applicants and for his high fees. In the divorce register entries, he frequently gave as his grounds for granting a *ta'alik* or *fasah* decree the fact that the applicant wife had sworn that she had not been maintained over a period of months (or years) and that witnesses – whose names and addresses were not mentioned, and whose signatures did not appear – had corroborated her statement. Moreover, he made no reference to a Report Book where the details of the enquiry should have been recorded in full. Other, more conscientious, kathis did so. They also granted very few *ta'alik* or *fasah* decrees.

I also examined every entry in the marriage registers for 1957. This same kathi frequently omitted to fill the entry requiring 'evidence of divorce' if the bride alleged she was a divorcee (and thus free to remarry). Indeed he sometimes did not trouble to specify whether she was a widow or divorcee, contenting himself with the statement '*Janda*'. *Janda* is a Malay word for a woman who has been married and whose marriage has been dissolved by divorce (*janda cherai hidup*) or by death (*janda cherai mati*). This kathi is said to have attracted many women who had deserted (or had been deserted by) their husbands, had not in their possession a divorce certificate, and wished to marry again. Some told him that they were widows, others that their divorce certificate had been lost, and he made a note to this effect, without apparently asking the women concerned to obtain another copy of the death or divorce certificate, or to produce a statutory declaration. Others, again, stated that they were spinsters, and had run away from home to get married; he then noted in the marriage certificate that the bride had no *wali*, and he acted as her *wali hakim*. Other Singapore kathis also acted as *wali hakim* in cases where the bride had eloped, but it is said that many of them did make some enquiries before agreeing to solemnize a marriage without a *wali*'s presence or consent.

The 1957 Ordinance (Section 7, subsection (3)) gave to the Chief Kathi the exclusive right to act as *wali hakim* when the bride had no *wali*, or when the *wali* refused his consent 'on grounds which the Chief *Kathi* does not consider satisfactory'. There was a great deal of opposition to this clause on the grounds that it would lead to much inconvenience, especially if the wedding was scheduled to take place in a remote village and the Chief Kathi found it difficult to get there at the time fixed for the ceremony. However, the argument in favour of restricting the power to act as *wali hakim* to one man only was very strong. If a young girl eloped, her father or *wali* could at once get in touch with the Chief Kathi and warn him; before the Ordinance came into force, he would have had to approach every kathi in Singapore, or else to request the Chief Kathi to do so, and by then the eloping couple might well have been married.[1]

Singapore kathis were not appointed on the basis of theological

[1] Some Singapore couples now run away to States in the Peninsula and succeed in persuading a kathi there to marry them.

or other academic qualifications. When I was in Singapore in 1950 one of the twelve kathis was a retired police corporal who was barely literate. On the other hand, nowadays both Court kathis are graduates of the famous centre of Muslim theology, Al Azhar University in Cairo, while the President of the Shariah Court has both a first and a higher degree from Al Azhar. Most of the outside kathis, however, do not enjoy a reputation as men of learning, or as leaders of the Muslim community; many Muslims have voiced forceful criticisms of kathis' standards of responsibility. When the Select Committee of the Legislative Assembly was hearing witnesses about amending the *Muslims Ordinance, 1957*,[1] the President of one of the Muslim Associations stated, on 11 March 1960, in the course of a discussion on the subject of brides who have no *wali*:

> I am not satisfied that a Kathi should be given the final authority to act as a *wali* where there is no *wali*, because that is a miscarriage of justice. From my 35 years' experience in Singapore, I have found that it is an injustice to the persons concerned and also to the good name of Islam, because Kathis are not relatives of the parties concerned and they do not care what happens to them the next day.

When this issue was being considered on 20 March 1956 by the Select Committee on the Muslims Bill (which later became the *Muslims Ordinance, 1957*) the then Vice-Chairman of the Muslim Advisory Board, Inche Ahmad Ibrahim, had stated:

> . . . we find from experience that this right given to the Kathis has been abused in the past. Just to take an example, a boy brought a girl at 2 a.m. to a Kathi's house saying that a *wali* could not be obtained and the marriage was performed. We feel that the only way to control the matter is to place the authority on one responsible man.[2]

In 1961, when only the Chief Kathi could act as *wali hakim*, he did so in 214 cases. In that year, 1,560 marriages were registered, and the percentage of brides who had a *wali hakim* was thus 13.7. In 1957, the last full year in which any kathi could act as *wali hakim*, there were 2,303 registered marriages;[3] a kathi acted as *wali hakim* in 722 cases, or for 31.4 per cent of all 1957 brides.

[1] *Report of the Select Committee . . .*, L.A. 14 of 1960.

[2] *Report from the Select Committee on the Muslims Bill*, L.A. 5 of 1957, Singapore, 1957.

[3] The decline in the number of marriages is discussed below at pp. 143 ff.

The 1960 Amendment[1] introduced a severe restriction on polygynous marriages. Since it came into operation in May 1960 only the Chief Kathi may allow the registration of a polygynous union, and before doing so he is required by Section 4 of the Amendment to 'satisfy himself after inquiry that there is no lawful obstacle according to the law of Islam to such marriage'. In 1960 he allowed the registration of only three polygynous marriages, and the same number in 1961, while in 1962 he allowed four.[2]

Moreover, since it was generally believed that members of the Armed Forces and of the Police often entered into polygynous marriages in Singapore and lightly abandoned a wife married in Singapore if they had another wife and family in the Peninsula, a special directive was issued to all kathis. The latter, before they consent to marry a member of the Forces or a policeman, must have a letter from the prospective groom's superior officer stating that according to the records the man is unmarried. (If he is married, he is referred to the Chief Kathi.) These letters are later deposited in the Registry.

To judge from the evidence in one case, the Army pays family allowances in respect of one wife only: in September 1962 a private in the Army was ordered to pay maintenance to his wife for herself and for their child. The Court approached the defaulting husband's colonel, and the following month received from the Regimental Pay Office a letter which stated: 'The orders were made in respect of a second wife . . . and under army regulations only the first wife is recognized for pay purposes.'

Another innovation brought about by the 1960 Amendment (Section 12 (2)) was to grant to the Shariah Court the power to order a husband to pay to his divorced wife a consolatory gift or *matta'ah*:

> A woman who has been divorced by her husband may apply to the Court for a consolatory gift or *matta'ah*, and the Court may after hearing the parties order payment of such sum as may be just and in accordance with the law of Islam.

Kathis are instructed by the Registrar to attempt a reconciliation before granting the registration of a divorce by mutual consent,

[1] *The Muslims (Amendment) Ordinance, 1960*, no. 40 of 1960.

[2] See State of Singapore, *Annual Report of the Registry of Muslim Marriages and the Shariah Court 1962*, Singapore 1963.

but there is no fee payable to a kathi who has reconciled a couple. When giving evidence to the Select Committee on the 1950 Amendment, one lady pointed out on 31 March 1960:

> . . . all Kathis may be interested parties. Every time they marry a person or divorce a person, they get a financial gain from it. But the Chief Kathi does not. He is a judicial officer – at least he is in the position of a judicial officer.[1]

When kathis register a divorce they are required to ensure that there is a note in the application form regarding the conditions of the divorce. A husband may offer, and his wife accept, $30 or $20 per month for three months as *iddah* maintenance;[2] in most cases the man does not have the total amount readily available, and the wife agrees that the allowance be paid to her at the end of every month either directly, or through the good offices of the kathi. The husband may then default, and if the kathi fails to persuade him to comply with the condition of the divorce, the wife is referred to the Shariah Court. In May 1963 the President of the Shariah Court very kindly sent at my request the following questions to every Singapore kathi:

> In most cases is *iddah* maintenance paid to the wife direct, or through you? Do you receive many complaints from wives that husbands do not pay the amount of *iddah* maintenance which they had undertaken to pay?

Among the outside kathis there is one who refuses to register divorces on a point of principle. He is said to be of Indian descent and to refuse to register divorces because he promised his father on his deathbed that he would never do so. He has been a kathi since 1941 and has never registered a divorce. The nine other kathis replied that some husbands pay *iddah* maintenance direct, and some through the kathi; they added that on the whole there were few complaints that husbands defaulted.

The Chief Kathi of Singapore in 1963 had been appointed in August 1960, and the other Court Kathi in March 1961. One of the eight outside kathis, of Indian descent (he is not the kathi who refuses to register divorces), was granted leave of absence for one year to visit India and a kathi was appointed on a temporary basis to replace him during his absence. The other seven kathis were

[1] See *Report of the Select Committee*, paragraph 966. [2] See below, p. 87.

respectively appointed in 1930, 1938, 1940, 1941, 1955, and two in 1960.

Although the letter of appointment of a kathi specifies the district or 'particular school of law' for which he is appointed,[1] it appears that a kathi may register a change in the marital status of any Muslim in Singapore irrespective of district of residence or allegiance to any particular school of law.

Outside kathis come to the Registry at the beginning of every month to deliver copies of the entries in their registers of marriages, divorces, and revocations for the previous month. Each kathi numbers his own entries serially, and must hand over exact copies of his entries to the Registry. Similarly, the two Court kathis must hand over formally to the Registry copies of the entries in their own registers.

When all the entries from all the kathis have been received in respect of a calendar year,[2] a Registry clerk re-numbers them in pencil serially, starting with the figure 1. The copies are then bound so that all the January entries from all the kathis come first, then February, and so on until December. This is so for all marriages, divorces, and revocations registered by kathis. However, divorces registered by order of the Shariah Court are entered in a separate register, and are separately numbered. Each filled stamped application form for marriage or divorce is bound together with the marriage or divorce entry to which it refers, in the registers kept in the Registry. Kathis do not retain copies of the application forms.

Each of the eleven States in the Malay Peninsula has its own separate legislation concerning Muslim marriage and divorce. In addition, there are unpublished directives to kathis, emanating from the Religious Affairs Departments, which advise on points of interpretation of the law.

In 1963 there were informal reciprocal agreements between Singapore and three States in the Peninsula (Johore, Malacca, and Selangor); these three States agreed not to register the marriage or divorce of a Singapore resident without prior reference to the Singapore Registry. However, I was informed that in several

[1] See *The Muslim Marriage and Divorce Rules, 1959*, rule 3 (1) and 3 (2), Government Printing Office, Singapore, 1959.

[2] The Gregorian calendar is observed in all Government Departments. However, kathis usually note in the entries the Muslim date, as well as the date according to the Gregorian calendar.

cases the registration of a divorce or of a polygynous marriage of a Singapore resident did in fact take place, in spite of a request by the Singapore Registry not to effect such registration. Kathis in these three States considered the Singapore Registry's views, but apparently they were not bound to act on them. The same, *mutatis mutandis*, applied to marriages and divorces in Singapore of residents of these three States.[1]

A Singapore resident, wishing to enter into a contract of marriage in the Federation of Malaya and reluctant to wait for official enquiries to proceed between a State in the Federation and Singapore, may obtain from the Singapore Chief Kathi a 'Letter of Authority' stating that there is no objection in Singapore to the marriage of this resident elsewhere. In 1961, thirteen such Letters were issued, while in 1962, 257 were issued. The Chief Kathi told me this was because the reciprocal agreement had come into effect late in 1961.

THE SHARIAH COURT

The Shariah Court is housed in an old two-storey colonial house. On the ground floor are verandahs, the offices of the Registry of Muslim Marriages and Divorces, and the clerical offices of the Court. In a back room of the Registry are stored large bound Registers of Marriages, Divorces, and Revocations. A kathi is legally required to surrender his books and notebooks to the Registry, as soon as they are completed; he must also return all such books when he ceases to be a kathi; and after his death his next of kin are required to return them. However, these

[1] In 1962, *Kaum Ibu* (the women's section of U.M.N.O.—United Malay National Organisation—a Malay political party in the Federation of Malaya) submitted a memorandum to the Conference of Rulers of Malaya, in which they asked for a unified, and stricter, law of Muslim marriage and divorce to cover all the States.

In July 1963 a Johore State Assemblyman told the Johore State Assembly that the 1957 Census revealed that there were 20,000 more Malay women than men in the country. He was reported (in *The Straits Times* of 23rd July 1963) as saying '. . . that in view of the excess number of Muslim women the men should marry more than one wife'. He himself had two wives. The Acting Chairman of *Kaum Ibu* on the following day replied that the Assemblyman was 'deliberately trying to make excuses for preserving the existing marriage and divorce laws which are unfair and unjust to Muslim women'. She added that Selangor had introduced legislation restricting polygyny, 'But this does not prevent a Selangor man taking a second or third wife in another State. . . . What we really want is marriage and divorce laws based on the real precepts of Islam.' (*Ibid.*)

regulations have not been rigidly observed in the past, and many kathis' personal records are missing.

Court sittings take place between the hours of 10 a.m. to 1 p.m., and 2 to 4.30 p.m. Mondays to Thursdays. On Friday mornings the Court rises at noon but sits in the afternoon; and there are no sittings on Saturday afternoons. Pious Muslim men join in communal praying in mosques at midday on Fridays. Singapore Government offices generally close on Saturday afternoons.

An applicant for divorce or other Court Order must be referred to a Court Kathi. On the first floor, there are the offices of both Court kathis, the office of the Lady Social Worker,[1] the room of the President of the Court, and the Courtroom itself. There are benches on the verandahs of the first floor and in corridors, where people sit while waiting to be interviewed, and where witnesses wait to be called into the courtroom to give evidence. There is one Court policeman who sees that order is preserved. The Court Usher sits during Court hearings at a table facing the public and with his back to the bench. He swears in the witnesses and ensures that Court procedure is observed; for instance, he sees that witnesses are not present in the courtroom before they are due to give evidence.

The President of the Court sits on a chair on a raised platform, and on his right is a witness-box. There are chairs immediately facing the Court Usher, on which the petitioner and respondent sit, and chairs are also used by lawyers, on the rare occasions when counsel are engaged by litigants. Immediately behind these chairs are rows of benches on which the public may sit.

Court hearings rarely attract the Press or general public; on the whole, it is only the kinsmen or close friends of the litigants who attend. However, when there is a long queue of people waiting to be interviewed by the kathis, whose offices are across the landing from the courtroom, and the benches on the landing are fully occupied, some of the men and women who are waiting sit on the benches in the courtroom. The atmosphere in the building is generally informal, and children are frequently seen sitting with their mothers outside the courtroom; they are not allowed inside, although I have witnessed exceptions to this general rule.

[1] See above, p. 22, n. 1. In October 1962, she was temporarily transferred for further training to the Department of Social Welfare and had not returned to the Court when I left Singapore at the end of July 1963.

Muslim women in Singapore are not veiled, but wear a long narrow scarf when they go out.[1] The scarf is usually of net or some other transparent material, and those careful of the proprieties wear it to cover their hair; most women, however, are content to drape it around the neck, leaving the hair exposed. I was somewhat surprised to observe that petitioning wives often did not trouble to put a scarf on their head when giving evidence. Some of the younger women, moreover, wore blouses with a scooped out neckline and short sleeves, while their faces were heavily made up with rouge and lipstick; these were not all women of unsavoury reputation. Many respectable young Muslim women in Singapore now dress boldly and use make-up, but one might have expected ligitants to present in Court a particularly modest and sober appearance. The men were usually dressed in clean neat clothes; if a witness had carelessly left a button of his shirt unfastened, the Usher before swearing him in usually asked him to fasten it, and he sharply rebuked him if his hands were in his pockets.

When a litigant or a witness is sworn in before giving evidence, he or she is cautioned in very simple language about the necessity of telling the whole truth, and of the penalties that may be inflicted for giving false evidence. The inadmissibility of hearsay evidence is also explained: 'You may not use statements you have heard from others – you must state here only what you yourself know, what you yourself have seen or heard directly from the parties to the dispute.' Court procedure is explained also in simple terms: 'First, your spouse gives evidence. You listen carefully, but you may not interrupt. Later you may ask questions, but not now; just listen now.'

The language used in the Court is usually Malay, but the Usher speaks to the President in English. When lawyers are present they use English only, and their questions are interpreted in Malay by the Court Usher for the benefit of the witness and of the litigants; this is so even if the lawyers are Malay-speaking. If any of the litigants or any witness knows no English or Malay,[2] an interpreter is called in order to translate the Indian or Chinese dialect into English, and this in turn is translated into Malay by the Court

[1] See my *Malay Kinship*, p. 6.

[2] Section 23 (1) of the *Muslims Ordinance, 1957* states: 'The languages of the Court shall be English and Malay'.

Usher in case one of the litigants speaks only Malay. Thus, in one case in 1963 involving a woman of Indian descent (who spoke Malay) and her Chinese husband who had become a Muslim convert in order to marry her, there were two witnesses: a Chinese (Teochew) shopkeeper; and a Tamil woman, both of whom spoke too little Malay to give evidence in that language. Arrangements had to be made for special interpreters to be called. On the whole, however, most litigants and their witnesses are Malay-speaking.

The President writes in longhand in the Jawi script a record or a summary of the litigants' allegations and counter-allegations, and of the witnesses' evidence. He exhibits remarkable patience and courtesy, and in every case makes an attempt at reconciling estranged couples. Before a witness proceeds to give evidence in support of either a husband's or a wife's petition, he enquires whether the witness has ever been at enmity with the spouse who has not called him. As a general rule, witnesses affirm that they have never quarrelled with the spouse in question. However, in one case which I heard in February 1963, when a woman was petitioning for divorce on the grounds of desertion without maintenance, one of her witnesses replied to the usual question from the President, 'Yes, I did once quarrel with the husband.' When he was asked to give details, he said: 'I rebuked him on one occasion for neglecting his wife.' The President declared: 'This cannot be called a quarrel, it was just that you gave him proper advice. But was there any real animosity between you, did you have a personal quarrel with him?' The witness replied in the negative, and his evidence was then recorded. The woman obtained the registration of her divorce at the end of the hearing.

Section 27 (1) of the 1957 Ordinance states:

> The Court shall observe all provisions of the law of Islam relating to the number, status or quality of witnesses or evidence required to prove any fact. Save as aforesaid, the Court shall have regard to the law of evidence for the time being in force in the Colony, and shall be obliged to apply the same strictly.

In divorce petitions, witnesses are generally male Muslims. There are exceptions, such as the case of the Teochew shopkeeper and the Tamil woman, and the President has discretion to decide in what circumstances the evidence of non-Muslims is admissible. A woman who petitions for the registration of a divorce must produce at least two witnesses, and she is warned that her father is not eligible; I heard the President tell a young woman, 'You may call your brother, or a brother of your father or mother, or some other kinsman, or a friend or neighbour – but not your father.'[1]

There is a right of appeal against the decisions of the Shariah Court to an Appeal Board.[2] Appeals are rare. The Annual Reports of the Shariah Court for 1960, 1961, and 1962 state that no appeals were heard in 1960 and 1962, while one appeal was heard in 1961. As far as I could discover, only two appeals were heard in 1959.[3]

[1] Cf. *Minhaj et Talibin*, p. 516: '. . . one cannot depose in favour of one's ancestors or descendants, though one may legally do so against them, . . .'

[2] See section 37 of the *Muslims Ordinance, 1957*.

[3] See below, pp. 73 f. and pp. 153 ff.

2

Ta'alik

It has been the practice among Singapore Muslims since the early days of marriage registration, if not before, for a bridegroom to utter a formula by which he binds himself to divorce his wife if he should leave her for a specified period without maintenance. In the marriage registers of the 1890's the following clause was often inserted:

> . . . *bin* . . . states: 'If I should leave my wife without maintenance for three months while I am journeying inland, or six months while I am on a sea journey, a one-*talak* divorce will befall her.'

In the 1920's the usual period was three months' absence 'whether inland or at sea'. Moreover, the clause has always been taken to apply equally to those wives who, although they are not physically abandoned by the husbands with whom they may still be cohabiting, have been given no maintenance by them or their agents. The husband has a duty to provide his wife with the minimum amount of food she requires, or he may give her money with which to buy it.

The entries in the marriage registers of the 1950's and early 1960's which have a *ta'alik* clause no longer make mention of travel inland or at sea. They simply mention 'three months or longer' (*tiga bulan atau lebeh*), but are more legalistically phrased than in earlier decades, for they state:

> If I should leave my wife . . . *binte* . . . without maintenance for a period of three months or longer, and she decides she cannot endure it and states her case to a kathi and the kathi finds the case proven, then a one-*talak* divorce will befall her.

Unlike some States in the Federation, Singapore does not provide for marriage certificates to have a printed *ta'alik*.[1] Each kathi who registers a marriage, after having solemnized it, makes the

[1] Except for a few cases when an 'unauthorized' printing of a *ta'alik* occurred—see below, pp. 48 ff.

entry in long-hand under the printed heading of 'Special Conditions'. By the terms of the *Muslims Ordinance, 1957* only the Shariah Court can register a *ta'alik* divorce, after a hearing by the President of the Court. Accordingly, some Singapore kathis now register a *ta'alik* formula which specifies:

> . . . if she decides she cannot endure it and states her case to a kathi or to the Shariah Court . . .

It may be that they retain the reference to a kathi because it is possible for a Singapore wife to seek a *ta'alik* divorce outside Singapore by pleading for it before a kathi. On the other hand, most kathis record only '. . . and states her case to the Shariah Court . . .', omitting reference to a kathi.

Up to the 1940's in Singapore it was rarely stated in the *ta'alik* that the wife must establish to the satisfaction of a kathi that her husband had contravened the condition of the *ta'alik* before the divorce could become operative. The usual formula was that if her husband failed to maintain her over a specified period of time, 'a one-*talak* divorce would befall her'; so that in Islam she might be considered to have been *automatically* divorced, even against her wish, as soon as her husband had infringed a condition of the *ta'alik*. In point of fact, of course, a Muslim woman did go before a kathi to prove her case, and did not consider herself a divorced woman until she had her divorce duly registered by him and a copy of the divorce certificate in her possession; and only then was she considered by other Muslims to have established that she was a divorcee.

Nowadays, however, with increasing legal sophistication and awareness of the Muslim law of marriage and divorce, the kathi registering a *ta'alik* sees to it that the husband's *ta'alik* formula includes the stipulation that the aggrieved wife must first establish her case, and that only when it is established will a *ta'alik* divorce be registered. Indeed, when in the course of time the divorce is registered by the President of the Shariah Court in Singapore, it is specifically stated that it results from 'the *ta'alik* uttered by . . . *bin* . . . and recorded on . . . by Kathi . . . in his marriage register No. . . .'

Some *ta'alik* contain two clauses: no maintenance for three months or longer, and injurious beating. An examination of marriage registers reveals that some Singapore kathis register more *ta'alik* clauses than others, and that they decide upon the exact words the bridegroom utters when the *ta'alik* is registered. The then Chief Kathi of Singapore, for instance, in November 1959 and in succeeding months registered identical *ta'alik* formulae, varying of course only the name of the bride concerned. He registered that the bridegroom had uttered: 'Whenever I should fail to fulfil my financial obligations towards my wife . . . *binte* . . . for three months or longer . . .'. During that same period other kathis recorded that bridegrooms had uttered: 'Whenever I do not give my wife . . . *binte* . . . maintenance for three months or longer . . .', while one kathi consistently recorded that the bridegroom had said: 'If I do not give my wife . . . *binte* . . . sufficient maintenance (*nafkah yang chukup*) for three months or longer or if I beat her cruelly . . .'. The kathi officiating at the marriage ceremony usually asks the bridegroom to repeat after him the words of the formula.

The President of the Shariah Court favours 'Whenever' (*Apabila*), for apparently it has been contended in some cases that the formula beginning with 'If (*jika, kalau*) I do not give . . .' grants a wife only once the right to plead for a divorce on the grounds of the *ta'alik*. The argument is that if, after the granting of such a *ta'alik* divorce, the divorce is revoked and a fresh *ta'alik* is not registered at the time of the revocation, and the husband again leaves his wife for three months without maintenance (or beats her cruelly), she has no right to plead that the *ta'alik* originally uttered still applies. However, if it is registered that the husband said '*Whenever* I . . .' such a *ta'alik* is absolutely clear and unambiguous and can be held to apply to *any* occasion when he is proven guilty of not having provided maintenance for (or of beating cruelly) the wife mentioned in the original *ta'alik*.

Although a kathi can advise a bridegroom to utter a *ta'alik*, he cannot force him to do so; and some kathis will register a 'no maintenance for three months or more' *ta'alik* in marriage after marriage, and then register a marriage with no *ta'alik*. It is, of course, the duty of the *wali* of the bride to persuade the groom to utter at least a non-maintenance *ta'alik*; and indeed he may insist that unless the groom is willing to do so he will refuse his consent to the marriage. However, there are situations when the *wali* is in no position to impose his will, as when the bride is already pregnant or heavily compromised and the groom has not been eager to marry her. Indeed, if the couple marrying are Singapore Malays (Indians are said to have resorted less frequently to the use of the *ta'alik*),[1] Court officials and kathis think it not unreasonable to suspect that the marriage was hastily arranged and that the bridegroom was reluctant.

In order to check this assumption I examined every entry in the marriage registers for 1961. There were 1,560 marriages registered in that year, and only in 23 cases was there no *ta'alik*. In

10 cases the bride and groom were Malays (out of a total 1,256 unions of Malays);
8 cases the bride and groom were Indian (out of a total 117 unions of Indians);
3 cases the bride and groom were Arab (out of a total 16 unions of Arabs);
1 case the bride was Malay and the groom Indian; while in
1 case the bride was Indian and the groom Malay (out of a total of 170 'inter-racial' unions).

The following is a brief analysis of these 23 cases.

Malay cases, no ta'alik. (1) Only in one case did the bridegroom make no marriage payment whatsoever: there was no *belanja kahwin* (marriage expenses); there were no gifts; and even the *mas kahwin* of $22.50 was recorded as owing (*hutang*). The groom was a bachelor whose age was not stated and the bride a divorcee aged 24 years; she was given away by her father. (2) In another case the groom paid no marriage expenses and made no marriage gifts, but he paid the *mas kahwin* of $22.50 in cash. He was 18, the bride 15 and a spinster, and her brother gave her away in marriage. Against the entry 'marriage expenses' the kathi recorded that none was paid and stated '*suka sama suka*'.[2] (3 and 4) In two cases (both brides were spinsters) the amount of marriage expenses was considerably lower than that usually paid when the bride is a spinster: one groom paid $20 and the other $50; however, both men paid a *mas kahwin* of $22.50 in cash at the time of the wedding. There were no marriage gifts; in each case the bride's father gave her away. (5–9) In five cases there were substantial payments by the bridegroom: $300; $401; $500; $601;[3] and $1,200. In four out of

[1] Mrs M. Siraj in 'The Shariah Court of Singapore' states: '*ta'alik* . . . is not popular with Indians and Pakistanis in Singapore . . .'.

[2] See above, p. 17.

[3] There seems to be a traditional dislike among Malays for the amount of the marriage expenses to be in round figures. (This is also true of Indians, see below,

the five cases the bride was a spinster, while in one case (where the groom paid $1,200 – $600 as marriage expenses, and gifts costing $600) the bride was a divorcee. (10) The tenth case is a peculiar one: it was registered as being the couple's 'renewal of their marriage' (*membahrukan nikahnya*). The man was 37 and the woman 27 years old. There were no marriage expenses and no gifts, but a *mas kahwin* of $22.50 was paid in cash. I was told by the Singapore Chief Kathi that such wedding ceremonies occur if the couple come to learn that there was a flaw in the solemnization of their marriage which would invalidate it in Islam. Thus, there was a man who, when he gave his adopted daughter away in marriage, stated her to be his own, i.e. begotten, daughter. Many years later, after the daughter had already given birth to four children, the man came to learn that Islam does not recognize adoption as conferring on an adopted child the rights and duties of an 'own child', and that an adoptive father cannot, unless he also happens to be the girl's closest available agnate, act as her *wali* or guardian for marriage. In 1963 he came to consult the Chief Kathi about the matter, and it was arranged then that the couple should enter into a properly solemnized form of marriage. Since the whereabouts of the woman's natural *wali* were unknown, the Chief Kathi became her *wali hakim*[1] and gave her away in marriage. He registered the union as a 'renewal of marriage', the technical term for this being the Arabic *tajdid al nikah*, lit. 'renewal of the marriage contract'.

On the other hand, an 'outside' kathi I interviewed in July 1963 in the presence of the Registrar, told me that he registered 'renewals of marriage' when couples came to him to say they had been married several years or decades earlier, often in Indonesia, but did not possess a marriage certificate. For a variety of reasons, mainly connected with employers' requirements and also pension rights, they needed such a certificate, and he was happy to be of

p. 44.) In my *Malay Kinship* I stated (p. 81) that a groom is expected to pay $101 to $301 for a virgin bride. Moreover, at all the weddings I attended in 1949 and 1950 an odd cent was ceremonially added to the sum of the marriage expenses when they were formally handed over: $101 and one cent; $121 and one cent; $201 and one cent. I was never able to obtain any explanation for this custom other than that 'it has always been so, this is the way Malays like to pay marriage expenses'. Some kathis dutifully record the odd cent when they fill in the entries relating to marriage expenses in the marriage registers.

[1] See above, p. 16.

service to them. I had arranged to interview him because I had noticed that over a period of years he had registered a much greater number of 'renewals' than other kathis; for instance, in 1957 there were seven kathis who registered a total of 52 'renewals', this particular kathi being responsible for 25. In 1961, only three 'renewals' were registered, all three again by this same kathi.

It seems that some couples do not find that a Statutory Declaration fully replaces a marriage certificate. In one case in August 1957 an Indian kathi in Singapore wrote the following details in English in the marriage register:

> Renewed the marriage because their certificate of marriage has been lost. They married first time in February 1948 in Ipoh according to Statutory Declaration of 24.8.57.[1]

To return to the cases of no *ta'alik* among Malay couples: in seven out of ten cases the bride was a spinster, and if we do not consider the couple who had already been married and were simply 'renewing' their marriage, only in two cases had the bride been married before. It is tempting to conclude that a woman who had been married once is less agreeable to consent to a marriage with no *ta'alik*. However, brides are rarely present when the marriage contract is discussed and registered, and they sign the register *after* the solemnization. Further, in the application forms for marriage there is no mention of whether or no there shall be a *ta'alik*.

When women come to the Shariah Court to plead for a judicial divorce, they are (according to Court officials) rarely aware that there was a *ta'alik* registered at their marriage, even if they have a copy of their marriage certificate in their possession. Few of them, in any case, know what a *ta'alik* means. The majority of women seeking a divorce after 1961 were born before 1945 (when it was not common for Muslim girls to go to school) and are illiterate.

The kathi solemnizing a marriage normally suggests a *ta'alik*, but if the groom refuses to utter it the bride's father may be reluctant to create a scandal by threatening not to proceed with the marriage. I was informed that it is unknown for a *ta'alik* to be discussed when the couple are formally engaged: the conditions

[1] Ipoh is the capital of the Malay State of Perak.

of the marriage usually discussed at that time are the financial payments to be made, the penalties for breach of promise, and sometimes the place of residence of the couple after marriage.

Indian cases, no ta'alik. There were eight cases. In five there were substantial marriage payments; and the bride was a spinster in all five. The payments were: \$201; \$301; \$401; \$501; and \$1,001, as marriage expenses. The groom who paid \$201 also gave gifts worth \$22, and paid the *mas kahwin* of \$22.50. The groom who paid \$301 made no gifts, but bound himself to a *mas kahwin* of \$101 (owing). The man who gave \$401 also made no gifts, but paid the *mas kahwin* of \$22.50. The man who gave \$501 also made gifts worth \$92.40, and paid a *mas kahwin* of \$51; while the groom who gave \$1,001 made no gifts and registered a *mas kahwin* of \$101 payable within three months of the marriage.

In one case (of the remaining three Indian unions with no *ta'alik*) there was no money paid as 'marriage expenses'. Under that entry the kathi noted '*suka sama suka*'; under the entry 'marriage gifts' the kathi recorded that the bride had received a necklace worth \$401; the groom, moreover, bound himself to a *mas kahwin* of \$101 which was registered as 'owing'. The bride was a spinster aged 22 years, and she was given away by her father. Under the heading of *ta'alik* the kathi entered *tidak mahu* (lit. 'does not want', i.e. refuses); as a rule, kathis enter simply *tiada* (none).

In the two other cases, the bride again was a spinster, and no marriage expenses were paid ('*suka sama suka*' was recorded by the kathi), and no gifts made. But in each case the groom paid a *mas kahwin* of \$22.50 in cash.

Arab cases, no ta'alik. In all three cases the bride was a spinster. In two cases there were no marriage expenses and no gifts; one groom paid a *mas kahwin of* \$5, and the other \$22.50; in both cases the bride's father gave her away. In the third case, the groom paid \$1,001 as marriage expenses, but he made no gifts, and gave only \$5 as *mas kahwin*. The bride was given away by her younger brother.

In the two cases of *mixed Indian-Malay* marriages, there was a substantial payment by the groom. Again, both brides were spinsters. The Indian groom gave his Malay bride \$500 as marriage expenses, and as *mas kahwin* a pair of earrings costing \$101; while the Malay groom gave his Indian bride $501 as marriage expenses, gifts costing $72, and registered a *mas kahwin* of $101 as 'owing'.

It is clear from these 23 cases that it is wrong to assume that the absence of a *ta'alik* at marriage implies that the union was hastily arranged and that the bridegroom was either reluctant or impecunious. In 1961 there were 1,560 marriages registered in Singapore; 1,070 of the brides were spinsters, while 490 were either widows or divorcees (*janda*). Of the spinsters, 139 received no marriage expenses whatever; while the comparative figure for *janda* was 230. Thus, a total of 369 brides in 1961 (or 23.7 per cent of all brides) received no marriage expenses, yet nearly every one of them (98.5 per cent) had a *ta'alik* registered at her wedding.

Traditionally the cash payment of marriage expenses (as distinct from *mas kahwin* or *mahr* which may be registered as 'owing') is considered a sine qua non for a 'proper marriage' (*kahwin betul*). This payment by the bridegroom or by his kin helps to provide for the feast and other ceremonies which follow the marriage contract. The presence or absence of a *ta'alik* at the time of the contract appears to be no guide as to whether the union was or was not a 'proper marriage': of the 23 grooms who registered no *ta'alik* in 1961, only 6 paid no marriage expenses.

It is not only at the solemnization of his marriage that a Muslim husband in Singapore registers a *ta'alik* divorce. The use of a *ta'alik* is encouraged as a means of conciliation by the two kathis of the Shariah Court, as well as by the President in his attempts to effect a last minute reconcilation. Such 'conciliation *ta'alik*', as I shall call them, tend to be specific. For instance, in one case before the Court a wife sought a *ta'alik* divorce on the grounds that her husband gave her no maintenance whatever, but had taken her to live in the house of his sister, where she had to eat whatever the sister provided. She added that she felt very ashamed at being dependent upon her sister-in-law. The husband, although he did not deny the general statement made by his wife, argued that he had not left her without maintenance: she had been fed and sheltered. Eventually in December 1962 the couple agreed to the terms of a conciliation *ta'alik*, which were to be far more specific than the original non-maintenance marriage *ta'alik* (registered in the nearby State of Johore, where the couple had married in June 1959). This fresh *ta'alik* bound the husband (1) to give his wife not less than $90 p.m.; (2) to find her separate accommodation; and

(3) not to beat her cruelly (*pukul bantai*). Three weeks later the wife proved to the Court's satisfaction that her husband had not provided her with independent accommodation. The husband did not deny the allegation, and the wife was accordingly granted a *ta'alik* divorce.

There was another case of a woman who had a maintenance and injurious beating *ta'alik* registered at her marriage. She came before the Court to seek a *ta'alik* divorce, saying that her husband frequently used to get drunk on arak and then became violent and beat her.[1] The couple were reconciled with a fresh *ta'alik* which to the former two conditions added a third that if he drank arak and this was proven, his wife would succeed in her plea for a *ta'alik* divorce. (Islam strictly prohibits intoxicating drink.) Six months later the wife came into Court and alleged that her husband had broken all three conditions: (1) he had beaten her; (2) he had given her nothing that could be reasonably called maintenance (this was a polygynous marriage, both wives living under one roof harmoniously – it would appear – and the wives had between them seven children by the common husband; the petitioner stated that the man had for several months given $20 p.m. maintenance for the two wives and seven children; the defendant stated he had in fact given $30 p.m., but even $30 p.m. would not be sufficient to provide such a large household with the bare minimum required for subsistence); and (3) he had drunk arak.

The Court enquired from the husband whether he had in fact drunk arak, and it was clear from his demeanour at the hearing (as his wife was quick to point out) that he was not even on this occasion entirely sober. He stated that after a recent conjugal quarrel he had drunk arak, but only a little. The Court found it unnecessary to establish that the other two conditions of the *ta'alik* had been broken. It ruled that since the husband had himself admitted he had drunk arak, the wife's case was proven and a *ta'alik* divorce would be accordingly recorded. Neither party could pay the fee required to register the divorce, and the President of the Court agreed to waive it.[2]

In yet another case which came before the Court in 1961, the couple (Indians) had married in 1947, the husband giving marriage

[1] See below, p. 71.

[2] There were only two cases in 1961 when the President consented to waive the registration fee.

expenses of $500 and registering a *mas kahwin* of $251 as 'owing', but no *ta'alik*. The union was stormy, there were violent quarrels, and the then Chief Kathi of Singapore eventually succeeded in June 1960 in effecting a reconciliation. In that month the husband bound himself to a *ta'alik* with four clauses, stating that if he broke any of these, and his wife established the fact that he had done so, a one-*talak* divorce would ensue. These were the stipulations:

(1) He would not beat her.

(2) He would allow her without hindrance to give cookery lessons in the conjugal home.

(3) He would allow her to go to English classes in the evening.

(4) He would not rent out any room in the matrimonial home.

A year later the wife came before the Court to seek a *ta'alik* divorce on the grounds that (1) her husband had constantly and harmfully beaten her (*selalu pukul bantai*) since the registration of the *ta'alik*; (2) he had given her no maintenance; (3) he was excessively jealous; (4) he had a Chinese mistress, with whom she had frequently seen him (and she produced photographs showing her husband and the Chinese woman together); (5) he rented out a room in the matrimonial home to a Chinese hairdresser, and an endless stream of people came in and out of the house.

The husband defended the action, and it was necessary for him to show that his wife's allegations only in respect of the *ta'alik* clauses were unsubstantiated. Thus he (*a*) denied beating her; and (*b*) although he had to agree that he did rent out a room, he contended that she had given her consent to this. The case was adjourned, and the wife was then able to establish to the satisfaction of the Court that her husband had harmfully beaten her on several occasions. The Court accordingly found that since a clause of the *ta'alik* had been infringed a one-*talak* divorce ensued, and duly registered the divorce. It further ordered the husband to pay:

(1) the *mas kahwin* of $251 which he still owed;
(2) a consolatory gift (*matta'ah*) of $15;[1]
(3) *iddah* maintenance of $33 p.m. for 3 months;
(4) maintenance of $20 p.m. for a child in the wife's custody;
(5) the fee for the divorce registration and one copy for the wife, $22.

[1] See above, p. 30.

The same day he paid into Court $341, of which $53 were the first monthly payments in respect of the wife's *iddah* maintenance and the child's maintenance, and $266 the payment of the *mas kahwin* he still owed her, and the consolatory gift. In addition, he paid $22 to the Registry.

Soon after the Shariah Court had been constituted many Singapore Muslims were of the opinion that the entries in the Marriage Registers (i.e. the marriage certificates) should have a *ta'alik* clause printed as a reminder to kathis to ask the bridegroom whether he was willing to utter a *ta'alik*. The matter was discussed by the Muslim Advisory Board; those who argued for the printed *ta'alik* stated that the kathi – if the groom objected – could cross out the *ta'alik*; but that if the groom agreed, the kathi would only have to fill in the names of the parties and would be spared the laborious process of writing out a *ta'alik* in longhand. Further, printed *ta'alik* were no innovation among Malayan Muslims, for they existed in the Malay States. The printed *ta'alik* placed before the Singapore Muslim Advisory Board, however, was not limited to the usual non-maintenance and harmful beating clauses common both in printed *ta'alik* in the Federation and in *ta'alik* registered in longhand by Singapore kathis. In addition to these two stipulations it included a clause by which the husband allowed the wife he was now marrying to claim a divorce if he took another wife (i.e. if he entered into another, polygynous, union).[1] In *ta'alik* printed in some Malay States, e.g. in Kelantan, the non-maintenance and

[1] Imam Nawawi in *Minhaj et Talibin*, p. 308, states that such a condition is unlawful. In India, however, it has been held to be lawful: see R. B. Sethi, *Muslim Marriage and Dissolution*, second edition, Allahabad, 1961, p. 198. With reference to Singapore, see E. N. Taylor, 'Mohammedan Divorce by Khula', *Journal of the Royal Asiatic Society, Malayan Branch*, vol. XXI, Part II, 1948. A. K. Nazmul Karim in his contribution 'Changing patterns of an East Pakistan Family' in Barbara E. Ward (ed.), *Women in the New Asia, The changing roles of men and women in South and South-East Asia*, Paris, 1963, quotes the stipulations in the marriage contract of his parents. He says that the Deed was registered in Feni (in what is now East Pakistan) in 1899. His father bound himself to abide by several conditions, two of which read (p. 314):

'*Condition* 7. I shall not marry a second time without your permission, nor keep any concubine. If I do so, they will be considered as divorced, once, twice, thrice, i.e. finally. Children born of them will not be entitled to inherit my property. *Condition* 8. God forbid, if I become mad, untraced, imprisoned or impotent or fail to perform my matrimonial obligations for a period of one year, or if there persists ill-feeling between you and me, or if I am otherwise considered unsuitable by you, you will be able to divorce me once, twice, thrice, i.e. finally (by virtue

injurious beating clauses are printed, and there are in addition several blank lines which may be used to insert additional clauses. Moreover, there is nothing to stop a kathi, at the request of the bridegroom, from deleting any or all of the printed clauses. Indeed, many kathis do so.

Towards the end of 1959 in Singapore, when the matter was still under discussion by the Muslim Advisory Board, the then President of the Shariah Court ordered the *ta'alik* to be printed, and distributed the forms to Singapore kathis. The kathis registered marriages on these forms, but in all the entries containing printed *ta'alik* which I saw in the bound registers kept in the offices of the Shariah Court, the kathis had crossed out the polygyny clause. The maintenance clause in the printed *ta'alik* stated, 'If I . . . *bin* . . . do not give sufficient maintenance (*nafkah yang chukup*) to my wife . . . *binte* . . . for a period of three months or more . . .'; some kathis crossed out the whole of the printed *ta'alik* and wrote in longhand a non-maintenance clause similar to the above, except that the word 'sufficient' was omitted. The printed *ta'alik* also stated that if the husband threw his wife out ('*Jika saya . . . halau akan dia*') and the Court found this proven, the wife would be entitled to seek a one-*talak* divorce. Singapore kathis also struck out this clause.

When it became generally known that marriage forms containing the *ta'alik* still under discussion by the Board had been printed, distributed to, and used by, Singapore kathis, a storm broke. *The Straits Times* of 9 January 1960 carried the following headlines:

> 'UNAUTHORIZED' CLAUSE IS FOUND. MARRIAGE LAW SHOCK FOR MUSLIMS. PRESIDENT OF THE SHARIAH COURT REPLACED

The newspaper stated that the President (who, as we know, is also the Registrar of Muslim Marriages and Divorces) who had ordered

of the delegated power with which I hereby empower you) whenever you wish or wherever you may be.

The bond of matrimony between you and me will thereupon stand dissolved, and you will be free to choose another husband. I shall no longer be entitled to demand any matrimonial duty from you.'

Professor Nazmul Karim comments (p. 313): '. . . the husband has to accept certain self-imposed conditions in the marriage deed or contract. He remains honour bound to respect those conditions (although they may not be always legally valid). These conditions also reflect the social status which a woman enjoys.'

the printing of these forms was no longer in office. His appointment, which was a temporary one, had been terminated, and since the beginning of the month of January his Deputy had been acting as President.

Ten days later, on 19 January 1960, *The Straits Times* printed a long letter written by the former President. In it he stated:

> The 'unauthorized' clause was a 'ta'lik' or special condition of marriage printed in the new Muslim marriage certificate thus: 'Should I . . . (the husband) fail to maintain my wife sufficiently for three consecutive months or more, or beat her . . . or marry another wife, or drive her out of the house, and should she lose her patience to the extent of lodging a complaint to the Shariah Court and claiming for a divorce, the court shall, on her claim being proved, award her a 'ta'lik' divorce'.
>
> In the past this 'ta'lik' was not printed in the marriage certificate. It was left to the Kathis themselves to write down in their own handwriting. Sometimes it was not properly written and sometimes some of the terms or clauses were inadvertently omitted.
>
> Thus by having it ready printed, it acts not only as a reminder to the kathis and simplifies their task, but serves as a warning to husbands not to ill-treat their wives as they please.
>
> Again, should the 'ta'lik' be omitted, the wife might not be awarded a divorce, but because she has been very severely ill-treated she might refuse to return to her husband under any circumstances. Thus 'nushuz' might be pronounced against her, i.e. she could not obtain a divorce and yet could not get any maintenance from her husband, besides committing a major sin. And this 'nushuz' might last for life.
>
> It has been the practice for many years in the Federation, Indonesia and other progressive Muslim countries, to have the 'ta'lik' printed on marriage certificates.
>
> One of the causes of the high rate of divorce among Muslims here is the abuse of polygamy, bringing about a very undesirable social condition.
>
> Polygamy is permitted in Islam only under certain conditions – as it is sometimes beneficial – but irresponsible and uncontrolled polygamy is certainly contrary to the teaching of Islam. It is a sin.
>
> . . . The Advocate-General stated that the printed 'ta'lik' was not provided for in the Muslim Marriage and Divorce Rules. I have shown that the ready printed 'ta'lik' has many advantages. Therefore the rules should be revised as early as possible to include the above clauses. . . .

A few days later, the Select Committee on the Muslims

(Amendment) Bill received a letter[1] written by a watchman at a Malay Girls' School, in which the writer said that he was responding to the invitation extended to the public to make representations to the Committee. Among several other matters, he raised the question of the printed *ta'alik*.

> . . . the State Advocate-General stated that the Singapore Goverment had withdrawn all documents for the registration of marriage which have written on them the words of the *Taalik* . . . I am not satisfied; the demand is very erroneous. . . . I would suggest that the withdrawal be revoked and that the words of the *Taalik* be reinstated, so that it would be convenient for the Kathis without wasting time at the house of the party or at the Kathis' house and at the Shariah Court.

The writer of the letter attended two meetings of the Select Committee and was examined about several matters he had raised in his letter. The Chairman told him[2] that the question of a printed *ta'alik* 'is a matter which is covered by the Rules which are made under the Ordinance. This select Committee is not looking into the Rules.'

Up to July 1963 there was no printed *ta'alik* in the marriage forms, and none appeared to be under active consideration.

Husbands eager for a reconciliation with their estranged wives are not always willing to bind themselves by *ta'alik*. They sometimes, however, agree to make a verbal or a written promise to abide by certain stipulations, and the wife may then consent to resume cohabitation. If the husband breaks his promise the marriage persists in law.

An Indian couple married in Singapore in 1958 when they were both about forty years old. The woman was a widow with two children. There was no *ta'alik* at marriage. In October 1960 the wife came to the Shariah Court and reported to the Social Worker that her husband beat her savagely and gave her practically no maintenance. The husband was called for an interview, and at first adopted a threatening attitude towards his wife. Later he promised verbally to treat her well, and she withdrew her complaint. But she returned in May 1961 to say that her husband had beaten her again, that she went in fear of her life, and that she sought the protection of the Court. She was admitted on that very

[1] Dated 2 February 1960, and printed in the *Report of the Select Committee* (L.A. 14 of 1960).

[2] *Ibid.*, p. 144.

day to the Muslim Women Welfare Home (run by the Social Welfare Department of the Singapore Government) and took out a divorce summons against her husband, alleging non-maintenance over a long period (which, if proven, might result in a *fasah* decree).

The husband was a self-confessed thug, and he admitted when he came to see the Court Social Worker that he had gone to the home of his wife's sister and smashed up some furniture there, in retaliation for his wife's divorce plea and the support given her by her sister. At the first hearing in Court, in June 1961, the wife admitted that her husband had last beaten her in October 1960, and that after she had withdrawn her complaint and they had become reconciled he had not beaten her again. But, she added, he had frequently threatened to beat her.[1] She had received practically no maintenance from him since early in their marriage, and moreover he had taken her jewelry and that of her children by her earlier union, and pawned it. In the course of a lengthy cross-examination he denied these charges.

The Court then appointed two *hakam* (arbitrators), one on behalf of the husband, and one on behalf of the wife. On their recommendation the husband agreed on 1 September 1961 to a reconciliation on the basis of a *ta'alik*, containing the following four clauses, which he duly uttered:

'(1) I shall give my wife $90 per month maintenance.
(2) I shall not go to her elder sister's house.
(3) I shall never gamble.
(4) I shall never beat my wife.

If I should fail to fulfil any one of the four stipulations, my wife upon proof of it may be divorced by one *talak*.' This was duly recorded, and the husband signed the *ta'alik*.

At a hearing in Court on 16 January 1962 the wife stated that since 1 September 1961 her husband had given her only $45, once, and she now sought that a *ta'alik* divorce be proven and registered. The husband admitted that he had given only $45 since 1 September, but pleaded that this was because he was now unemployed. He had gone to seek help from the Public Assistance

[1] The man was obviously given to uttering such threats, for he threatened the Court Social Worker with violence, and he also repeated this threat to the Social Welfare officer in charge of the Home where his wife had been admitted, and the Police were duly informed.

Section of the Social Welfare Department and explained he needed a minimum of $90 p.m. to save his marriage, but he stated that Social Welfare officials had assured him that if he told the Shariah Court he was unemployed, the *ta'alik* would not be proven, 'because Muslim law would not allow such a *ta'alik* to be implemented in respect of an unemployed husband'.

The wife replied that she had, however, other grounds for seeking a *ta'alik* divorce proven, namely that, firstly, he had gone to her elder sister's house on six occasions since registering the *ta'alik* and created a disturbance. He denied this, admitting only that he had gone to visit a friend who was a neighbour of the elder sister; he persisted in this statement, even after his wife had sworn that he had actually entered her sister's house. Secondly, she added, he had gambled on at least two occasions since 1 September, and she gave the addresses of the houses where the alleged gambling had taken place.

The Court found that since the husband himself had freely acknowledged that he gave his wife only $45 in all the months since 1 September 1961, whereas he had promised $90 per month in the *ta'alik* he had registered on that day, it was proven on the husband's own admission that he had failed to keep one of the conditions of the *ta'alik* (*telah melanggar satu daripada ta'aliknya dengan pengakuan sendiri*). A *ta'alik* divorce was accordingly registered. There is, of course, no record in the Shariah Court of whether the husband went to seek redress from the Social Welfare official who had, according to his allegations, so grievously misdirected him.

PROCEDURE TO OBTAIN THE REGISTRATION OF A TA'ALIK DIVORCE

Before the establishment of the Shariah Court a Muslim woman could apply to any kathi in Singapore to register a *ta'alik* divorce, and before he consented he had to satisfy himself that her plea was a valid one. It is alleged that some kathis were less stringent than others in their requirements as to the degree of proof necessary, but that on the other hand they insisted upon an advance payment of a large sum of money 'to conduct the necessary enquiries'.

Since the establishment of the Shariah Court in November 1958, no Singapore kathi may register a *ta'alik* divorce, or indeed any divorce other than one by mutual consent of the spouses. Only the Shariah Court, after a hearing, may effect such registration. The complainant wife is first seen by one of the two Court kathis, and is then referred to the summons clerk. Upon payment of the prescribed fee,[1] a date is fixed for the hearing. If the husband resides in a State in the Federation and his address is known to the wife, the Chief Kathi of that State is requested by the Shariah Court to serve the summons on the husband. In a great number of *ta'alik* pleas, however, the man is said to have disappeared without trace. If the wife declares that she does not know his present whereabouts, a notice is inserted in a Malay newspaper (at her expense) by a Court official stating that . . . *bin* . . . is to attend at the Shariah Court at such an hour on such a date, when there will be a hearing of a plea for divorce by his petitioner wife . . . *binte* . . ., and that if he fails to appear the Court may proceed with the case in his absence.

There were at least two cases in 1962 of husbands who appeared in Court as a result of such an advertisement. If the husband chooses to contest his wife's *ta'alik* divorce petition, the President first hears her sworn evidence, and asks the husband whether he wishes to cross-examine her on it. Later the husband gives his own sworn evidence and the wife in turn may, if she chooses, cross-examine him. If the President considers that the evidence before the Court is not conclusive, and either spouse offers to substantiate his or her plea by producing witnesses, the latter are heard. (This may require the fixing of another hearing.) If the witnesses' evidence is inconclusive, and the wife persists in her plea, i.e. refuses the Court's repeated attempts at conciliation;[2] and if the husband, on his part, refuses to divorce her of his own free will, e.g. by uttering and registering the *talak* formula, the Court may adjourn the case for two or three months for tempers to cool. The hope is that eventually either the woman will agree to a reconciliation or else the husband will consent to utter and register an ordinary repudiation. There have been cases, however, where the deadlock has persisted, and as a last resort the couple submitted to their case being placed before arbitrators (*hakam*). Recently, it has

[1] See above, p. 23.

[2] E.g., by asking the wife whether she would agree to a reconciliation on the basis of a new, more specific and stringent *ta'alik* such as in the case mentioned above.

been the practice for one of the two Court kathis to be appointed as arbitrator for the husband, and the other for the wife; after the spouses sign an undertaking to abide by their decision, the President of the Court fixes a date and hour at which the decision will be made known in Court.

In the majority of such cases, the *hakam* decide that the wife may be divorced by 'redeeming' herself from the marriage, by *khula*. It is thus that some of the divorces registered as *khula* by order of the Shariah Court President originated as *ta'alik* summonses. For if a couple agree to divorce by *khula* in the first place, they need not come into Court at all, since any Singapore kathi is empowered to register a *khula* divorce. However, in cases where the couple agree to register a divorce by *khula* but disagree about the material consideration the wife must pay to redeem herself from the marriage, the woman often issues a summons pleading either for a *ta'alik* or (if this is inapplicable) for a *fasah* decree. She will do so, however, only after one of the Court kathis has attempted – but failed – to patch up the marriage; and after he has failed again to persuade the couple to agree to an amicable divorce.

Similarly, some of the divorces registered by the Shariah Court as *talak* divorces (i.e. when the husband has apparently uttered a repudiation formula at his own wish) arise from cases where the wife had originally issued a summons pleading for a *ta'alik* divorce to be registered, but before (or after) she had proceeded to give evidence the husband had of his own free will consented to divorce her, and uttered a repudiation in Court. In other cases, the husband hotly contested his wife's *ta'alik* petition, and produced evidence to show that he was not guilty of contravening a *ta'alik* clause; but when faced with her determination not to resume cohabitation, even after her plea failed in Court, he graciously consented to utter a *talak* and thus release her. In 1961 there were two cases of *talak* divorces registered by the Court which had originated with a wife's *ta'alik* summons; in 1962 there were thirteen such cases.

In many *ta'alik* divorce hearings the husband is absent either because, although he has received the summons, he does not choose to appear; or, when his address is not known to the wife, because he has not seen (or if he has seen, has ignored) the notice in the newspaper requiring him to appear at the hearing. In such a case the wife must first give her own sworn evidence in support of her plea; and then produce two male adult Muslim witnesses who come into Court later, one by one, to give evidence and answer the Court's questions about their evidence. The witnesses are asked by the President whether they have ever quarrelled with the husband, for they must not be prejudiced against him by personal enmity.[1] I was present in 1963 at many such hearings. I now give a summary of cases which illustrate the various issues to be settled before a *ta'alik* plea is granted or dismissed.

The names I mention here are not the names given in Court. In every case the wife was a Malay, and in every case there had been a three-months non-maintenance *ta'alik* uttered at the time of the marriage contract.

I. February 1963. *Asmah* was sworn in, and cautioned that if she told lies in the witness-box, and the Court came to know of it, she might be punished. If the Court did not find out, God certainly would know, and He would punish her – if not immediately, certainly at some time in the future. Finally she was warned in simple language that hearsay evidence was inadmissible: 'You can only say things which you yourself know; not what other people have talked to you about, because this cannot be taken into account.'

Her husband was not in Court. Notice of the hearing had been served on him through a Malay newspaper. She handed her marriage certificate to the Court. (She had forgotten to bring it when her case came up for hearing, and the Court had been adjourned for an hour to enable her to fetch it.) The President verified that the information relating to date of marriage, and to payments made by the bridegroom, was as stated in the certificate before him. She confirmed that she had been a *janda* when she had married him in 1957; that her groom had made no payment whatever as 'marriage expenses' (*belanja kahwin*), had given her no marriage gifts; and that the *mas kahwin* of $22.50 was not paid at marriage. The *mas kahwin*, moreover, had not been paid at a later date. The President remarked that her husband's name was very unusual, and asked her whether she knew anything of the man's family or place of origin; she replied that he was of the Malay 'race' (*bangsa Melayu*), and that she did not know whether

[1] See above, p. 36.

he came from Indonesia or elsewhere. The President commented that she had obviously married after only a casual encounter, and that since there had been no marriage payments it was clear that this had been a *suka sama suka* match.[1] Asmah did not deny this.

Continuing her evidence, Asmah said that within a month or so of marriage she suspected she was pregnant. A few weeks later, for no reason she could think of, her husband left one morning and did not return home for some days. He knew she was pregnant. She went to look for him at the food stall where he worked, and asked him why he had abandoned her, and he returned home that evening. But the next day he left, never to return. In reply to the Court's questions, she said she took no steps to trace him; she had no money to conduct elaborate searches. She had delayed for more than four years her application for a *ta'alik* decree because she had no money to institute proceedings. Her husband had sent her 'not a single cent' since he had deserted her, for neither her nor their child now four years old. She persisted in her story that she had had no quarrel or argument with her husband before he had deserted her; she had been neither disobedient to his lawful commands ('for instance, did he ever order you to pray, and you refused?' enquired the President, to which she replied firmly, 'Never!'), nor had she been a recalcitrant wife (e.g. unreasonably refusing to live with him in the conjugal home). She was further asked whether her husband had left behind any material possessions such as clothes in good condition, or a bicycle (which she might have sold in order to buy food), and said that he had not.

Her first witness was called and sworn in. He had been a witness at the marriage, stated that he had known Asmah since she was a child, and lived near her house. He knew she had been deserted for four years, he often visited her in the home she shared with her elder sister, and had never seen her husband there during that period. Moreover, the home was a poor one; he had never seen a sign of her husband's possessions, and from her style of living it was obvious that she was without means. He concluded from all this that she had never received an allowance from her absent husband. He could not, however, be certain that the man had never sent money by post, for he was not in the petitioner's home on every occasion the postman called.

The second witness was then called and sworn in. He too had

[1] See above, p. 17.

known the wife since childhood, he lived near her home, and confirmed that the husband had not been seen for four years. He had made some effort to trace him, however, having gone to the district where the man used to work, but had failed to find him. He could not state categorically that the husband had never sent money by post; he had no means of knowing this.

The President then considered the evidence before him, which he had taken down in longhand in his record-book. He commented that the witnesses' evidence was not fully conclusive. Eventually he told Asmah to listen carefully to what he was about to say, and he read to her a summary of the facts that she had given in her evidence. She confirmed that the summary was indeed correct, and agreed to swear a solemn oath that it was. She then stood up and swore, repeating word for word after the President:

> In the name of Almighty God, in the name of Almighty God, in the name of Almighty God (*Wallahi al Azhim*), I have been abandoned by my husband without maintenance for the past four years, although I was neither disobedient nor recalcitrant (*saya tidak ada ingkar atau nushuz pada prentah-nya*). He left behind no material possessions which I could have sold to provide maintenance for myself.

The President then announced that he found, taking into account the wife's evidence and her swearing of a 'special oath' (*sumpah khas*) that the husband had contravened the *ta'alik* which he had uttered on the day of the marriage, and that accordingly the wife was entitled to a one-*talak* divorce, which the Court duly ordered to be registered. The court then rose.

II. The petition of *Rabiah* was also heard in February 1963. Again, notice of the hearing had been inserted in a Malay newspaper. She said she was eighteen years old, and confirmed the entries in her marriage certificate that she had been married the previous June, in 1962. This had also been a *suka sama suka* marriage, although Rabiah had at least been paid the $22.50 *mas kahwin* in cash. But she had received neither marriage expenses nor gifts. In her sworn evidence she stated that her husband had told her before they married that he had a job, but after their marriage it was evident he was unemployed. They lived with her mother. She herself had some savings, for she used to work as a domestic servant, and she it was who gave her husband pocket-money for cigarettes, snacks, etc. Then one day, about three months after their marriage, he just disappeared. He said nothing to her before he left, there had been no quarrel or argument, he left no address, sent no letter or news. He just disappeared without trace, and left no clothes or other material possessions behind. The Court questioned her closely about the circumstances of the man's desertion: if he had had it so good, if he was in a home where he had shelter, food, and pocket-money and did not go out to work, and there were neither quarrels nor arguments, why did she think he deserted her? She said repeatedly, 'I don't know'. The President asked her what she knew of the man's background and family, and she replied that he was a Malay, and that he had told her he was from Kuala Lumpur. The President commented that she had obviously married a man '*dari tengah jalan*' (lit. 'from the middle of the street', i.e. after a casual encounter), that husbands should be carefully selected, and that as a result of her rashness she might well find herself a *janda* after less than one year as a married woman. She smiled at that – for indeed her whole purpose in coming to Court was to obtain a decree which would make her officially a divorcee. The President rebuked her for smiling, saying this was no laughing matter, it was a matter of great concern, and the Court frowned upon the break-up of marriages. He added that since she had married only at the end of the previous June, and claimed that her husband had left her in September, she seemed in a great hurry to dissolve the union. Would she not consider waiting, in case her husband returned to her? She replied that she did not want to wait any longer, for there was no prospect of her husband returning, since he had told her that he wished to divorce her.

President: 'Then there was a quarrel?'

Rabiah: 'No, no quarrel, just talk, he used to like to say such things.'

Her first witness was called, and sworn in. He said that he was the uncle (*pa' saudara*) of the petitioner, whom he had known from her childhood. He gave evidence that the husband had been unemployed, and had left no material possessions. Asked by the Court whether he knew anything of the circumstances of the desertion, he replied that he only knew that about a month after the marriage the husband had taken the wife to Malacca to stay at his elder brother's house, and that a few days later the wife returned alone to Singapore, and the husband had not joined her.

Invited, as usual, to question her witness, the wife replied that she had no questions to put to him. The President asked if the evidence he had given was true, and she said it was. She was silent, however, when asked why she had made no mention of the Malacca journey during her evidence. The President insisted: 'Did you have a quarrel in Malacca before you left?'

Rabiah: 'No, there was no quarrel. He told me to return to Singapore and that he would join me later. He took me to the bus stop, and when I got on the bus, I asked him to get in too and return to Singapore with me, but he declined and assured me that he would join me later.'

The second witness was called. His evidence confirmed that of the earlier witness; he also mentioned spontaneously the Malacca journey; and again the wife said that she had no questions to put to the witness.

The President adjourned the Court for twenty-five minutes. When the hearing was resumed, he read his verdict. The Court was not satisfied with the evidence presented in respect of the contravention of the maintenance *ta'alik*; it was further not satisfied that serious attempts had been made to trace the husband and serve a summons upon him, in order that he might defend the petition if he wished to do so. Accordingly the Court made no Order in this case. The Court then rose.

I was told later by a Court official that the wife could come again within a few months, show proof that she had attempted to trace her husband, and present a fresh petition. Or, of course, she might find it simpler to go to a Malay State where a *ta'alik* divorce might be granted by a kathi without very strict enquiries.

III. *Mariam*'s petition was heard in March 1963. Her husband was not present at the hearing, although the summons had been served on him. The process-server was called and gave sworn evidence that he had served the summons upon the husband in person. The wife then went into the witness-box and was sworn in. She said she was now 17 years old, and had married in June 1960. There was one child of the union. She declared that her husband was rarely in regular employment. For the first two months after their wedding he had had a job, and had given her an adequate sum for her maintenance. In the third month he said he had lost his job and had no money, and he took her to live with his parents; they lived with his parents for four months. She was then six months pregnant, and with her husband's consent her mother came to fetch her and she went to stay in her mother's home. Her husband did not join her then, but when the child was about six months old he came to live at her mother's home, and stayed for six months. For the first three months of that period he gave her \$30 a month for their food and other domestic expenses, but in subsequent months he gave nothing at all. In December 1962 they had a quarrel, he hit and wounded her, and she reported the matter to a police station. Later he asked her whether she liked him, '*Ada suka sama saya?*', and she had replied that she did not. So he told her, 'Well then, go to the Court'. She came to the Court, and was seen by a kathi. The latter attempted a reconciliation without success, because her husband did not appear before the kathi when requested to do so, or, as far as she knew, at any later date.

When the President asked her whether she was now willing to return to her husband she declared firmly that she was not. Her first witness was called. He was sworn in, and said that he knew the couple well; the husband was lazy and irresponsible, and would not listen to his friends when they explained to him that now he was a married man he had duties towards his wife and child and must work regularly to support them. The President asked the witness how it was that a young girl was allowed by her parents to marry a man with a reputation for laziness and irresponsibility. The witness replied that the girl had no father, and the young couple had *suka sama suka*. The President commented on the evils of this type of union, and the witness dutifully agreed, adding that today's youth wanted to be 'modern'.[1] The witness further confirmed that the husband had left no material property in the conjugal home (i.e. in his wife's mother's home), and stated that the man had so few possessions that all of them including his clothes could be packed into a bundle 'that big' – and with his two hands he made a gesture such as would encompass a football.

The evidence of the second witness closely confirmed that of the first witness. Again the President enquired how it was that a young girl was given in marriage to such a lazy and irresponsible man, '*Siapa kasi kahwin?*' (who allowed this match? i.e. whose

[1] The witness, who said he was 29 years old, spoke Malay, and used the English word 'modern', which is often used in Malay in the same sense as in English.

responsibility was it?). At this there was a loud groan from the back of the Court, where the girl's mother sat with two other women. The witness replied, '*suka sama suka*'. The President asked further, 'Do you know of any reason why the husband left the home in which he lived with his wife?' The witness replied, 'Perhaps because he felt ashamed that he could not support her'.

The President adjourned the Court for a few minutes. When the hearing was resumed, he read the Court Order. The Court was satisfied with the wife's evidence and that of two knowledgeable witnesses that the husband had contravened the terms of the *ta'alik* he had uttered at their marriage, i.e. he had failed to maintain his wife for three months and more, and a *ta'alik* divorce was accordingly recorded. As the President rose he told the wife, 'You have a three months' *iddah*; don't go out and about' ('*Awak ada tiga bulan iddah; jangan keluar jalan jalan*').[1]

IV. *Habsah*'s case, which was heard in April 1963, illustrates some of the difficulties experienced by the Shariah Court in dealing with some illiterate and unsophisticated wives, who are obviously greatly puzzled by Court procedure.

Habsah was a middle-aged woman, and looked slightly apprehensive. She was sworn in and gave the following evidence. She had married in January 1942; her husband was a Malacca man, and she was a Singaporean. She had been deserted by her husband for six years now, and he had sent her no maintenance whatever since.

President: 'What year was it then, the year your husband deserted you?'

Habsah: 'I don't know, I never went to school.'

President: 'Do you know what year we are in now?'

Habsah: 'No, I don't know.'

President: 'Are we in the year '60, or '61, or '62, or '63, or '64?'

Habsah: ''63.'

President: 'Well then, if we are now in the year '63, and you say your husband left you six years ago, what year was it he left you?' Habsah looked blank, and he patiently advised her, 'You can subtract, count back, we are now '63, count back six years.'

Habsah: 'I never went to school.'

[1] N. E. Baillie, in *A Digest of Moohummadan Law*, vol. 1, p. 360, states: 'When a woman is in *iddut* for a valid marriage, and is absolutely free, adult, sane, and a *Mooslim*, and has freedom of choice, she ought not to go out by night or by day, whether the repudiation were triple, irrevocable or revocable.'

The President gave up, suggested to her that the year was probably 1957, and she promptly agreed. She proceeded to say that her husband was a 'soldier'. They had no quarrel, and one day he just left home and did not return. She did not know why he went, could think of no cause. She had not looked for him because she had not known where to look; she did not know what kind of soldier he was, she just knew he was a soldier. Her husband had sent her no letter, and no money, since his desertion. He had left no possessions she could have sold to buy food. The President enquired ,'No sewing-machine, no motor-cycle?'. Shaking her head, she said, 'No'.

Before calling the first witness the President made the usual formal attempt at persuading the wife not to proceed with the divorce petition. 'Are you sure you want to proceed with your case, you do not want to wait a little longer, have more patience?' She firmly replied, 'No'.

The first witness said that he had known Habsah for fifteen years, and lived close to her house. He knew that her husband had deserted her twelve to thirteen years ago, he did not remember the exact year, but believed it was about 1950. He could not say categorically that the husband never sent money by post, or that he left no material possessions before he deserted, but to judge from Habsah's style of living and home it seemed unlikely that she was in receipt of funds.

Habsah, invited to question her witness, said she had no questions to put to him.

President: 'But you must ask him at least one question. He has said that your husband deserted you twelve to thirteen years ago, while you said it was only six years ago.'

Habsah: 'Yes, my husband did desert me about twelve years ago, but then he returned home for a short while. He left me again, and since his last desertion six years ago he has not returned.'

President: 'Then you must put the question formally to the witness, "Do you not know that . . ."'

After a little coaxing, Hasbah did so.

The second witness confirmed the wife's evidence, and in answer to the question about material possessions the husband might have left behind, said 'The only things he left were worn clothes'. He added that he had attempted, but failed, to trace the man, who had no known relatives in Singapore.

The President told Habsah that her witnesses' evidence was not fully conclusive, and inquired whether she was willing to swear a special oath, of which he would now read the words. He proceeded to read the same oath which he had administered in earlier, similar, circumstances,[1] varying the formula only as to the period of non-maintenance, in this case 'about six years' (*kira kira enam tahun*). She consented to swear to this, and repeated the words after him.

The President ordered the registration of a *ta'alik* (one-*talak*) divorce. He added, 'You have an *iddah* of three months. Do not go out of the house if it is not necessary for you to do so (*jangan keluar rumah kalau tidak perlu*)'.

INTERPRETATION OF THE NON-MAINTENANCE TA'ALIK

We must now summarise and clarify the manner in which the Court interprets the non-maintenance *ta'alik*.

(1) There must be a minimum *continuous* period of three months (or any other minimum period specified by the *ta'alik*) during which the husband provides for his wife nothing which could reasonably be called maintenance.

(2) It is immaterial to the wife's *ta'alik* petition whether she has in fact suffered any hardship during that period. She might have been adequately maintained out of her own capital or her own earnings, or had assistance from her own kinsmen. It does not exonerate her husband, who is bound by the terms of the *ta'alik* to provide her with maintenance, and must do so either himself or through his agents.

(3) Unemployment, or sickness, or any other circumstance within or beyond the control of the husband, is no valid excuse for contravening the non-maintenance clause in the *ta'alik* he has uttered – as we saw in the case of the Indian couple above.[2]

However, if the husband has not provided his wife with maintenance over the period specified by the *ta'alik*, and she has not petitioned for a decree but endured the situation, and later he has been able to maintain her and she has continued cohabitation, she cannot invoke the *ta'alik* to seek a decree. For in a non-maintenance *ta'alik* the man as a general rule states (or if he does not do so, is taken to mean) that if he fails to maintain his wife 'over a period

[1] See p. 58 above. [2] pp. 51 ff.

of three months or longer and she can endure it no longer and goes before a kathi or the Shariah Court and her claim is proven . . .' Thus if the wife has not lodged a plea in the course of a period of non-maintenance or immediately after such a period, she is deemed to have condoned the offence and to have been able to endure it. However, this does not bar her, if her husband at a later period is again guilty of non-maintenance over the minimum period stated in the *ta'alik*, from instituting proceedings. The fact that she has condoned the offence once does not mean she is bound to condone it again. On the contrary, the Court takes into account the fact that the wife has already shown commendable patience, and is not seeking to dissolve her union at the first opportunity.

(4) Singapore *ta'alik* do not as a rule explicitly state that the wife who has been undutiful, or disobedient, or recalcitrant, is barred from seeking a *ta'alik* decree. Nevertheless the Shariah Court has taken such a proviso to be implicit in the general condition of a *ta'alik*. A wife guilty of adultery, or of contravening a lawful command of her husband, or of having deserted her husband without proper cause, is not entitled to plead for a *ta'alik* decree; or if she does so plead and the Court establishes or suspects strongly that her behaviour was conducive to her plight, her petition may be rejected.

What is a Muslim husband's lawful command? All Muslim jurists agree that a man who orders his wife to pray, or not to eat pork, is issuing a lawful command. Further, I was informed by the President of the Shariah Court that, according to a strict interpretation of Shafi'i law, a Muslim wife may not leave the conjugal home without her husband's permission unless she is in peril of her life – e.g. if the roof is about to collapse on her head.[1] Singapore Malay women, however, have customarily enjoyed a much greater degree of freedom than many of their Muslim sisters in other lands (e.g. Arabia, or Middle Eastern countries), and indeed than Indian Muslim women in Singapore itself.[2] They consider it unbearably oppressive if their husbands order them to remain indoors. One woman did not deny in Court her husband's allegation that when he had rebuked her for going out without his prior

[1] Cf. *Minhaj et Talibin*, p. 386: 'Leaving the conjugal domicile without first asking permission also contitutes a fact incompatible with a wife's submission to marital authority, unless the house is threatening to fall down.'

[2] See my *Malay Kinship*, p. 12.

consent she had told him, 'Wherever I choose to go, I can go (*kemana saya suka pergi saya boleh pergi*)'. They normally go out shopping, and so long as they do not indulge in provocative behaviour or conversation with other men, and do not associate with women of loose morals, while out on an errand, they consider themselves blameless. Moreover, they deem it a solemn duty to pay, on the day of the burial, a visit of condolence to the bereaved household of a kinswoman or of a close friend; as Muslims are usually buried within a few hours of death, and it may not be possible to obtain one's husband's consent to go on such a visit, a Malay wife feels that in such circumstances she has a right to dispense with the consent. (In one divorce hearing the husband claimed his wife went out with other men while alleging she had been on a visit of condolence. He had more than once discovered that there had been no bereavement in the homes she had said she had been visiting.)

As we saw, the Shariah Court, in seeking to establish whether a non-maintenance *ta'alik* has been proven, enquires of the petitioner wife – especially if her husband is absent from the hearing – whether she has been disobedient or recalcitrant in the period immediately preceding that of her husband's failure to maintain her. The wife is asked '*Awak ada ingkar atau nushuz?*' ('Have you been disobedient or recalcitrant?').

In all the cases I heard in 1963 the petitioner wife was further asked by the Court, 'Did you have a quarrel before your husband deserted you?' Most wives declared that there had been no quarrel; but some admitted that there had been a quarrel because they had complained to their husbands that they had no money whatever with which to buy food and that the local shopkeeper would give no further credit. Such a quarrel is not deemed to prejudice a wife's case, for it provides further proof that she registered her proper complaint (of not being maintained) to her husband.

Further, if a wife has left the conjugal home because the landlord has evicted the household for non-payment of rent, and the husband has been unable or unwilling to provide other accommodation, and she has gone to live with her kin, she is held to be blameless. Nevertheless, Singapore Muslim women have become increasingly aware that in order not to prejudice their case in any matrimonial proceedings which might arise at a later date, they should as soon as possible establish the propriety of their action in deserting their husbands. Consequently many of them come to see one of the two kathis in the Shariah Court to report that they have left the conjugal home because their husbands have been excessively brutal (and in support of this they may show bruises or cuts, or a copy of their report to the local police station), or have ordered them out of the house, or because they have failed to provide the minimum amount of maintenance necessary for survival. At this stage a woman may not seek a *ta'alik* decree, or indeed may not be eligible for one, but she comes to report the matter to one of the two Court kathis as an act of self-justification. The Court kathi then writes to the husband to ask him to come for an interview, and if he does come, an attempt at reconciliation is made. But if he does not, the wife feels free to remain separated from him. However, if at a later stage she issues a summons for a *ta'alik* decree and her husband defends the petition, and is able to prove that his wife's statement to a Court kathi that she had been driven by him to leave the conjugal home was false, the Court will consider his argument.

Can a wife invoke the non-maintenance *ta'alik* only if she has received no food or money whatsoever from her husband or his agents during the minimum specified period? The answer, as given by Shariah Court decisions, is that whether the *ta'alik* specified 'sufficient maintenance' (*nafkah yang chukup*), or only stated 'If I give no maintenance', the clause is interpreted to mean 'a minimum amount necessary to appease hunger'. Thus, at a hearing in April 1963 a man declared that he had given his wife *some* maintenance, an average of \$7 a month over a period of the six months in respect of which she was invoking the *ta'alik* clause. The Court ruled that so small a monthly allowance could not properly be called 'maintenance' and granted the wife a *ta'alik* decree. In another case, the husband admitted that he had given his wife \$30 p.m. and that she had to pay \$15 p.m. rent out of that amount, and also feed him, herself, and their four children. Again, the monthly allowance made by the husband was deemed by the Court not to constitute maintenance.

Here it must be stated that the general non-maintenance *ta'alik* uttered and registered when a couple marry applies only to a *wife*'s right to maintenance. That is to say, if the couple later have children and the impoverished husband decides to put such children in the care of friends or relatives who take responsibility for their support, and manages to give the wife sufficient maintenance for her own minimum needs, she is unlikely to be successful in her plea for a *ta'alik* decree. On the other hand, if husband, wife, and their children live in one household and the husband makes his wife an allowance for food and rent, he cannot later plead that although the allowance was insufficient to cover rent and food for the whole household, nevertheless it was sufficient to pay for his wife's food and shelter, and that she could have refused to feed their children or her husband out of that sum.

However, where the couple have been residing with the wife's kinsmen and have paid no rent, the husband is held to have failed to comply with the maintenance *ta'alik* if he has not given her the minimum amount necessary to pay for the food they both consume; or, if he takes his meals out, for the food she herself needs to consume.

A man, as was said earlier, may not expect his wife to support herself out of her own earnings or other income. Indeed, a dutiful Muslim woman has an absolute right to be maintained by her husband, and Singapore Muslim women – whether Malay or Arab or Indian – are fully aware of this right. When they recite the grounds on which they seek a *ta'alik* decree, many wives allege in a tone of righteous indignation: 'When I complained to my husband that he gave me no money and that we could not buy even plain rice to eat [i.e. merely rice, let alone fish or vegetables, or coffee and sugar], he told me to go out to work!' I heard others state: 'He told me to make and sell cakes to pay for our maintenance, and I replied that it is a man's duty to go out to work and bring food, and that a woman's duty is only to look after the home. A woman knows only how to eat, not to provide the food. A husband has no right to order his wife to go out to work.'[1]

Nevertheless, the issue is not always as clear as may appear at first sight. At the end of April 1963 a wife came before the Court to plead for a non-maintenance *ta'alik* decree. Her case was that her husband had not been in regular employment for nine years, and that although he had now and then given her $10 or $15 per month out of his earnings as a casual gardener, this could hardly be called maintenance considering they had four children, three

[1] The 1957 Report on the Census notes, in chapter 15, on 'Economic Characteristics': 'Malaysians had the lowest percentage of persons economically active on account of the small number of females in the labour force.'

of whom went to school and needed to be decently clothed and supplied with bus fares and exercise books. She declared that she had been the main supporter of the household, for she made snacks, cakes, and fried bananas for sale, and also took in washing.

The husband rose to question her, and alleged he played the major share in earning the household's living. He declared that it was he who went to market to buy the raw ingredients, that he also often did the actual preparation or cooking of the cakes, and that he it was who hawked the articles for sale. His wife, he stated, often helped in the preparation; this was a joint enterprise, and usually a harmonious one, as befitted a loving husband and wife. The woman did not refute these statements, and the Court accordingly was unable to establish that the husband had contravened the maintenance *ta'alik*.

Finally, it is necessary to point out that even if a husband leaves material possessions, the wife is not barred from seeking a *ta'alik* decree. If she proves that she sold these possessions and maintained herself with the proceeds over a period, but that there was a further period during which she was left without maintenance, and that such a further period extended over the minimum amount of time specified in the *ta'alik*, she may rightly seek a *ta'alik* divorce.

PUKUL BANTAI (*Injurious beating*)

Next in frequency to the maintenance *ta'alik* is a *ta'alik* relating to injurious beating. This latter is a *ta'alik* of comparatively recent introduction. It occurs only very rarely in the Singapore registers of marriage in the decades before 1950. In the 1950's, however, nearly every other entry records such a *ta'alik*; moreover, it occurs as a subsidiary clause immediately following a maintenance clause. Thus:

> If [or 'Whenever'] I should leave my wife . . . *binte* . . . without maintenance for a period of three months or longer, or if I should strike her so as to cause her injury [or 'so as to bruise or wound her'], and she should be unable to endure it and plead her case before a kathi,[1] and her plea is established, a one-*talak* divorce will befall her.

The wife's name is specifically mentioned in full – e.g. Rabiah

[1] From 1959 on, the *ta'alik* usually states 'before the Shariah Court'. See above, p. 39.

binte Ali – presumably because a Muslim may have more than one wife and may have registered a *ta'alik* in respect of only one of them.

I never came across a Singapore marriage certificate[1] which registered a *ta'alik* only relating to injurious beating; in every case in the entries in the marriage registers, or individual copies of marriage certificates produced by wives petitioning for a *ta'alik* decree, if there was such a clause, it was recorded immediately following the maintenance clause. On the other hand, there are many cases where the only *ta'alik* relates to maintenance. I was told by senior Government officials in charge of Muslim affairs that in recent years Singapore kathis have been advised to suggest the insertion of an injurious beating clause in a *ta'alik* when they solemnize and register a marriage. However, as we know, they have no authority to compel a bridegroom to utter a *ta'alik*.

In March 1961 (just over a year after the uproar created by the unauthorized printing of a *ta'alik*), 85 marriages were registered in the State by eleven kathis. Eight kathis recorded in every case a maintenance and beating *ta'alik*, two recorded in every case only a maintenance clause, while one kathi who registered seven marriages during that month recorded only a maintenance *ta'alik* in six cases, and no *ta'alik* whatever in one case. This last kathi is Indian and deals largely with Indians. In December 1962 he registered nine marriages, and in every case he recorded a *ta'alik* binding the groom to both maintenance and beating clauses. It can be safely assumed, therefore, that kathis – if they choose to do so – are able to exert a great deal of influence in this matter when they solemnize a marriage.

The injurious beating *ta'alik* is not always easily proven. Some wives have alleged that they were brutally beaten late in the evening or at night, that they were afraid to go out alone in the dark (or were bodily prevented from doing so), and that when on the following morning they had gone to a police station to report the beating, the swelling or other bruise or mark inflicted had disappeared or become less clearly visible. Others, when they have been more successful in conclusively establishing the fact that they were badly bruised or cut, and that the local police station, as well as the General Hospital where they had gone for treat-

[1] I examined some ten thousand marriage entries.

ment, had made a record of their having presented such an appearance, failed to prove that the injury had been inflicted by their husbands. For instance, in a case before the Court in April 1963 I heard a wife allege that her husband had struck her so brutally that he had cut her upper lip, and she had gone with her face bleeding to the nearest police station, then to the General Hospital, where the cut had been stitched, and thence straight to the Shariah Court where she saw a Court kathi and reported the matter. In cross-examination her husband stated that she had first attacked him, he had exerted the minimum degree of violence necessary for him to free himself, and his wife then lost her balance, fell against a pedal sewing-machine and cut her lip in the process. The case was adjourned for the wife to produce witnesses to corroborate her story; and as one of the witnesses was a Tamil, and another a Teochew Chinese, and neither spoke Malay or English (the two languages of the Court), the Court adjourned the case to such a date as it could secure the services of two Court interpreters. Eventually, after further hearings, the case was referred to arbitrators and the wife obtained a *khula* divorce in July 1963.

In another case the wife alleged that her husband had beaten her on 'hundreds of occasions', and that once when the beating had been particularly savage and her face was swollen and bruised she had reported the matter to a police station and to a Court kathi. The husband, who contested her plea for a *ta'alik* decree, said that on the occasion his wife made the reports she had deliberately inflicted these bruises on herself by striking her face against the bedstead. The woman had also invoked the maintenance clause in the *ta'alik* and eventually was granted a decree on the grounds that her husband had not maintained her.

Wives who invoke the beating clause sometimes explain that the husband is brutal either because he is excessively and irrationally jealous ('*chemburu buta*', blindly jealous), or else because he gets drunk and becomes violent when drunk. In the disputed divorce cases before the Court in 1961 and 1962, both Malay and Indian wives alleged that the brutality was often a result of excessive jealousy; but of the eight wives who alleged that alcoholic drink (arak or beer) was the immediate cause, only one was in respect of a Malay husband. The remaining seven related to Indian husbands. Four of the seven wives declared that their husbands were friendly with non-Muslim Indians, such as Hindus or Sikhs, and that it was the latter who were a bad influence.

Sometimes, when a wife gives sworn evidence of her husband's brutality, her case may appear unanswerable. Thus one woman alleged that her husband had, in the course of a violent beating, smashed four of her teeth and that she had reported the matter the same day to the nearest police station. When invited to question her, he said: 'I agree I did smash four of your teeth on that occasion. But these were false teeth, and I took them from you and smashed them on the floor with a stone. Moreover, it was I who had paid for these false teeth, they cost me $80.' The wife: 'They did not cost $80, they cost only $40'.

There are many women who come to the Shariah Court to petition for a divorce on the ground that their husbands are brutal. Some of these wives were married before the insertion of a beating *ta'alik* became general in Singapore, and are not entitled to a *ta'alik* decree since none was registered by the husband with regard to injurious beating. However, they refuse to resume cohabitation, and usually go to live with their mothers or some other close kinswomen. The husband ceases to maintain his deserting wife, and may either petition the Court to 'advise' her to return to him; or he may be served after some months with a summons issued by his wife who has petitioned the Court to register a *ta'alik* decree (if there had been a maintenance *ta'alik* recorded at their marriage); or, if there was no *ta'alik*, she petitions for a *fasah* decree also on the ground of non-maintenance.

In such cases it is not always easy for the Court to determine whether the wife's desertion should be classified as recalcitrancy, and thus bar her from pleading successfully for a *ta'alik* or *fasah* decree. If the husband firmly refuses to divorce her, and shows himself eager for a reconciliation, the Court may persuade the couple to resume cohabitation on the basis of a new specific *ta'alik* relating to beating. However, if the wife refuses to return to her husband, and he continues to refuse to divorce her, the Court may appoint arbitrators to settle the matter.

Among Singapore Muslims a *ta'alik* is usually taken to refer to a conditional divorce uttered by a man *in favour* of his wife. As we saw, a husband declares, for instance, that if he should be guilty of failing to provide her with maintenance over a specific period of time, or of beating her, or of failing to secure independent accommodation for her, or if he should drink alcohol, or gamble, and it is proven that he has contravened such a *ta'alik*, a one-*talak* divorce will ensue.

Islam, however, allows a husband to utter (and if he so chooses, register) a conditional divorce which becomes operative if his *wife* commits any action which he specifies; thus a man may say, 'If my wife goes to visit her parents, she is divorced with one *talak*'. Whether the wife is or is not aware of the fact that he has uttered such a statement, if she goes to visit her parents, the divorce at once becomes effective in Islam. Modern jurists, however, have ruled that frivolous conditional divorces are invalid.[1] It was not unknown in Egypt (I witnessed myself more than one such occasion in the 1940's) for a host to press his guests to eat all the food he had piled on their plates with the threat that if they did not eat it his wife would become automatically divorced with three *talak*.

Frivolous conditional divorces appear to be extremely rare among Singapore Malays. I neither saw nor heard of any case of a *ta'alik* being registered by a husband to the effect that his wife would be automatically divorced if she performed or failed to perform a specific action. On the other hand, in the records of conciliation attempts by the Shariah Court there are cases when husbands are said to have warned their wives: 'If you continue to gamble I'll divorce you', or 'If you go out of the house without my consent I'll divorce you'. Such threats have never been registered as conditional divorces (it is arguable whether they could, in such a form, for traditionally they would be effective only if phrased thus: 'If you go out of the house without my consent you will be automatically divorced with one [or two, or three] *talak*'). Moreover, to the best of my knowledge, there has been only one case of a wife coming before the Court seeking that a divorce be registered because her husband uttered such a conditional divorce, and she has fulfilled the condition, and is now consequently entitled to a registration of the divorce.

The couple were Arabs, and cousins. The husband was 31 years old, and the wife a year younger. The wife's case was, briefly, as follows, On 1 January 1956, her husband took leave of her, before starting on a journey to Indonesia, and cautioned her: 'If you go to see your mother, a three-*talak* repudiation will befall you.' He returned to Singapore four weeks later, and enquired

[1] See Ahmad Ibrahim 'Muslim Marriage . . .'.

whether she had visited her mother, and she replied that she had done so on two occasions. He remarked, 'You are therefore divorced!' Nevertheless, they did not separate, and neither of them mentioned the matter to anyone.

About six months later, the husband approached a kinsman who was the headmaster of a religious school. The headmaster was a first cousin of both the husband and the wife. The husband put to him the hypothetical case of a man who uttered a triple repudiation conditional upon his wife visiting her mother, and enquired whether, if the wife fulfilled the condition, the divorce was operative. The headmaster unhesitatingly declared that it was, and the husband then confessed that the case was not hypothetical, but concerned him. The headmaster warned him at once that if he still lived with his wife he was committing adultery, but the husband asserted that since his return from Indonesia they had slept apart.

He then went to see another religious teacher (also an Arab), repeated the question and received an identical reply and again confessed that he was the husband concerned. When told that if he wanted to resume a lawful union with his wife she must go through a *China buta* marriage, he replied, 'Who wants to put up with a *China buta?*'[1] The headmaster and the religious teacher then informed the wife's older brother. The latter went to his sister's house, asked her to pack her belongings, and took her to his house. This was in July 1956.

Two years later, in August 1958, the Chief Kathi – at the request of the wife – registered the *ta'alik* divorce after enquiries, and after seeking the opinion of the Muslim Advisory Board. The husband appealed to the newly constituted Shariah Court, and at a Court hearing in February 1959 he denied that he had uttered the *ta'alik*, although he himself did not go into the witness-box; he made his denials in the course of cross-examination of his wife and her witnesses. He admitted that he had put the question to the headmaster and to the religious teacher, but alleged that he had done so on behalf of a friend. The 'friend' could not corroborate the story. The Court found the divorce valid.

The husband went to the Appeal Board, which confirmed the Court ruling, and the *ta'alik* divorce, registered in August 1958, was declared valid on 16 September 1959 by the Appeal Board.

[1] Cf. above, p. 20.

Although a man, in order to save his marriage, may agree to bind himself by a specific conciliation *ta'alik*, he sometimes does so only on condition that his wife also make some concessions. A case of this kind occurred at a hearing in May 1963. The dispute was a long and bitter one. Both husband and wife were still in their twenties, and their respective kin also became deeply involved. There were two young children of the marriage. The wife had applied to the Shariah Court for maintenance at the end of 1962 (when the President of the Shariah Court also sat as a magistrate to hear maintenance cases involving Muslims). The case was postponed at the request of one or other of the parties on several occasions and was eventually heard in April 1963, each spouse being represented by a lawyer. The two lawyers announced in open Court that there had been an amicable settlement: the couple had agreed that as soon as the husband secured independent accommodation the wife would resume cohabitation. The wife said she must first view the accommodation to see whether it was suitable, and the President ruled that 'the minimum for a Muslim wife is one room, with a separate bathroom, and a separate kitchen'.[1] The case was adjourned for one month, and in May the couple came again before the Court. The husband had secured accommodation, which the wife had approved, but she had not as yet resumed cohabitation. After some discussion, and with help and advice from the Court, the couple agreed to a reconciliation on the following conditions. The husband said, and this was duly recorded by the President: 'Whenever (*bila bila*) I wake up my wife . . . *binte* . . . in the middle of the night in order to scold or insult her; or allow my male or female kin to come into our home, if my wife lays a complaint regarding the matter, and this is proven, she will certainly be divorced with one *talak*.' The wife said: 'If I should receive into our home my male or female kin, or a man by the name of . . . *bin* . . .; or if I should leave the house in order to visit any person, including my parents, without my husband's permission, then I shall be at fault and shall be deemed guilty of recalcitrancy (*gugor-lah hukum nushuz atas saya*).'

Both before and after each spouse uttered the binding promise, the President succinctly explained to them the duties of a husband and wife in Islam. He told the husband that he had the right to scold his wife if she behaved badly, but there was a difference

[1] Cf. *Minhaj et Talibin*, p. 374. Also Vesey-Fitzgerald, *Muhammadan Law*, p. 44.

between polite rebuke and bitter insult. His wife was neither his servant nor his slave, and she must be treated with kindliness and respect. If she wanted to visit her family, he should not forbid it; she should be able to do so; although she should formally ask his consent, he should not refuse it. 'If she wants to visit her parents, she may do so.'

To the wife he said that she must try to put aside the bitterness of the past and start afresh; her primary duty was to her husband and young children. When the Court Usher enquired whether the maintenance summons was to be struck off, the wife insisted that her husband pay her arrears of maintenance in respect of the past seven months. Eventually it was agreed that the husband would pay half the amount she claimed, i.e. in respect of three and a half months, and the summons was then struck off.

3

Fasah

Fasah (or *faskh*, or *pasah*) is the dissolution of a Muslim marriage by judicial decree, and according to the Shafi'i school a spouse may apply for such a decree on the grounds of impotence, insanity, or a serious and repellent disease such as leprosy or venereal disease. Further, a Muslim wife is entitled to seek a *fasah* decree if her husband is insolvent and unable to maintain her.

An application for *fasah* by a husband is unknown in Singapore, since a man has an unconditional right to utter a repudiation, and the *Muslims Ordinance, 1957* (Section 32) provides that only a woman may petition for a *fasah* decree.

It was the practice in Singapore at the end of the last century and in the early decades of this century for kathis to grant a decree of *fasah* on the grounds of non-maintenance only after the husband had abandoned the complainant wife over a period of years and left her without maintenance throughout that period. This was probably the reason why *ta'alik* clauses specifying three to six months of non-maintenance by the husband became so popular.

A Shafi'i wife is entitled to be provided with either the raw materials for her sustenance (e.g. flour, or bread, or rice), or with a sum of money with which she can purchase such materials; and if she is given less than half the usual amount of food (or half the usual amount of money her husband gives her to purchase such food), she is entitled to report the matter to a kathi, and plead for a *fasah* decree. The kathi must then summon the husband and grant him three days' grace during which he must find enough food to feed his wife for one day. If he fails, the kathi gives him a further day's grace, and only if he has failed again is this taken as proof that the man is in veritable truth a pauper, and the kathi dissolves the marriage by *fasah*.[1]

In Shafi'i law a *fasah* decree cannot normally be granted for lack of maintenance when a husband has means to support his wife

[1] See *Minhaj et Talibin*, pp. 382–9.

but does not choose to do so although she is blameless (i.e. has not committed any conjugal offence); for in such a case a kathi in a Muslim State is presumed to have power to compel the husband to support his wife. Nevertheless, some Muslim jurists allow a kathi to grant a *fasah* decree where the husband is solvent but either cannot be traced, or else is outside the jurisdiction of the Muslim authorities. The jurists base themselves on a *fatwa* by Ibn As-Salah, and under the umbrella of this *fatwa* several *fasah* decrees have been granted by the President of the Singapore Shariah Court in cases where the husband is not a pauper. The *Shorter Encyclopaedia of Islam*[1] defines a *fatwa* as

> a formal legal opinion given by a *mufti* or canon lawyer of standing, in answer to a question submitted to him either by a judge or by a private individual. On the basis of such an 'opinion' a judge may decide a case, or an individual may regulate his personal life.

There are numerous collections of *fatwa*, and in 1935 Al Azhar University in Cairo established a *Fatwa* Council, which has published an average of about 350 *fatwa* every year.[2]

Ibn As-Salah (A.D. 1181–1245) was an eminent Shafi'i legal scholar who taught in colleges in Jerusalem and Damascus. One of his pupils has said:

> This doctor was one of the most eminent men of his time by his deep acquaintance with the sciences of Koranic interpretation, traditions, jurisprudence, . . . His *fatwas*, or legal opinions, were considered of great validity, and he was one of the masters from whose tuition I derived great profit.[3]

Two *fasah* decrees were registered in Singapore in 1961, and eight in 1962. The 1961 decrees were granted on the ground that the husband had failed to maintain his wife over a number of years. In both cases the husband had registered no *ta'alik* at the time of the marriage, and the wife stated that she had no knowledge of his present whereabouts. In the first case (heard by the Court in March 1961) the couple had married in 1944, the husband

[1] Edited by H. A. R. Gibb and J. H. Kramers, Leiden and London, 1953.

[2] See S. and N. Ronart, *Concise Encyclopaedia of Arabic Civilization*, Amsterdam, 1959, p. 173.

[3] See *Ibn Khallikan's Biographical Dictionary*, translated from the Arabic by M. G. De Slane; 4 vols., Paris, 1842, 1843, 1868, 1871; vol. II, p. 188. De Slane's translation into English was printed in Paris for the Oriental Translation Fund of Great Britain and Ireland.

leaving unpaid the *mas kahwin* of $22.50 but giving marriage expenses of $151. The wife, on oath, stated that her husband had first deserted her in 1951, after four children had been born of the union. Early in 1956, however, he returned to Singapore and told her that he was now working in Trengganu (on the East Coast of Malaya) and wished her to join him. They went to see the then Chief Kathi, who told the husband that he was liable for his wife's maintenance during the years of his absence, and asked him whether he proposed to pay her these arrears. The man is said to have replied that he had no intention of doing so, since such a large sum would enable him to marry afresh not only one woman but two. He did, however, pay the $22.50 *mas kahwin*. She had not seen him since, but in October 1956 she had received a letter from him informing her that he had repudiated her with two *talak* and that he did not acknowledge the four children as his. The following month she went to see the Chief Kathi and asked him to grant her a *fasah* decree, but she did not show him the letter she had received. She added that the Chief Kathi said that she would need to pay a fee of $35 to register the *fasah*; but as she was then a domestic servant and earned only $40 per month she was in no position to pay this fee, and accordingly did not pursue the matter.

She produced two witnesses in Court who were able to confirm that her husband had sent her no money since 1955, and had left no material possessions in the conjugal home which she could have sold to maintain herself. The Court ruled that her petition would be granted, and the President said: 'I, in my position as judge (*hakim*)[1] of the Shariah Court, Singapore, declare: "I dissolve the marriage between . . . *binte* . . . and . . . *bin* . . .".'

In November 1961 the Court allowed another *fasah* application. In this case the couple were both Indian, and the marriage had taken place in 1952. It had been a *suka sama suka* match; this was stated in the marriage certificate after a note that there had been no payment of marriage expenses; a *mas kahwin* of $22.50 was entered as 'owing', and there was no *ta'alik*. There had been no children of the union. The wife, on oath, declared that her husband had left her to return to his native land; he used to run a business in Singapore with two nephews, and the latter had also returned home. She had no address at which she could reach her

[1] Not to be confused with *hakam*, arbitrator.

husband, and he had sent her neither a letter nor money since his desertion. She was now thirty-one years old. To a question from the Court, she replied that she had not sought a *fasah* decree earlier because no man had expressed a desire to marry her; but now she had a suitor. Two witnesses gave conclusive evidence that she had been left without maintenance for three years, and the President made a formal declaration in Court that he dissolved the marriage.

In 1962, out of eight *fasah* decrees registered by order of the Court, four were granted on the ground of non-maintenance; two were granted because the husband was insane; and one because the husband was impotent. The eighth *fasah* was registered by order of the Appeal Board; the case is discussed below.[1] In six of the eight cases the petition was undefended. One of the defended petitions had odd features. The couple were married in December 1959, when the bride was fifteen years old and the groom twenty-seven. There was a substantial sum paid for marriage expenses ($501), a *mas kahwin* consisting of (*a*) $22.50 paid in cash and (*b*) a gold chain. There was also a three-months maintenance *ta'alik*.

In October 1960 the husband petitioned the Court to 'advise' his wife to return to him. He stated that his wife's mother had come a few days earlier to fetch the young woman, alleging that the latter's father was very seriously ill; the wife had not returned to the conjugal home, in spite of her husband's repeated invitations to do so, and of advice which a Court kathi (at the request of the husband) had given her; finally, he and his wife were on good terms, he still loved her, and he wanted her back. At the first Court hearing the wife declared that her husband was impotent, and that there had been no intercourse – 'not even once' (*walau sekali*). She now pleaded that the marriage be dissolved.

The husband, on oath, insisted that the marriage had been consummated, and freely consented to both him and his wife being examined medically. This was arranged by the Court which, a few weeks later, received a medical report (in English) stating that the wife was virgo intacta, and that the husband was 'not completely impotent', but that his semen was sterile and that treatment could 'improve the semen analysis'. The report added that the husband 'should also be taught regarding the physiology of normal sex life, the ignorance of which may be the cause of non-consummation of marriage in this case'.

[1] pp. 127 f.

In January 1961 the Court ruled that the wife must wait for a year from the date her husband's impotence had been established;[1] she should return now to live with her husband, and if he were not cured of his impotence at the end of the year she would then be entitled to a *fasah* decree. The wife did not resume cohabitation despite representations by a firm of lawyers acting on behalf of her husband in May 1961; the lawyers further stated that the husband intended to take legal proceedings in another Court against his wife's parents for enticing her away from him.

Hearings were fixed at the Shariah Court, at which the husband failed to appear and was not represented, and letters from the Court requiring him to state whether he had been cured of his disability were left unanswered; but his elder sister came at the last hearing (in March 1962) and declared that the husband was ill in hospital. She stated that his illness was caused by his anger and bitterness (*sakit hati*) at his wife's behaviour, and that he also had gastric disorders as a direct consequence; she told the Court that he had gone into hospital the previous month, but she failed to produce a medical certificate.

The wife pleaded that she had waited for one year and two months since her husband's failure to consummate the marriage had been medically proven, and that she now sought to dissolve the union. There is no reference in the Court record to the fact that the wife had not resumed cohabitation when advised by the Court to do so. The Court Order states that the husband had been requested by letter to produce medical evidence that he had been cured, but had failed to do so; that it was now over a year since the non-consummation of the marriage had been established; and that accordingly the marriage would be dissolved by a *fasah* decree.

It is important to note here that when the President ruled in January 1961 that the wife must wait for a year, he had quoted a Shafi'i authority; the words he quoted, however, made no reference to the need for such a wife to resume cohabitation with her husband. Nevertheless, the President had said that the wife must live with her husband for a year and be patient (*sabar*), and that if at the end of the year he had still failed to consummate the

[1] Cf. *Minhaj et Talibin*, p. 300: 'In whatever manner impotence has been proved the Court cannot immediately pronounce dissolution of marriage in consequence, but must grant the husband a year's delay in which to acquit himself of the physical obligations resulting from marriage. On its expiry the wife may summon her husband a second time . . .'. See also above, p. 48 n.

marriage she would be entitled to a *fasah* decree. It is possible, of course, that the President had before him evidence (which is not available in the Court records) which satisfied him that the wife was entitled to refuse to return to the home provided by her husband; for the conjugal home had been shared with her husband's elder sister.

In one of the two cases in which a wife was granted a *fasah* decree on the grounds of her husband's insanity, the man was living with his father. The wife was 29 years old, and had been married for ten years. She had seen the Chief Kathi before petitioning the Court for a decree. The Chief Kathi reported that the husband and his father had come for an interview; the husband had been silent throughout, but the father had told the Chief Kathi that he admitted his son had lost his mind, and that he had been trying to cure him with the help of healers. The father added that he had himself no objection to an amicable divorce (*dengan baik*); the husband had remained silent.

The wife, at the Court hearing, gave evidence on oath. She said that her husband had been 'a little mad' (*gila sidikit*) for four years; and later, two years ago, he had become seriously mad (*gila kuat*). She was told by the Court that a woman is entitled to a *fasah* decree on the grounds of her husband's madness if she seeks such a decree soon after the madness is apparent; otherwise she is deemed to have accepted the situation. She replied that she was ignorant of the law, that she had had only a sketchy religious education, and had never heard of *fasah* before coming to Court. She then swore a solemn oath that she had indeed been totally ignorant of matters entitling a Muslim woman to a *fasah* decree, and the President dissolved the union.

In the second case, the husband had been in a State mental hospital for three years, and the wife also had to swear a solemn oath that she had not earlier petitioned for a decree because she was totally ignorant of the Muslim law of *fasah*. She had been married in 1945, and there was one child of the marriage, a boy aged eleven.

Of the four decrees granted for lack of maintenance, one was in respect of a comparatively brief period of non-maintenance. The couple had married in June 1960, when the bride was stated in the marriage certificate to be a spinster aged thirty-two years. There had been a sum of $501 as marriage expenses; a *mas kahwin* of $22.50 paid in cash; gifts costing $40; but no *ta'alik*. The wife declared that she had lived in an independent home with her husband until she was seven months pregnant, when the couple had moved to her mother's house. She had a baby in September 1961, and the following month they had a quarrel because she had rebuked him for not coming home regularly. He used to be absent for two or three days at a time, and give no explanation. After the quarrel he packed his clothes and before he left told her: 'Only when my parents rise from their grave will I cross the threshold of your mother's house.'

She had neither seen nor heard from him since, and he had not sent her maintenance. She did not know his present whereabouts. (The summons had been served through a notice in a Malay newspaper in May 1962.) Her first witness, a retired schoolteacher, said he had seen the husband only a few days after he had deserted his wife; the man had given him $10 to pay for religious prayers and a meal, as is customary when a child is forty-four days old,[1] and another $10 for the child's mother. The witness said that he advised the husband to agree to a reconciliation, or at least to send maintenance regularly to his wife, but he had refused to do so. The second witness said he advised the husband to return to his mother-in-law's house, and when he had refused, he had offered him his own house as a conjugal home. The man again refused, and gave no reason for deserting his wife. He did not know his present whereabouts; he thought he was a native of Johore, although he had been a Singapore resident.

The case was adjourned for a week, to 17 August 1962, and the Court then asked the wife whether she had been guilty of disobedience or recalcitrancy either before or after the occasion on which her husband had deserted her. She said she had not, and agreed to swear a solemn oath to that effect, and to repeat that he had not maintained her since his desertion, had empowered no agent to do so, and left no material possessions she could have sold to provide herself with maintenance; and that she was ignorant of his whereabouts. The Court then granted her a *fasah* decree, ten months after her husband had deserted her.

In another case of *fasah* on the grounds of non-maintenance, the marriage had taken place in 1959, when the bride was a girl of fourteen. There had been $400 as marriage expenses, gifts worth

[1] See my *Malay Kinship*, pp. 91 f.

$50, and an unpaid *mas kahwin* of $22.50. Again, there had been no *ta'alik*. The husband had been a sailor, and for a year the union was harmonious: 'there had never been a single quarrel', according to the wife's sworn evidence in Court. She added that one day she was speaking to a young kinsman, when her husband rebuked her for doing so; they quarrelled and he beat her. In the middle of the night, while she was asleep, the husband packed his clothes and left, and she had neither seen nor heard from him since. He had not maintained her since his desertion, nor had he left material possessions for her to sell. She produced two witnesses, whose evidence the Court found inconclusive. The case was adjourned for a month, when the wife swore a solemn oath that her evidence was indeed true to the facts mentioned above, and a *fasah* decree was registered.

In the other two cases of *fasah* on the grounds of non-maintenance, the period of non-maintenance was considerable: ten years in one instance, and nineteen in the other. In the former case the husband was Indian and had returned to India; in the latter, the husband was a Boyanese sailor who had deserted his Singapore wife only a month after their marriage in 1942. In each case the wife declared she had had no news of her husband since his desertion.

The Indian husband left his wife in 1952, two years after they had been married. There was one child of the marriage. At a Court hearing in September 1962 the wife said on oath that one day in 1952 her husband told her he had heard his father was very seriously ill in India, and he had to go immediately to see him. Before he left, he bought about fifty pounds of rice, some tinned milk for the child, and gave her $15 in cash. He promised he would be back in Singapore within two months. She had not heard from him, or of him, since. He had sent neither a letter nor money. He had, however, left some material possessions in the conjugal home; a sewing-machine and a wireless set. She had sold the former for $90 and the latter for $75. There were also a bedstead, a table, and some chairs, but these she had not sold.

The two witnesses who gave evidence on her behalf were unable to satisfy the Court, for they could not state categorically that the husband had failed to send his wife money; they had no direct proof. The wife was therefore required to repeat a summary of her evidence, swearing a solemn oath that she had told the truth, and a *fasah* decree was registered.

The other deserted wife was able to have her evidence confirmed by two witnesses. They had known the husband, and they stated that the man had never been seen in Singapore after he had deserted his wife. When asked by the Court why she had waited for nineteen years before asking for the registration of a *fasah* decree, she replied that she was always hoping he would return to Singapore and come to her. Now she had finally given up hope. After ascertaining from her that she had been guilty of neither disobedience nor recalcitrancy, the Court granted her petition and registered in January 1962 a *fasah* decree 'in accordance with the *fatwa* of Ibn As-Salah which has been followed and approved by many of the later jurists'.

4
Khula

Khula is divorce by redemption. A Muslim wife, eager to dissolve her marriage, may persuade her husband to release her by offering him some monetary or other material compensation; Malays refer to this form of divorce as *tebus talak*. *Tebus* means 'to redeem'; it is the term used when one redeems a pawned item.

When a Singapore Muslim couple have reached agreement to register a divorce by *khula* there is a formal exchange, verbally, of the conditions of the divorce. Thus, husband Ali addresses his wife Patimah: 'O Patimah, if you surrender your claim to the *mas kahwin*, $22.50, I owe you, and to your *iddah* maintenance, i.e. $90, making a total of $112.50, I shall divorce you with one *talak*.' Patimah replies: 'O Ali, I surrender my claim to $112.50.'

As soon as she says this, the divorce becomes operative and may be registered. This exchange is often also recorded in full in the divorce certificate; some kathis, however, only record the terms of the *khula* (e.g. 'the wife surrenders her claim to the *mas kahwin* and to her *iddah* maintenance, worth $112.50'), without quoting the actual words uttered by the spouses.

In some *khula* divorces the wife redeems herself by making an actual payment in cash to her husband, as well as by surrendering her *iddah* maintenance and any claims she may have in respect of the *mas kahwin*. In such a case the formula will be: 'O Patimah, if you surrender your claim to the *mas kahwin*, $22.50, I owe you, and to your *iddah* maintenance, i.e. $90, making a total of $112.50, and if you give me $50 in cash, I shall divorce you with one *talak*.'

Patimah replies: 'O Ali, I surrender my claim to $112.50, and I give you now $50 in cash.'

This formal exchange of the terms of the bargain struck between a man and his wife is the essence of *khula*. The financial consideration may be very slight, and an examination of Singapore divorce registers reveals that many wives divorced by 'ordinary' *talak* – i.e. neither *ta'alik*, nor *khula*, nor *fasah* – agree to surrender amounts as large as, and in some cases larger than, those surrendered by wives who obtain a divorce by redemption. For instance, in 1961 and 1962 there were numerous cases of *khula* registered by kathis where the *mas kahwin* was not mentioned (because it had usually been already paid at marriage) and the only consideration for the divorce was the wife's surrender of her *iddah* maintenance 'worth $90'. On the other hand, many divorces registered as ordinary *talak* record that the wife surrenders both her *iddah* maintenance and the *mas kahwin* which her husband had not paid at marriage.

Although in *khula* divorces registered after a hearing in Court the value in dollars of the forfeited *iddah* maintenance is usually stated, in *khula* divorces registered by kathis this is often not so: many kathis simply note in the relevant section of the entry in the register 'the wife surrenders her *iddah* maintenance'. One Singapore kathi is of the opinion that since no *iddah* maintenance is due until after a divorce, the surrender of *iddah* maintenance cannot be properly a consideration for divorce; consequently, he refuses to register a divorce as *khula* when the only consideration is the surrender of the *iddah* maintenance. The amount of *iddah* maintenance mentioned in a *khula* divorce certificate may not be identical either with the amount the husband concerned would have paid, had he also been eager to dissolve the union, or with the amount he might have been ordered to pay after a contested hearing in Court. In 1961 and 1962, however, the amount of *iddah* maintenance which the two Court Kathis and the President of the Court most frequently mention as actually due to be paid by a husband is '$30 per month for a period of three months'. There were rare exceptions to this, as when a husband earning a high salary ($500–$600 per month) and eager to repudiate a reluctant wife finally agreed to pay her $50 per month *iddah* maintenance. In another case the husband paid $60 per month, and in yet another[1] $90 per month. On the other hand, there are men casually employed, or who earn less than $60 per month as part-time gardeners or labourers, who pay only $15 per month.

A couple may agree in the privacy of their home to the financial conditions of a divorce, or they may do so after a considerable amount of discussion of the terms by their respective kinsmen or by unofficial arbitrators. The couple then go before a kathi –

[1] See below, p. 102.

usually either the same kathi who solemnized their marriage or the kathi nearest to their home – and state they wish to have their divorce registered. He may, after recording the financial conditions of the divorce, suggest that it should be properly registered as a *khula*; or he may simply register it as an ordinary repudiation. At least one Singapore kathi does not favour the registration of *khula* divorces; in an interview I had with him in the presence of the President of the Shariah Court, he stated that he registers divorces where the consideration paid by the wife amounts to only a few dollars as ordinary *talak* divorces. Nevertheless, the President and the Court kathis are of the opinion that if a couple go before a kathi and tell him that they wish to divorce but are not agreed on the terms; and the husband insists that he will not consent to the dissolution if it will involve him in any financial loss; and eventually the wife surrenders her claims to both *mas kahwin* and *iddah* maintenance and also agrees to pay for the registration of the divorce; the kathi should register the divorce as *khula* after requiring the couple to utter the appropriate formulae.

Although there may not be any difference between the financial arrangements reached before the registration of an ordinary one-*talak* divorce, and of a *khula* one-*talak* divorce, in at least one very important respect the two forms of divorce are fundamentally different. A one-*talak* ordinary divorce is revocable within a wife's *iddah* period (unless, of course, it is the third time that it has been uttered in respect of this wife by her husband) whereas a *khula* divorce, whatever the number of *talak*, is irrevocable. The reason for this is obvious, for otherwise a husband who has already obtained a consideration for releasing his wife might revoke the repudiation and demand a further consideration in order to release her again from the marriage. If a couple divorced by *khula* wish to resume married life, they must enter into another marriage contract, and the wife has then a right to a fresh *mas kahwin*. A *khula* divorce is a divorce *bain sughra*, i.e. irrevocable (*bain*) but allowing of remarriage by the same couple without the prior intervention of the wife's marriage to, and divorce from, another man (after due consummation of the marriage to this intervening husband). Such an intervening marriage, of course, is essential before a couple divorced by three *talak* (*bain kubra*) may marry again. (*Sughra* is the Arabic for 'small' or 'little' while *kubra* means 'big' or 'great'.)

I examined all the available records of divorces registered in 1961 and 1962 by the President of the Shariah Court after a hearing, and found that in 1961 there were 18 *khula* divorces registered by order of the Court, and in 1962, 21. (These figures differ slightly from those mentioned in the Annual Reports of the Shariah Court, which give 17 for 1961 and 20 for 1962.) In no case did I see a summons issued by a woman in which she explicitly petitioned for the registration of a *khula* divorce. Divorces which were eventually registered as *khula* resulted as a rule from an original petition by a wife seeking either the registration of a *ta'alik* or *fasah* decree, or, when she had no grounds for claiming either, by a petition which merely stated in the summons initiating the proceedings her reasons for her prayer that the Court dissolve her union. Moreover, there were cases when a hearing was fixed as the result of a husband's petition to the Court to 'advise' (*nasehat*) his wife to resume cohabitation. The wife refused to return to her husband, and in the course of time he agreed to a *khula* divorce.

I now give some instances of matrimonial proceedings which ended with the registration of a *khula* divorce.

I. The couple, both Indians, had been married in 1956 and had two children. There was no *ta'alik* either at the time of the marriage or later. In May 1961 the husband issued an 'advice' summons, and at the first Court hearing in June he stated that his wife had deserted the conjugal home, taking their two children with her, and had gone to live in her mother's home. He had pleaded with her to return on no fewer than eight occasions. He had also taken her to see the *imam* of the Cross Street mosque (where many Indian Muslims pray) who had advised her to return to him, but she had refused. He had also gone to seek the help of the Social Welfare Counselling Section,[1] who had also advised her to return to her husband, but again she had refused.

He had then come to see a Court kathi, who had also failed to effect a reconciliation, and as a last resort he had issued a summons. In a letter to the Court, written in English, he submitted: 'I am ashamed to say she refuses because she wants to marry someone

[1] This is the only case on record, in the Shariah Court documents I examined, of a couple who went to the Social Welfare Counselling Section before coming to the Shariah Court.

else', and he named the man, whom I shall here refer to as Ibrahim. He added that his wife had been cohabiting with Ibrahim 'for the last four months'.

At the hearing in Court, when he gave evidence on oath, he repeated these statements. The wife stoutly denied the allegations. She claimed that Ibrahim had been introduced to her by her husband, who often brought him to the conjugal home, and that on more than one occasion her husband had ordered her to seek a loan from Ibrahim. She once obtained a loan of $100, and her husband had not kept his promise to repay it; when he told her to borrow yet another $100 from Ibrahim she refused, and he became so angry that he beat her savagely. The husband did not deny that he had beaten her on one occasion, but he alleged that he did so in the course of a quarrel, when he had accused her of provocative behaviour with Ibrahim, and after she had hit him first; he had only hit back in self-defence.

On oath, the wife stated that she found married life intolerable because:

(1) her husband drank beer, usually on his pay day, and brought home a sum pitifully inadequate for buying food and other essentials;

(2) her father-in-law lived with them, and his manner and interference in the day-to-day life of the household were offensive to her;

(3) her husband's jealousy and his allegations that she was or had been Ibrahim's mistress were equally offensive, and totally unfounded.

After she had given evidence and been lengthily cross-examined on it by her husband, she said that she wanted the marriage dissolved. The husband said he did not agree to this, for he was eager to have her back; and the Court attempted to persuade her to agree to a reconciliation. At first she declared that she would on no account return to him, in view of the disgraceful allegations he had made against her in open Court. Eventually she said she would agree to a reconciliation on the following terms:

(1) he would come to live in a room (now vacant) in her mother's house;

(2) he would regularly hand over his salary to her (he had declared on oath, earlier, that he always had done so when they lived together);

(3) his father would not live with them, and would come to visit them only occasionally.

The husband refused to agree to the conditions. The Court then appointed arbitrators to settle the issue, after the couple had agreed to this course of action and had bound themselves in writing to abide by the decision of the arbitrators.

Three weeks later the decision was announced. A *khula* divorce was recommended, the terms being that the wife surrender:

(*a*) her right to the *mas kahwin* ($75) which had not been paid at the marriage;

(*b*) her right to her maintenance in respect of the past few months when she had deserted her husband and not been maintained by him; and finally

(*c*) her right to *iddah* maintenance.

Khula formulae in these terms were exchanged in open Court by husband and wife, and the same day she paid the divorce registration fee.

II. The couple were Malay. They had been married in 1944, and again in this case no *ta'alik* had been registered; but the husband had paid a *mas kahwin* of $2.50 in cash on the day of the wedding. There were seven children of the marriage.

Early in November 1960 the wife was seen by a Court kathi. She told him that she had been beaten by her husband on the previous day and had already reported the matter to her local police station. She had left the conjugal home, and her seven children were still in it, in the custody of their father. She was now living in her mother's home. The Court kathi failed to effect a reconciliation, and the wife issued a summons in which she pleaded that the Court dissolve her marriage on the grounds that:

(1) her husband has beaten her so brutally that she bled from the wounds he inflicted on her, and she has been compelled to run to her mother's house for protection;

(2) he is unemployed, makes no serious attempt to find a job, and has given her no money for four years;

(3) he is in receipt of $61 per month allowance from Public Assistance funds, but has given her no part of this allowance, either for her own maintenance or for the maintenance of their children;

(4) he gambles with his Public Assistance allowance.

At the first hearing in Court, she repeats these accusations on oath. Her husband, in the course of cross-examination, generally denies her allegations. He admits that he did beat her on one occasion, but claims this was because he had heard she was engaged in an affair with another man. He says that he does give her a regular amount of money for household expenditure. She insists that he gives her nothing, and that for the past four years she has maintained the household with financial help from her mother and brothers and with her earnings from the sale of cooked food which she hawks in a large commercial building. The husband refuses to agree to a divorce and the case is adjourned.

At the second hearing the husband persists in his refusal, and repeats that he does maintain his wife adequately. He offers to bring witnesses to prove that he does so, and the case is accordingly adjourned.

At the third hearing, however, he reports that his witnesses are unable to attend. The case is further adjourned.

At the fourth hearing, due to begin at 10.30 a.m., the husband fails to appear by 11 a.m. and the case is further adjourned.

At the fifth hearing the husband produces witnesses, who do not give conclusive evidence in support of his contention, and the case is further adjourned.

At the sixth hearing the Court makes a final attempt to persuade the wife to agree to a reconciliation. The Court suggests to the wife that she might consent to a reconciliation with a *ta'alik*: her husband would declare that if

(1) he beats her, or

(2) fails to maintain her over a period of three months or longer, or

(3) gambles,

upon proof of his having broken any one of these conditions the Court would decree that a one-*talak* divorce be registered.

The wife refuses to be reconciled, even on these terms. She declares that if she had thought she could bear to live again with her husband she would not have been so persistent in her petition to the Court to dissolve the union. The husband, on the other hand, still refuses to utter a repudiation. Arbitrators are appointed and at the seventh and final hearing the arbitrators state that the spouses have now agreed to a *khula* divorce on the following terms: the wife is to surrender her claim to past maintenance, and to *iddah* maintenance; and she will pay the divorce registration fee.

The appropriate *khula* formulae are exchanged by husband and wife, and the latter immediately pays $22 and secures the registration of the divorce and a copy of the divorce certificate.

From the record of the proceedings in this case, it appears that the arbitrators consulted the couple before stating the terms of the *khula* in open Court. However, such consultation need not take place after the arbitrators have reached a decision based on the evidence before them. Arbitrators, before reaching a decision, may feel the need to question the parties; but, once satisfied that they have all the relevant facts before them, they may reach a decision and not communicate it to the spouses until the date and hour of the formal hearing in Court. In 1963 in some cases of bitterly contested divorces the arbitrators have been the two Court kathis. The parties heard the verdict of the arbitrators only when the latter were formally invited to come into Court and read their decision.

III. I was present in March 1963 at such a hearing. The case concerned two Indians. The wife, a Hindu who became a Muslim in order to marry, had left her husband and gone with the two young children of the marriage to live with her mother and stepfather. One of the Court kathis had vainly attempted to reconcile the couple, and he had then suggested that the marriage be dissolved amicably, by mutual consent. The husband had replied that if his wife paid him one thousand dollars to redeem herself he would agree to a *khula* divorce. She rejected this proposal outright, arguing that she was penniless. Eventually the case came before the Court, and after several hearings the two Court kathis were appointed as arbitrators. In March 1963 they came into Court and one of them read their joint decision in the presence of the husband, the wife, and the wife's stepfather, who throughout the case had acted as her protector and spokesman. The kathi stated that the couple would be divorced by *khula* if the wife:

(1) surrendered all claims to past maintenance and *iddah* maintenance;

(2) paid her husband $50 in cash; and

(3) paid the divorce registration fee.

A Tamil interpreter explained this to the parties, and the woman's stepfather at once protested that he had had no prior notice of this decision, and that neither she nor he had any money at all; but he could manage to raise $22 by 2 p.m. the same afternoon to register the divorce and obtain a copy of the certificate. He was told by the Court that the arbitrators' decision was binding, since both the wife and husband had given in writing full authority (*kuasa penoh*) to their respective arbitrators to settle the matter, and had further agreed to be bound by such a decision. The stepfather nevertheless continued to object to the verdict, while the young wife remained silent and motionless, huddled in her cotton sari. Eventually the Court Usher stated bluntly: 'No $50, no divorce.' The President then agreed to a plea on behalf of the wife that time be given for the sum to be raised, but warned the girl and her stepfather that he would brook no endless delays, and that the case would be struck off if it were not settled soon.

Nevertheless, there were no fewer than three further postponements of the payment. On one occasion the stepfather pleaded to be given another week in which to find the money, and the husband raised no objection; a week later the stepfather came into Court to state that the wife was ill in bed with a temperature; on the third occasion the wife came to say that she was a destitute woman, and where could a person like her find $50? By July 1963 she had still not paid the price of her redemption and was still a married woman. The Chief Kathi, commenting on the case, said to me after the hearing at which the arbitrators' verdict had been announced: 'The whole point of putting a case before arbitrators is to end the deadlock. If arbitrators discussed their decision with the spouses, the matter might never be settled, for the same arguments would be advanced again and again.'

IV. The couple had been married in 1948, and when they came before the Shariah Court in 1961 they had seven children. There had been no *ta'alik* at marriage or later, and the wife sought a *fasah* decree. She complained that her husband used to give her a very inadequate amount of housekeeping money up to 1960 – an average of only $50 per month, and a maximum of $60 in any one month. He had told her he could afford to give her nothing more because he paid $50 per month rent. In 1960 they moved to her mother's house, but although he paid her mother no rent, he did not increase her housekeeping allowance. In the end she felt compelled to take maintenance proceedings against him, and was awarded $160 per month in respect of the seven children. He had then already moved out of her mother's house. She was unable to obtain an order of maintenance for herself from the Court because he had stated that he was willing to support her if she resumed cohabitation and she had refused then to live with him.

At the first Shariah Court hearing she states that she will not agree to a reconciliation, that she has no faith in her husband because he has taken all her jewelry (worth $935) and pawned it, and because he has been unfaithful to her: she has seen him frequently in the company of another woman and a small child; he was with them that very morning. Her husband denies the allegation that he gave her an insufficient housekeeping allowance when they lived together; and he declares that the woman she has referred to is no stranger; she is his first cousin.

At the second hearing there is again a lengthy catalogue of complaints by the wife, who claims that her husband took away a radio and refrigerator which were her own property. The case is adjourned for three months in the hope that the parties may become reconciled. At the third hearing, however, the deadlock persists, and arbitrators are appointed.

At the fourth hearing the arbitrators recommend that a *khula* divorce be registered on the following terms. The wife is to surrender her claims to:

(1) her jewelry, worth $935;

(2) eighteen months' past maintenance, which at $30 per month would have amounted to $540;

(3) *iddah* maintenance; and

(4) the radio and the refrigerator.

Moreover, if at some later stage she decides she is willing to marry the husband again, she will not revive her claims to any of the above items, but will return to the husband unconditionally.

The wife agrees to all these conditions, and she also pays the divorce registration fee on the same day. In this case the price of the wife's redemption is the highest amount of all *khula* payments recorded in the registers of 1961 and 1962. It is also the only case when the conditions of the *khula* contain a reference to the wife's possible claims if she should choose to marry the same husband again.

Not all *khula* divorces registered by the Court give rise to such bitter arguments, nor do all *khula* divorces get settled only after the intervention of arbitrators. In 1961, out of a total of 18 *khula* divorces registered by the Court, only 8 required the appointment of arbitrators. In 1962, out of a total 21 *khula* decrees, only 7 did so.

In some cases a *khula* divorce was registered at the first Court hearing of the case. Some husbands consider it futile to prolong the dispute when faced with a wife who is so determined in her refusal to resume cohabitation that she has taken the bold step of instituting legal proceedings to secure a dissolution of the marriage. The following case was settled at the first hearing.

V. A man, aged thirty-five years, married a girl of seventeen in September 1961. He gave marriage expenses of $201, paid a *mas kahwin* of $22.50, and gave his bride presents worth $24.90. The total payments made to her, and duly recorded in the marriage certificate, thus amounted to $248.40. (In addition, he must have incurred other expenses in connection with the wedding ceremonies, but these are not recorded.)

On oath he declared that his wife had refused to consummate the marriage. Although they had slept alone in the same room for one week he had been unable to persuade her to yield. She then left the conjugal home, returned to her parents, and told him that she wanted him to repudiate her. He was willing to agree to the divorce only if he were repaid the sum total of the marriage payments he had made. The wife, after being sworn in, admitted: 'All that my husband has said is true. I do not like him. Before we married I saw him and I liked him, but later, after the wedding, I did not like him any more.' She added that there was another man whom she had also liked, and after she had refused to consummate the marriage and had returned to her parents, this other man had promised to find $500 to compensate her husband handsomely for her refusal, and so redeem her from the marriage. The suitor, however, eventually produced only $250, and she had lost patience with him too, for he had not been faithful to his promise. She concluded: 'Now I don't want to marry this other man because of his false promise (*kerana dia janji bohong*) and neither do I wish to return to my husband.'

At the end of the hearing the couple agreed to a *khula* divorce: the wife paid half the total amount of the marriage payments she had received, i.e. $124.20.

It is impossible to tell from the available records of *khula* in registers of divorces recorded by outside kathis whether there has been a great deal of haggling before the couple have exchanged *khula* formulae 'by mutual consent'. Moreover, although the terms of the *khula* divorce should be entered in the divorce register, it may well be that all the details of the financial settlement are not revealed to the kathi; or, if they are revealed, that he does not think it necessary to enter them in full in the register.

The one safe assumption which may be made, however, is that before a *khula* divorce is registered as a result of a Court Order (after at least one Court hearing), the following steps will have been taken:

(1) One of the Court kathis has attempted a reconciliation, and failed.

(2) The kathi has then sought to persuade the husband to agree amicably (*dengan baik*), without bitterness, to the divorce.

(3) The kathi has failed in this again, and either the wife has petitioned the Court to dissolve the union, or else the husband has petitioned the Court to advise his wife to return to him.

VI. I know of only one case of a *khula* divorce registered by the Court which did not have such a history. It occurred in 1962, when a husband came to see a Court kathi and said that he had been separated from his wife for two years, that she had been guilty of disorderly behaviour during that period, and that he did not know her present whereabouts and wished to repudiate her. He then issued a summons, served by way of a notice in a Malay newspaper. On the day fixed for the hearing the wife appeared in Court and said she did not wish to contest the divorce. She further agreed to surrender her *iddah* maintenance. An exchange of *khula* formulae was then recorded, and the divorce duly registered. On the basis of the evidence in the record-book, I suggest with great respect that this case might well have been registered as an ordinary repudiation, without requiring the parties to utter *khula* formulae, but simply recording that the wife surrendered her right to *iddah* maintenance. In this case the wife was not, properly speaking, redeeming herself. It was the husband who had initiated the proceedings and it was he who was eager to have the divorce registered.

With very rare exceptions, such as the one just mentioned, *khula* divorces are divorces registered at the wife's request; and in order to obtain such registration she may agree, as we saw, to make a specified payment to her husband, or to forfeit her right to a sum of money which normally would have been due to her when the marriage was dissolved.

In Islam there is traditionally no provision for a husband to redeem himself from a marriage, since a man may pronounce a repudiation whenever he pleases. However, since the establishment of the Shariah Court in 1958, a Singapore Muslim cannot, as in the past, go before a Singapore kathi and simply upon payment of the prescribed fee ask him to register the repudiation he has uttered. Since Singapore kathis no longer have the right to register divorces other than those reached by mutual agreement, a novel and rather piquant situation has arisen whereby a wife may refuse her consent to her husband's proposal that they end the union. He may then have to agree to such terms as she imposes before she will sign both the divorce application form and the entry in the divorce register in the presence of a kathi. It is impossible to tell how many of the ordinary repudiations (i.e. not *khula*) registered by kathis are divorces recorded only after the husband has yielded to special conditions imposed by the wife.

Moreover, since it is only in very rare cases and after a searching enquiry that the Singapore Chief Kathi grants a man permission to enter upon a polygynous union,[1] a husband eager to marry another woman cannot, as in the past, simply go before any kathi and ask him to solemnize and register a polygynous union. The ordinary man, therefore, who knows that his salary is too small for the Chief Kathi to allow him to enter into such a union, but who is desperately keen to take another wife, may decide to persuade his wife to agree to a divorce and may yield to her terms in order to secure a speedy dissolution and be free to remarry. Some women, however, ask a price which the husband deems exorbitant, and he then petitions the Court to register the repudiation he has already uttered, or is eager to utter.

VII. An interesting case came before the Court in 1962. A couple had had their marriage solemnized in October 1961, the groom being then twenty-three years old and the bride nineteen. It was agreed to postpone the actual wedding celebrations and the consummation of the marriage until such time (a period of twelve months was mentioned) as the groom had saved the amount of

[1] See above, p. 30.

marriage expenses which he bound himself to pay (and which was entered as due) in the marriage register: $350. When the marriage contract was signed, he paid the *mas kahwin* in cash, $22.50. Moreover, he bound himself to pay his bride an allowance of $20 per month while she continued to live with her parents, and until such time as the wedding ceremonies took place. This was a *nikah gantong*, lit. 'a suspended marriage contract'.

A *nikah gantong* usually occurs when the bride is very young, especially when she has not yet reached puberty, and the wedding ceremonies are delayed (suspended) until she is considered fit for marriage. Meanwhile she continues to reside with her parents.[1] In recent years Singapore kathis have been instructed to refuse to register a marriage if the bride is under fifteen years of age; parents, however, may appeal to the Shariah Court President – who is Registrar of Muslim Marriages – and he may, if he thinks fit, consent to the registration of a marriage of a girl under fifteen years of age.[2]

Nikah gantong of brides aged nineteen years are rare in Singapore. One can only assume that in the *nikah gantong* of October 1961 the groom persuaded the bride and her parents to consent to such a contract in order to ensure that the girl would not be given away to another suitor. If she were bound to him only by an engagement, that might be broken far more easily than a registered marriage contract.

For several months the groom paid $20 pocket-money to his bride, as agreed. Then he and the bride's elder brother had a very serious quarrel, in the course of which bitter accusations were made. The groom decided he did not want to remain tied in marriage to such a man's sister. The latter, however, refused her consent to the proposed divorce. Eventually she told him she would consent only if he gave her *twice* the amount of the marriage expenses specified in the marriage certificate, i.e. twice $350.

The husband instituted Court proceedings, and there was a hearing at the end of July 1962. On oath, he said that he sought a divorce because:

(1) he could not put up with the arrogant and quarrelsome attitude of his wife's elder brother;

[1] See my *Malay Kinship*, p. 71.

[2] I am informed that, in effect, he does so only if the girl in question is already pregnant.

(2) as a result of his brother-in-law's behaviour there had been a quarrel.

The Court attempted a reconciliation between the spouses, but the husband stated, 'I do not like my wife any more'.

The wife admitted that her husband's evidence accorded with the facts, but said that she was genuinely unwilling to end the marriage. She herself had had no quarrel with her husband, and she should not be held responsible for the quarrel between the two men. However, since he was adamant in his determination to dissolve the union, he must abide by the terms of the agreement entered into at the time of the marriage, that whichever party cried off before the wedding ceremonies would pay $700 as compensation to the other. Moreover, her husband must pay her $100 in respect of her monthly allowance of $20 which he had discontinued during the past five months.

Cross-examining her, the husband denied that such an agreement had ever taken place, and asked when she thought such a promise had been made – at the engagement, or at the *nikah* (marriage contract)? She replied that the witnesses at the *nikah* had heard (and informed her of) the agreement. Moreover, her father had also been present when the agreement had taken place. Her father then went into the witness-box and confirmed that there had indeed been such a verbal agreement, but that it was not put into writing (*tidak bertulis dengan hitam puteh*, not written in black and white). The husband declined to cross-examine his father-in-law in respect of this evidence.[1]

The Court made a final, but vain, attempt at reconciliation; and recorded the husband's hard (*keras*) determination to end the marriage. He uttered a one-*talak* repudiation in the presence of two witnesses. The Court ruled that since the husband had not consummated the marriage, and in the absence of a written contract that he had agreed – as alleged – to pay $700 if he cried off the wedding, the husband would now pay his wife only half the specified marriage expenses, half $350, i.e. $175.[2] It further

[1] See my *Malay Kinship*, pp. 74–5 and pp. 77–8, on the theory and practice of compensating a fiancé(e) for breach of promise or a husband for refusal to consummate the marriage.

[2] Such a decision is in accordance with Shafi'i law (see *Minhaj et Talibin*, p. 311) if the principle guiding the payment of 'dower' (Arabic, *mahr*; Malay, *mas kahwin*) may be extended to apply to the payment of marriage expenses in cases where the husband resiles from the contract before consummation.

ordered the husband to pay his wife $100 in respect of the past allowance due to her, and ruled that he was not entitled to recover any gifts he had made to the bride at the time of the marriage contract. On the other hand, since there had been no consummation there would be no *iddah*, and no *iddah* maintenance was therefore payable to the wife.[1]

The husband paid his wife $275 in open Court, and paid the divorce registration fee. The divorce was registered as 'one-*talak*, before consummation' (*talak satu, belum bersetuboh*).

VIII. That same year, another case came before the Court of a husband seeking a divorce from a wife who was reluctant to agree to the dissolution. He had married this woman as his second wife some years earlier, in 1957. His case was that after meeting her in a hotel in a Malay State where she was a hostess, he had a brief affair with her. When he returned to his first wife and to his job in Singapore she followed him and he agreed to marry her in order, as he said in Court, 'to help her to become a good person' – to make an honest woman of her. He explained that he had at first been reluctant to take a second wife, for his monthly salary in 1957 was only $400 (in 1962 he was earning over $1,000 per month), but eventually he had consented. She settled in a separate home, and the union was happy until 1959, when she suddenly became uncontrollably jealous. She nagged at him persistently to divorce his first wife, and he stoutly refused to do so, for he was attached to her; she was the mother of his children. (He had no children by the second wife.) Eventually he found her nagging intolerable, it was affecting his health, and he left her; but she begged him to return to her, promising she would be more reasonable in the future, and he agreed to live with her again (i.e. to share his days and nights again between the two wives), but she did not keep her promise. Indeed, she nagged him more than ever, and he finally left her in March 1962, and in May issued a divorce summons in which he stated he sought the registration of a divorce because his wife

(1) nags constantly;
(2) is disobedient;
(3) is a liar and a cheat;
(4) goes out late at night.

[1] See below, p. 139.

At the Court hearing the man repeated these allegations, on oath. The wife indignantly denied them. She admitted that she had rebuked her husband for spending very little time with her, for although she was legally married to him and entitled to the same consideration as his first wife, he visited her only occasionally. Moreover, on the odd evenings that he did come he would arrive very late, at about 10 p.m. She had been a dutiful, blameless wife and did not want to be divorced; she was very fond of her husband.

He, for his part, maintained that he was determined to end the marriage. She stated that, although he earned such a large salary, he had taken and pawned all the jewelry (worth $936) which she had bought out of her own earnings, before she had met him. He admitted this, but argued that it was at the beginning of their marriage, when his salary was modest, and she had herself consented to his pawning the jewelry so that she might use the money to set up an independent home. She reminded him that the jewelry had been redeemed; and that much later he had again taken it from her, saying he was momentarily embarrassed, and she had not seen it since. He confessed this was so, and further, that he had since sold the jewelry.

The Court adjourned for the lunch recess, and when the hearing was resumed the wife declared she was now resigned to the divorce, and the husband stated he undertook to repay the cost of the jewelry, $936. He uttered, before witnesses, a one-*talak* repudiation. In addition to the agreed payment of $936 to the wife, the Court ruled that the husband would pay *iddah* maintenance of $90 per month for three months.[1] Further, the husband was to pay the *mas kahwin* of $22.50 which he still owed to his wife; he was to give her a consolatory gift of $10; and he would pay the registration fee.

Before the establishment of the Shariah Court this marriage could have been dissolved by the husband merely going alone to any kathi to register the divorce. If his wife had wanted to claim the jewelry he had appropriated she would have had to take legal proceedings against him, and the procedure might have been

[1] This is the highest amount of *iddah* maintenance recorded in all the divorces registered in 1961 and 1962 in Singapore—i.e., 401 in 1961, and 449 in 1962— but of course the husband earned more than ten times the salary received by a large number of Muslims who were ordered to pay $30 per month for three months in respect of *iddah* maintenance.

lengthy and costly. Moreover, it is unlikely that she would have been able to induce him to part with $90 per month for three months as *iddah* maintenance, or with even one dollar as consolatory gift. Thus the terms of this divorce are very similar to those to which a wife, *mutatis mutandis*, consents in order to redeem herself from a marriage which has become intolerable.

IX. In yet another divorce petition in 1962 by a husband (earning about $600 per month), the wife argued that after thirteen years of marriage and three children the man was now eager to dissolve the union because he had taken a fancy to marry a young girl. She was unwilling to consent to the divorce, and as a blameless wife she felt she had good grounds for doing so. The husband contended that the sole reason for his seeking a divorce was that his wife was 'blindly jealous', and he found her attitude unendurable. He could not contemplate a reconciliation. He had left the conjugal home some months earlier, and had given her no maintenance since (probably in the hope that she might petition the Court for a *ta'alik* decree). She, on the other hand, had hoped that he would return to her, and she had not embittered matters by suing for maintenance, as she was entitled to do.[1] She had merely sold some of his possessions to pay for the household's food and other expenses.

When she realised that the Court was powerless to refuse the registration of a repudiation a determined Muslim husband had already uttered, or intended to utter,[2] she decided to settle the matter at the first hearing provided her husband agreed to her terms. These were that the conjugal home's entire contents (bought, it would appear, out of the husband's sole earnings) should be made over to her.[3] The man was so eager to have a divorce registered immediately that he agreed to this, adding only that he wished to have his camera, clothes, tape recorder, and books returned to him. She replied that she had already sold these items in order to pay for food and other necessary expenses during the five months he had deserted her. When he enquired, 'Whom

[1] See below, pp. 166 ff.

[2] Although it could delay the actual date of the registration by adjourning the case.

[3] A Singapore Muslim woman has no right to household chattels acquired by her husband during their conjugal life. This has been the law since the 1880 Ordinance, and contrasts with the situation in the Malay States. See above, p. 4.

did you sell the tape recorder to?' she replied, 'To my younger brother'. The husband then not only agreed to surrender all the items in the conjugal home, but also to pay his wife:

(1) $210 in respect of past maintenance;
(2) $60 per month for three months, as *iddah* maintenance;
(3) $25 as a consolatory gift.

In addition he paid the registration fee, after he had uttered a one-*talak* repudiation.

There are other cases when a husband wants a divorce and 'redeems' himself from the marriage, because his deserted wife has obtained a maintenance order against him. Some Muslims desert their wives and hope that the woman will eventually petition for a *ta'alik* or *fasah* decree. Instead, she applies for, and obtains, a maintenance order. The husband then finds himself without a wife's services, but compelled to pay her a fixed allowance. However, since he is a Muslim and since the Shariah Court 'has no power to prevent a husband from repudiating his wife' (a phrase which repeatedly occurs in the Court rulings, *keputusan Mahkamah*, the President reads when he delivers his judgment), a man may decide it is to his advantage to spend about $10 in order to issue a divorce summons, and later to pay the divorce registration fee of $22. He would, of course, have to pay three months' *iddah* maintenance, but after that period he would be relieved of all responsibility in respect of his divorced wife.

Several such cases came before the Court in 1961 and 1962, and it is likely that many more Muslim husbands ordered to pay maintenance to their wives will take advantage of the fact that they may release themselves from the burden by applying to the Shariah Court for the registration of a divorce.[1] One remedy which the President of the Court might then have would be to make an order for the husband to pay a fairly large amount of *iddah* maintenance and/or consolatory gift.[2] If the man earns a very small salary, he might be ordered to pay the amount in instalments. Of course, the man may default (as so many husbands do, in cases when they have been ordered to pay maintenance to a deserted wife); and the wife may find it more costly in time and transport expenses to issue a summons praying the Court to enforce the Order.

[1] See below, p. 144 f.

[2] See Ahmad Ibrahim, 'Muslim Marriage . . .'.

5

Talak, or 'Ordinary' Repudiation

We have so far considered divorces known as *fasah*, *ta'alik*, and *khula*, which are usually divorces registered by the Shariah Court at the request of a wife who wishes to dissolve her union. (*Khula* divorces, as we know, may also be registered by kathis by mutual consent of the spouses.)

Another form of divorce is that known as a *cherai biasa*, an ordinary repudiation, and entered in the divorce registers as a *talak* divorce – *talak satu*, or *dua*, or *tiga*, i.e. one, two, or three *talak* – without further specification. In the case of a *fasah*, *ta'alik*, or *khula* divorce, the entry specifies the number of *talak*, but in addition there is a further entry to the effect that the divorce is either a *fasah*, a *ta'alik*, or a *khula* divorce.

All 'ordinary *talak*' which are by mutual consent may be registered by any kathi upon payment of the official registration fee. However, if a husband wishes to utter and register a divorce and is unable to secure his wife's agreement, he must issue a summons petitioning the Court to order the registration. But it would be wrong to assume that all ordinary *talak* registered by the Court are the result of a petition by a husband whose wife has refused to consent to the divorce. The exceptions are many.

I. There is the man who has deserted his wife, or been deserted by her, and is later unable to trace her. He now wishes to marry another woman. In the old days, before the establishment of the Shariah Court, he could have gone to any Singapore kathi and simply registered a divorce; or else he might not even have cared to go to the trouble and expense of doing so, but merely entered into a second (and therefore polygynous) union. The first of these courses is no longer permitted to him; while it is only the Chief Kathi who may grant a man permission to register a polygynous marriage (under Section 21 of the 1960 Amendment to the Muslims Ordinance), and he does so only after a searching enquiry to ascertain that the man can provide for two wives and two households simultaneously.

A Singapore Muslim in such a situation therefore formally petitions the Court to register his divorce, and the summons is served upon his wife through a notice in a Malay newspaper stating the date and hour of the hearing at the Shariah Court. It may well be, of course, that the wife has meanwhile applied (and obtained) a *ta'alik* or *fasah* decree in another State in the Federation. Indeed, it is not outside the bounds of possibility that she may have obtained such a decree from a Singapore kathi before 1958, for there was not then a central indexed register of Singapore divorces which would make it possible to ascertain fairly rapidly whether a particular marriage had been dissolved. One would have to examine every entry in the registers. There is now an index of all cases decided by the Shariah Court.

The reverse is, of course, also true. A wife who has lost trace of her husband and petitioned for a *ta'alik* or *fasah* divorce may discover half way through her divorce proceedings that she has already been divorced by him. Indeed such a case did occur in 1962, when a wife attempted (through the good offices of the Singapore Shariah Court who approached the Chief Kathi of Kota Bahru in Kelantan) to serve a summons on her husband at an address in Kelantan. She was duly informed that he was no longer resident there, and eventually the summons was served on him through a notice in a Malay newspaper. A few days before the date of the Singapore Court hearing, in May 1962, the husband sent a letter saying he had already repudiated his wife several months earlier in Klang, Selangor, and the Shariah Court at the formal hearing duly decreed that it found it proven that the husband had divorced his wife in the previous August, and now ruled that the divorce (which had apparently not been registered in Selangor) be duly registered in Singapore.

II. There are men whose wives live outside Singapore, at a known address, but these women are unwilling or unable to come to Singapore in order to register before a kathi their consent to be divorced. In one such case, the wife lived in Bawean in Indonesia and had requested her husband (who had settled in Singapore) to repudiate her and send her a divorce certificate.

III. There are men who feel that according to Islam they are already divorced, for they have uttered a repudiation formula (usually outside Singapore) and informed their wives of the fact, but have never registered the divorce. They now require documentary evidence of this divorce, and therefore apply to the Shariah Court.

IV. There are men who issue a summons petitioning the Court to 'advise' their wives to resume cohabitation, but eventually these men utter a repudiation.

V. Finally, there are ordinary *talak* divorces registered by the Shariah Court when the original summons was taken out by the wife who sought a dissolution of the union. In one case, a wife successfully established that her husband had previously uttered a repudiation formula, and not revoked it.

In 1961, out of a total of 13 'ordinary' repudiations registered by the Court, 11 were in respect of husbands who petitioned for the decree; in the other two cases the wife was the petitioner. In 1962, out of a total of 34 ordinary *talak*, only 20 were the result of such action by the husband; in 13 cases the wife had petitioned the Court, and in one case the husband had issued an 'advice' summons.

I. *Desertion by the wife, and wife's whereabouts unknown*

There was one such case in 1961, and four in 1962, when the husband paid for a notice in a Malay newspaper to serve the summons on his absent wife. In the case before the Court in 1961 the husband, who was a storekeeper on a boat, said that on his return to Singapore in November 1960 from a trip to Australia he discovered that his wife had left home. Neighbours told him she had moved out two weeks earlier. His wife's kinsmen, including her father, vainly tried to trace her. He himself had gone to Malacca and Perak to search for her. They had been married only a year when she deserted him. He had now given up hope of her returning to him, and sought to register a repudiation. He produced two witnesses who confirmed his allegations, and then uttered a three-*talak* repudiation in their presence, and this was duly entered in the Register.[1]

In January 1962 there was a similar case. The husband returned

[1] The President in rare cases consents to register a three-*talak* repudiation uttered on a single occasion, when it seems clear that the wife has sinned gravely.

from a trip to India, after an absence of a year, to find that his wife (also an Indian) had left the conjugal home. Neighbours told him she had left some weeks after he had gone. In answer to a question from the Court he said he had given her no money before his departure, but had told her that if she needed funds she could apply to her kinsmen who owed him a substantial amount of cash; she had replied that this would not be necessary, for she worked as a domestic servant and was able to support herself. He had been back in Singapore for six months, she had failed to return to the conjugal home, and he was now eager to dissolve the marriage. The Court consented, and he uttered a three-*talak* formula before witnesses.

The second case of a wife's desertion was heard in March 1962. The couple were also Indian. The husband stated, on oath, that on a day in the previous October he had gone with his son to the barber, and on his return found that his wife had left the house, taking with her their other child, a young daughter, and all their clothes. He was amazed, for there had been no quarrel and they had spoken in friendly terms that very morning. He had heard gossip that his wife had been keeping company with a Hindu man, but he himself had never seen them together. He reported the disappearance to the police, and searched in vain everywhere for her and the child. He now wanted to end the marriage. He produced two witnesses who confirmed his statements, then uttered one *talak*, which was duly registered.

The third case was heard in August 1962. The couple had been married in a Malay State in 1956, and there were three children of the marriage. The husband, on oath, said that one day a young man came to the house from the Federation and stated he was the wife's brother by the same mother but a different father. His wife had previously mentioned to him that she had such a brother, and had welcomed the young man. The husband also welcomed him, and the 'brother' spent a week in their home. In Court the husband declared that he woke up one night to find his wife sleeping with her alleged half-brother; he said and did nothing about it, but simply left the house. In the course of the next afternoon, his wife and the man left, taking with them the youngest child, and leaving behind the older two children. Two witnesses confirmed in Court that the wife had indeed deserted him, and the husband pronounced a one-*talak* formula which was registered.

The last case was heard in November 1962. The couple had married in Kelantan in 1954. The wife was a native of Kelantan, while the husband was a Singaporean. On oath, the husband said that in 1960 his wife asked his permission to go to Kelantan to see her mother, who was reported to be very ill,

> . . . and she promised she would return to Singapore within a month. Four months later, she asked me to send her money for the return trip, and I sent her $50. She did not return, however, but sent another letter to say that she had spent the money, and to ask me to come in person to Kelantan to fetch her. I replied that my employers would not give me leave, and again asked her to return. But she wrote back to say that if I was unable to come to fetch her, she would ask me to send her a divorce certificate instead.

Meanwhile, the wife seemed to have moved, for the divorce summons could not be served on her at the Kelantan address, and a notice was inserted in a newspaper.

Two witnesses on behalf of the husband gave evidence that they had seen the wife off at the railway station when she had left for Kelantan, and she then wore several items of gold jewelry. (The implication seems to be that she could have pawned or sold the jewelry if she had been really eager to return to Singapore.)

The husband uttered a one-*talak* formula, and the divorce was registered.

II. *The wife lives outside Singapore*

She has acknowledged receipt of the divorce summons, but is unwilling to come to Singapore for the hearing of her husband's petition. She does not write to the Court to say that she objects to the divorce, or else she writes to say that she is willing (or eager) to be divorced.

In 1961 a Boyanese man issued a divorce summons, which was duly served on his wife in Bawean through the good offices of the Religious Affairs Bureau (*Kantor Urusan Agama*) of her district. He pleaded that he was in regular employment in Singapore and had written to his wife to join him, and on two occasions had sent her money for her fare. She had not come, and later she had acknowledged his numerous letters but not alluded to the likelihood of her joining him. He had now lost patience. The wife entered no defence, and the Court ruled that the husband was entitled to have a one-*talak* divorce registered.

In December 1962 another Boyanese husband came before the Court to seek the registration of a divorce from a wife in Bawean; he had been married in Bawean in 1945, and divorced in 1947 with a one-*talak* divorce. Some months later he remarried this same wife, and in 1948 a daughter was born. Later in that year the man left his wife and child and came to Singapore, where he took another wife by whom he now had six children. Early in 1962 a kinsman of his first wife approached him and told him she was eager for a divorce (presumably because she had another suitor). He came to the Shariah Court and said that he wished to end his marriage to his wife in Bawean, and the Court wrote to the Religious Affairs Bureau in the district where the wife lived, enclosing the summons. The Bureau returned the summons after it had been served on the wife (and duly acknowledged with her right thumbprint), and reported that the respondent begged her husband to send her a copy of the divorce certificate as soon as possible. She also asked him not to forget he had a daughter for whose maintenance he was responsible.

At the hearing in the Shariah Court the husband said that his daughter had recently married in Bawean and that he was accordingly no longer responsible for her support. He uttered one *talak*, which meant that his Boyanese wife was now divorced cumulatively with two *talak*, and accordingly the divorce was registered as *talak satu* (*jadi dua*), lit. 'one *talak* (become two)'. The Court ordered the husband to pay his wife $30 per month for three months as *iddah* maintenance, and he also agreed to pay in addition a consolatory gift of $10.

In April 1963 I heard the case of a young husband who sought a divorce because his wife refused to join him in Singapore. The couple had been married in 1957 in Malacca, and there were no children. The husband came to work in Singapore and his wife agreed to accompany him; later she said she wanted to return to her native village for a visit, and did so. He patiently waited for her to come back, and when she did not, he wrote to her. He sent the first letter in April 1962, and had since repeatedly requested her to come to Singapore. She had ignored his wishes, and he was now tired of waiting for her.

The summons had been returned by the wife who, in an

accompanying letter to the Court, stated she regretted she was unable to be present at the hearing and consented in advance to any ruling the Court chose to make.

The Court urged the husband to consider a reconciliation, even at this late hour. He replied very firmly that he *minta maaf* (begged pardon), his patience was utterly exhausted, he had waited a whole year for his wife to have a change of heart. The President replied that he fully appreciated the position, but that it was the Court's duty to make a final attempt at a reconciliation. He then enquired whether there were two men present who would be witnesses when he uttered the repudiation formula. The men were in Court, and were asked to come forward to sit on chairs in the front row and listen. The husband then stated, loud and clear,

'*Saya mencherai-kan isteri saya .... binte ... dengan talak satu*'. ('I repudiate my wife ... daughter of ... with one *talak*.') The President then asked: 'Have you divorced your wife before?', and when the husband said he had not, he declared 'This will be entered therefore as *talak satu yang pertama* (one *talak*, which is the first)'. Then he turned to the two witnesses and asked them, 'Did you hear him utter the repudiation?' They replied they had, and stated their names and addresses, which he wrote down.[1]

He now dealt with the matter of *iddah* maintenance. He asked the husband how much he earned, and was told, '$130 a month'. He declared: 'The Court rules that you pay $25 per month, for three months, as *iddah* maintenance. Then there is the matter of *matta'ah*, this is a consolatory gift a husband should make to his wife when he divorces her. There is no fixed amount, it can be $1,000, or $500, or $5, or $10. What will you pay?'

The husband said, '$5', and the President vainly attempted to coax him into raising the amount to at least $10, commenting: 'I know your wages are not high, and that is why I ordered you to pay only $25 per month *iddah* maintenance. I usually order $30 per month in the majority of cases. So, since you have been let off lightly in this respect, you might give $10 *matta'ah*.'

But the husband firmly replied he could not afford to do so. He was then told that he must pay, apart from the $5 *matta'ah*, $20 for the divorce registration fee, and $2 for a copy of the divorce certificate to be posted to his wife, plus the cost of postage.

The Court then rose. A few minutes later the husband went

[1] The divorce certificate requires the signatures of two witnesses.

with his father (who had been present throughout the proceedings) to see a Court official. He stated that he wished now to pay into Court, in advance, the whole amount of the *iddah* maintenance, i.e. $75, and $5 for *matta'ah*, and the registration total fee of $22, and he accordingly paid $102. He also gave an additional sixty cents to cover the cost of the registered letter for the Court to send his wife the sum she had been granted ($80). It was obvious that both father and son wished to walk out of the building with the matter completely settled.

III. *Men who are divorced according to Islam, but who have no official registration of the divorce they have uttered*

In April 1963 an officer on a merchant ship came before the Court to register a divorce he alleged he had uttered in 1950. Court officials told me that the background to this petition was a novel one. The man was born in Indonesia but had been domiciled in Singapore for many years. He now sought to acquire Singapore citizenship, and had been requested by the Immigration Department to fill in a form which required him to give details of any wives he had married. He had stated on the form that he had a wife (who had joined him from Jakarta some months earlier, with their three-year old child) living with him in Singapore, but that he had also been married before in Indonesia. He had been married in Java to a woman (whom I shall here refer to as Alijah) whom he later divorced. He had sent her a letter in 1950 to inform her he had divorced her. She had not replied, and he did not know her present whereabouts. He had registered this divorce neither in Indonesia nor in Singapore.

Apparently the Immigration authorities required him to produce such a document, i.e. an official copy of an extract from a Divorce Register, a divorce certificate. Accordingly, he had come to the Shariah Court. However, before a divorce summons is issued by the Shariah Court a copy of the marriage certificate must be produced. This the man did not have, so he made a statutory declaration giving details of the marriage, and this was accepted in lieu of a copy of a marriage certificate.

At the formal Court hearing in April 1963 the husband, on oath, stated he had sent a letter in 1950 to Alijah to tell her he had divorced her with one *talak*, and naming as a witness to the repudiation a friend from Pakistan. He had had no reply from Alijah and had never heard from, or of, her since; he had, moreover, lost touch with the Pakistani friend, but he had two witnesses ready to come into Court to testify that they knew the circumstances of the divorce. The first witness was the husband's younger brother. He declared he had never met Alijah, but had been told by his brother that he had married the woman when he had been to Java. Later, in 1950 or 1951, his brother had sent him a letter saying he had now divorced Alijah. Unfortunately, he had not kept this letter. He did remember, however, that his brother had referred to the matter again later, in a conversation between them.

The second witness was a Singapore postman. He too had never met Alijah, but had been told by the petitioner that he had married a woman in Celebes, when his ship had called at a port there. The President enquired whether he was absolutely sure the marriage had taken place in Celebes, and not elsewhere, and the witness replied that he was fairly certain of the fact. It was in 1950, or about 1950, that he had met the petitioner again in Singapore, and had been told by him that he had divorced that wife.

President: 'Did he tell you why he divorced her?'
Witness: 'He said it was difficult to have so many wives.'
President: 'How many wives did he then have?'
Witness: 'Seven.'

Answering a question from the Court, the husband stated that he had indeed had a total of seven wives, although not simultaneously of course, and that he had divorced several of them.

The President told the husband that the evidence given by the witnesses was not conclusive, *kurang kuat* (i.e. 'lacking in strength'), and he would have to swear a solemn oath that he had indeed repudiated his wife Alijah with one *talak* in the hearing of a witness called . . . *bin* . . ., whose present whereabouts he did not know, and that he had sent her a letter to this effect. The husband returned to the witness-box and repeated after the President the words of this oath. The Court then ruled that the repudiation, established to have been uttered in 1950, be now registered in Singapore.

A Court official later told me that the man was to go through the same procedure before the Shariah Court in respect of other wives whom he had in earlier years divorced in the same casual way. He added that one of them might well be the Celebes woman his second witness had referred to in his evidence. (A few days later the man was, in fact, granted the registration of a divorce from another wife.)

IV. *A husband requests the Court to 'advise' his estranged wife to resume cohabitation*

There was one such case in 1962, which ended in the husband agreeing to his wife's request to end the union, and uttering a repudiation formula in Court; the divorce was registered as an ordinary *talak*. Usually, when a husband issues an 'advice' (*nasehat*) summons, and the wife resolutely refuses to return to him, the case is eventually resolved by the wife redeeming herself from the marriage, and a *khula* divorce is registered. In the 1962 case the husband alleged that his wife had deserted him in order to live with another man, and that he was willing to take her back; indeed he was eager to do so if she promised she would be faithful in the future.

The wife denied the adultery and alleged that she had left her husband because of his brutality. She had earlier been called to see one of the Court officials who had advised her to return to her husband, but she had explained she could no longer endure the man's violent temper. She was still of the same mind now, and she added, 'All I want is a divorce'.

The husband announced that, in the circumstances, he was willing to grant her wish, and he uttered a one-*talak* repudiation. The wife then surrendered her right to *iddah* maintenance, and paid for the registration of the divorce. (Of course, had the husband made his divorce *conditional* upon her surrender of the *iddah* maintenance, and said, 'If you surrender the *iddah* maintenance, worth $ . . ., I will divorce you with one *talak*', and she had replied, 'I hereby surrender my *iddah* maintenance worth $ . . .', the divorce would have been registered as a *khula* decree.)

V. *The case starts with a summons issued by the wife who wishes to dissolve the union*

There were two instances in 1961, and thirteen in 1962. Sometimes the wife petitions for a *ta'alik* decree, but is unable to produce conclusive proof that her husband has contravened the terms of the *ta'alik*; at first he contests the application, but when he sees she is determined not to return to him he utters an ordinary *talak* repudiation.

In one case, the couple had been married for seven years and had four children. The wife invoked the maintenance *ta'alik*. She stated on oath that for the greater part of their married life her parents had maintained her husband, but that he had once taken a job on Christmas Island. Before he left, he promised that as soon as he settled there he would send for her; and eventually she joined him, with their children. She then discovered that during her absence he had been living on the Island with another woman. After his Singapore family joined him, he continued to visit his mistress and ate most of his meals with her. This had created a local scandal. After ignoring the headman's repeated warnings, the husband was dismissed from his job, and the family returned penniless to Singapore. The wife refused to live with her husband's parents; taking with her three of their four children, she went to her mother's house. She now stated that she had not been maintained by him for more than four months.

He denied the allegation, and added that he had offered her a home in his parents' house. She replied: 'It is not sweet to be maintained (*bukan di-tanggong manis* . . .) by your parents.' She accused him of being generally lazy, reluctant to look for work, and irresponsible, and asked him: 'Why do you refuse to divorce me?' He replied: 'Because I love the children, and you also.' She declared: 'You love only yourself, you don't care for me or for the children.' She added that if he divorced her, he would be involved in no expense, for she would surrender her right to *iddah* maintenance and pay for the registration of the divorce. He then uttered a one-*talak* repudiation, and the divorce was registered as an ordinary *talak*.

Not all wives who petition for a *ta'alik* decree and obtain the dissolution of their marriage are women who have been much sinned against. A man came to see the Shariah Court Social Case Worker in 1961 to report that his wife had deserted him, leaving their six children in his care. They had married in 1947. Recently, she had obtained a job as a domestic servant, and had become the mistress of a young soldier. The husband said that he had gone one night to her quarters and through an open window seen her asleep with the soldier by her side, both covered only by one sarong. He had then fetched his wife's own mother and brother and when the three came on the scene the couple were still asleep. They were roused, and the soldier was warned to leave the woman alone. The husband then pleaded with his wife to return to him and look after their children, but she had refused. He later told the wife's employers what had happened, and they dismissed her. The wife went to live with her mother, and still refused to return to her husband; she was continuing to see her young lover. The husband was distraught when he came to see the Social Worker, explaining that his job required him to work at night, and that in his absence his eldest daughter, aged twelve years, had been raped one night by a neighbour. He asked if Court officials could exert pressure on his wife to return to the conjugal home, but he did not take out an 'advice' summons.

The wife came to see the Social Worker, in reply to a letter requesting her do to so; she brought her lover with her. She said she had no love left for her husband, that she was willing to take all the children and look after them herself, but she would on no account return to her husband. The soldier, who was a young bachelor, said he 'could not help it if she liked him', and he for his part would not give her up. Until such time as she found another job and had another home, he would continue to visit her at her mother's home; he had a right to do so for he was no stranger, being a kinsman of the woman. The wife then asked her husband to agree to a divorce in order to settle the matter, but he refused, saying he still wanted her back.

Five months later the wife issued a non-maintenance *ta'alik* summons, and there was a Court hearing three months after the summons was issued. By then the husband was resigned to the divorce, for after his wife agreed not to seek at any future date the custody of their six children (who were to remain with their father), he uttered a one-*talak* repudiation. The wife surrendered her right to *iddah* maintenance. In view of the bitter conjugal disputes which led to this dissolution, the statement in the Court record-book is worth quoting: 'The couple agree to divorce amicably (*cherai dengan baik*).'

There are cases where a husband in a fit of temper utters a repudiation in his wife's presence, and later regrets the action and refuses to register the divorce. If the wife, on the other hand, is eager to dissolve the marriage, she may petition the Court. One young woman did so in 1961: she claimed that her husband was violent and bad-tempered, and that after a quarrel he had told her

'Get out of here, I divorce you! (*Keluar angkau dari sini, aku cherai-kan angkau!*).'

At their marriage he had bound himself by *ta'alik* containing two clauses: non-maintenance over a period of three months or longer; and injurious beating. In her petition she also claimed that he had frequently beaten her, and that she had endured it on account of their three children. She had now, however, reached the limit of her endurance. She produced two witnesses who confirmed that they had heard the husband utter the repudiation; their evidence was conclusive, and the Court accordingly ordered the registration of the divorce as an ordinary *talak*. Had she been unable to produce these witnesses or to satisfy the Court in some other way that her husband had indeed uttered the fateful words, her alternative would have been to prove conclusively that her husband had been guilty of a breach of the injurious beating clause, in which case a *ta'alik* divorce would have been registered.

Although a Singapore Muslim woman is not entitled to seek a divorce on the ground that her husband has taken another wife, one young Indian woman did so in 1962. The Court, of course, did not order the registration of the divorce on account of the polygynous marriage – indeed it is not empowered to do so – but as a result of the husband eventually agreeing to pronounce a *talak*.

The couple were both Indian, and the wife was fifteen years old when she married in 1959. There was no *ta'alik*. They lived in her parents' house, and the union was at first harmonious. In 1961 her mother's first cousin (who had been married to her mother's brother and so was her aunt by marriage as well as her first cousin once removed) was divorced and came to live in the household. A few months later the divorcee left, saying she was going to stay with another kinswoman; but in fact did not do so. It was then the young wife discovered that her husband had been engaged in an affair with her aunt. The latter was now living in a rented room and the husband regularly visited her there; moreover, the aunt's close kinsmen were exerting pressure on the lover to marry her and regularize the position. (There is no indication in the available records of the case that the older woman was pregnant.) The young wife came to see the Social Worker in the Shariah Court and reported the situation in which she found herself. She added that her husband had now stopped coming home to her altogether and was openly cohabiting with her aunt, and she begged the Social Worker to advise her husband to break off the affair.

The husband was called for an interview, and came. He admitted that all the allegations were true and added that he was in a very difficult position because his mistress's kinsmen were threatening him with violence if he did not marry her. Yet he was reluctant to divorce his wife, and knew that the Singapore Chief Kathi would be unlikely to give his consent to his marrying polygynously since his earnings were modest. Eventually he declared that he would like to live again with his wife, but not in her parents' home. He would at once rent independent accommodation and fetch his wife to live with him.

Two weeks later the wife reported to the Social Worker that she had not seen her husband yet; but she had heard he had married his mistress in Kelantan, and that the couple were now back in Singapore. She added that he had ceased giving her money for maintenance. The husband, again called for an interview, adopted a 'very rude' manner, according to the report of the Social Worker. He admitted marrying his mistress in Kelantan and neglecting to maintain his first wife, and eventually agreed to the latter's request that he divorce her. The divorce was to take place 'amicably', i.e. by mutual consent, and a date was fixed for the couple to come before one of the Court kathis to register the dissolution.

On the appointed day the husband said he had changed his mind and was now unwilling to utter the repudiation. He claimed he was well able to maintain two wives. The young woman protested that he was barely able to make ends meet when they lived with her parents, that moreover she was convinced he would neglect her in favour of the older wife – since he had already done so even before the Kelantan marriage. She was only eighteen and not prepared to resign herself to such a miserable conjugal existence.

There was deadlock and the young wife on 17 August 1962 issued a summons petitioning for the registration of a divorce on the following grounds:

(1) My husband has another wife.
(2) I do not like to have a co-wife (*saya tidak suka bermadu*).
(3) He has deserted me since 11.7.62.

On the date fixed for the hearing the couple were both present, and the Court record-book simply states that husband and wife 'want to divorce amicably on the following conditions:

(1) The husband is to pay *iddah* maintenance of $30 per month for three months.

(2) The wife surrenders her right to the *mas kahwin*, $22.50.

(3) The wife will return his clothes to her husband.

(4) The husband will pay the divorce registration fee.

(5) The wife will make no other claims at any future date.'

The husband then uttered one *talak*, which was registered the same day.

When a man wishes to dissolve his marriage but fails to secure his wife's consent, his only remedy lies in issuing a divorce summons. It may be that the wife is resigned to the divorce but disagrees as to its conditions – we have seen earlier that some husbands eventually consent at the Court hearing to make substantial financial concessions to their wives in order to 'redeem' themselves speedily from the marriage.[1] Or it may be that the woman still cares for her husband, and is moreover unwilling to surrender lightly the security of a home and a regular housekeeping allowance. Or again, she may have forced him into marriage after he had seriously compromised her and she is reluctant to be divorced soon after the wedding.

There was one such case before the Court in 1961. The couple were married in the last week of 1960 and in February 1961 there was a divorce hearing in Court. The husband stated that a week after the marriage his bride had agreed to an amicable divorce, and then changed her mind; he, for his part, was still very eager to dissolve the union. The Court adjourned the case for two months and advised the husband to reconsider his decision. Two months later, however, he declared he was still very anxious to end the union. The wife, on oath, alleged he had been a friend of her elder brother and a frequent visitor to their home. Marriage had been discussed, but his parents did not approve of the match. He had seduced her, she had become pregnant and informed him of the fact, and he had then advised her to induce an abortion for otherwise 'the child would be born from sin'; and he promised her that if she did abort he would then marry her. He gave her some medicine, which she took, and she aborted. She then confessed the whole matter to her family; her brother and her

[1] Cf. above, pp. 98 ff.

sister's husband at once went to fetch her lover, who at first denied her allegations. He was then asked whether, since he was so emphatic about his innocence, he would agree to drink *Ayer Ya Sin*. This is a type of 'truth oath' current among some Singapore Malays: a verse of the Koran is recited over a glass of water and the person willing to swear to the truth of his version of an event drinks the water. If he has lied, he exposes himself to divine retribution in the (near or remote) future. The reluctant bridegroom replied that there was no need for him to drink *Ayer Ya Sin*, for he was now ready to marry the girl. He did so the very next day, paying the modest sum of $50 as *belanja kahwin*, and the usual amount of $22.50 as *mas kahwin*. He also bound himself to a three-months maintenance *ta'alik*.

A week after the marriage he persuaded her to accompany him to the Shariah Court to register a divorce, but when a Court kathi advised them to reconsider the decision she said she would be happy to do so. The husband did not deny the truth of his wife's evidence in Court, but insisted that he still wished to dissolve the marriage. The Court adjourned the case for another two weeks.

At the third hearing it became evident that the husband would not relent, and he was told that if he uttered a one-*talak* formula the divorce would be registered. He then proceeded to utter a three-*talak* repudiation. The President of the Court recorded that he had done so, but ruled that such a formula uttered on a single occasion would be registered as a one-*talak* divorce.

A similar incident occurred in Court in October 1962. The couple had been married in 1960 when the bride, described as a Malay, was fifteen years old and the groom, an Arab, twenty-six. They had lived with the husband's mother, and there were frequent quarrels between the two women. The husband had come into Court one day to issue a divorce summons, had been referred to a Court kathi, and had told the latter that his wife had left the conjugal home without his knowledge or consent on the previous day, and that he did not know her present whereabouts. The kathi asked for the address of the wife's parents, sent her a letter, and she came for an interview. She declared that she had left her husband's home because his mother had thrown her out, that she had had no quarrel with her husband, only with his mother, and that she had no desire to be divorced. The husband and his mother were also present at the interview, and the older woman observed that she had not actually ordered the wife to get out of the house; she had merely rebuked her for not paying attention to the advice of her elders and for being rude, and the young woman 'perhaps left the house as a result of this rebuke'. The kathi advised the husband to consent to a reconciliation, but he refused to do so, saying that his wife's mother had constantly urged him to release her daughter from an unhappy union, and he was now willing and eager to accede to his mother-in-law's request.

When the Court kathi saw that the husband was determined to end the marriage, he asked the wife whether in the circumstances she would now consent to an amicable divorce. She refused, and five months after he had first been interviewed by the kathi the man took out a divorce summons, stating he wished to divorce his wife because:

(1) My wife left the house on 29.11.1961 without my consent.
(2) My wife always abuses me in public.
(3) My mother-in-law is always asking me to divorce my wife.

The wife was, meanwhile, pregnant, and the hearing took place three months after the summons was issued, i.e. after the birth of the baby.

The husband and wife argued bitterly in Court, and eventually she said that she hoped the husband would pay $30 in respect of the midwife's fee and $20 for postnatal medicines as one of the terms of the divorce. He agreed to do so, and also to pay a consolatory gift of $15, and $30 per month *iddah* maintenance for three months. He was also ordered by the Court to pay $30 per month in respect of his child's maintenance and to pay this from the day of the baby's birth. The husband was a clerk, earning $252 per month.

He uttered in Court: 'I divorce my wife . . . *binte* . . . with three *talak*.' The President recorded this and ruled: 'This means one *talak* because he has uttered this divorce on one occasion, i.e. in Court.' The divorce was accordingly registered as a one-*talak* repudiation.[1]

[1] Ahmad Ibrahim, in his article 'Muslim Marriage and Divorce in Singapore', notes: 'Some jurists in the Arab countries and in Indonesia are of the opinion that it is unlawful to pronounce the *talak* three times at short intervals or in close succession and they hold that where a person pronounces the three *talaks* together this should only have effect as one *talak* . . . Recent legislation in the Arab countries based on the Muslim law have decreed that where the three *talaks* are pronounced at once, this will only take effect as one *talak* . . .' and he cites in support of this statement J. N. D. Anderson, *Islamic Law in the Modern World*, London, 1959, p. 56.

The Shariah Court registered three cases of three-*talak* repudiations (uttered on a single occasion, it would appear from the records) in 1961; and two cases in 1962 – one in January and one in February. In four of the five cases, the wife had deserted the conjugal home without trace; and there was conclusive evidence in two cases that she had left in order to live with a lover. (Moreover, both wives had non-Muslim lovers – one of the men was a European, and the other a Hindu.) The four deserting wives were not in Court at the hearing, and had been served with a notice to appear through the medium of a newspaper.[1]

In the fifth case, which occurred in June 1961, the wife was in Court. The husband had been sentenced to eight years' jail early that year, and the wife wanted to dissolve the union, because as she told a Court kathi who reported it to the President of the Court, 'she cannot wait such a long time especially since she is still young'.[2] The couple had three children. At the hearing, the husband enquired of his wife: 'Do you want to be repudiated even if my kinsmen provide you with maintenance?' She replied: 'Yes, even so, I still wish to be repudiated.' The husband at once uttered a three-*talak* formula, which was duly registered.

In July 1963 I was present at a hearing when a three-*talak* divorce was registered after a wife had been caught *in flagrante delicto*, and after she had admitted in Court that she had committed adultery. The husband was on a military course in the United Kingdom, and he had been informed by letter of his wife's unfaithfulness; he had uttered a three-*talak* repudiation in England in the presence of witnesses. An affidavit to that effect was produced in Court on his behalf.[3]

What are the grounds a Muslim husband gives when he petitions the Court for the registration of a divorce from a wife reluctant to agree to an amicable dissolution? An examination of the summonses taken out by such men reveals a variety of allegations ranging from adultery to 'disobedience' ('my wife goes out of the house without my permission'). Sometimes, however, the man

[1] See pp. 107 f. above concerning the two deserting wives not accused of adultery.

[2] This was in English: one of the Court kathis often uses English when he writes a memorandum to the President about a matrimonial dispute.

[3] A three-*talak* repudiation is uncommon among Singapore Malays (see my *Malay Kinship*, pp. 112–13) and indeed among Singapore Muslims generally; see below, pp. 148 f.

gives no other grounds than 'I do not like my wife any more (*Saya tidak suka lagi kepada isteri saya*)'. Some husbands may in fact have serious cause to find the union intolerable, but may be reluctant to reveal it. In one such instance a man aged twenty-eight years simply repeated in the witness-box that he no longer liked his wife, and stated that after living with her for eighteen months he had left her. They had now been separated for two years and he sought to dissolve the marriage; he added, 'That is all I have to say'.

The wife, who was twenty years old, was invited to cross-examine him. She asked, 'What is the reason you do not like me?' He was evasive at first, saying he would willingly have offered her a substantial amount as a consolatory gift, because he wanted to settle the divorce amicably; but he had no ready money, and many debts. She persisted, 'But why do you not like me?', and at last he exclaimed, 'Because your body exudes a rotten smell, a smell quite out of the ordinary'. He added that he had endured it at first, hoping it was a passing ailment, but when it did not abate he could endure her proximity no longer. She did not deny his allegation, but commented: 'My body smells because you never bought me powder, or soap, or scent, or even clothes'. The husband then explained bluntly that her ailment sprang from more fundamental causes than lack of perfumed cosmetics or of change of garments. She had no further questions to put to him.

She then went into the witness-box and was sworn in. She declared she was still unwilling to be divorced, but that she would reluctantly consent to end the marriage if her husband paid her maintenance in respect of the past six months. Since he said he had no capital, she would agree to his paying the sum by instalments out of his monthly salary of $360. There was some haggling about the rate at which the total amount in respect of past maintenance would be paid off, and the case was eventually adjourned to the next day. At the second hearing the couple had reached agreement on the financial conditions of the divorce. The Court ruled that since there appeared to be no hope of a reconciliation, the divorce would be registered subject to the condition that the husband pay:

(1) *iddah* maintenance of $35 per month for three months;
(2) a consolatory gift of $10;
(3) the divorce registration fee of $22;

(4) a total of $210 in respect of six months' past maintenance, calculated at the rate of $35 per month. The instalments would be paid at the rate of $5 per month for the first three months, and afterwards at $15 per month until the debt was finally settled. He would bring the money into Court on the third of every month.

The husband then formally repudiated his wife in the presence of two witnesses.

In another case which came before the Court some months earlier, the husband gave no explanation whatever (or none that was recorded) of his desire for a divorce other than that he did not like his wife any more. The statement in the divorce summons reads: '*Saya hendak cherai isteri saya sebab: Saya tidak suka lagi dengan isteri saya* (I wish to divorce my wife because: I do not like my wife any more).' When he had come to say he wished to repudiate his wife, he had been, as usual, referred to one of the officials who had tried to dissuade him from ending the union. He was seen first by the lady Social Worker, and later by a Court kathi, and to neither would he state any reason to account for his dislike of his wife. They had been married for nearly two years and were both in their twenties; the wife had not been married before and it appears that it had also been the man's first marriage. The wife was called for an interview and she said that a year after the wedding she found herself pregnant, and told her husband, who left her when he heard the news. She still loved him and was unwilling to be divorced. The man, however, was adamant in his determination and eventually (six months after the conciliation attempts had failed) there was a hearing in Court. The President advised him to reconsider his decision and adjourned the case for two days, but at the second hearing the husband insisted on the divorce, which the Court finally consented to register. The husband formally uttered one *talak* and at once paid his wife a total of $177.50:

(1) $22.50 *mas kahwin*, which was owing;
(2) $20 as consolatory gift;
(3) $135 in respect of *iddah* maintenance (at the rate of $45 per month for three months).

In one case a husband came to seek the registration of a divorce on the grounds that he and his wife had no luck, were not well-fated in their union. He declared that she was of the same opinion and was also eager to end the marriage. They had not registered the divorce amicably before a kathi because the wife would not agree to the financial conditions of the divorce which he had suggested. They had been married for eighteen months and had a child four months old. At the hearing in Court the couple eventually settled on the terms and a repudiation was duly pronounced and registered.

This is the only case on record for 1961 and 1962 of a petitioner seeking a dissolution of his union on the sole grounds that it was not well-fated. I was informed by the Court kathis, however, that this argument is one which is very frequently advanced by husbands when they are first interviewed and asked to explain why they seek a divorce. Some state that they have been in ill-health since their marriage, or that they have had no success in their job, or that they have felt generally uneasy and restless, and believe that the remedy for their ill lies in dissolving the union which has been mysteriously responsible for this unfortunate state of affairs. Some of the husbands are persuaded to persevere in the marriage; others refuse and eventually take out a divorce summons in which they state more tangible grounds than ill-fate: the wife is quarrelsome; or a bad housekeeper ('does not look well after my food and drink'); or frequently goes out of the house without her husband's prior consent.

When such a husband eventually comes before the Court and gives sworn evidence of his wife's misdemeanours, she usually denies his allegations and says that 'the real reason' for his petition is that he now wishes to marry someone younger, or that his mother has made mischief, or that her co-wife has incited him. In two cases in 1962 (out of twenty when the husband had been the petitioner) the petitioning husband was polygynously married.

6

Rojo

Rojo (lit. in Arabic, 'return') means revocation of divorce. A Muslim may, within his wife's *iddah* period, revoke the divorce which he has uttered; he may do so only if he has previously divorced his wife with one or two *talak*. As we know, there is no revocation from a three-*talak* divorce; and there is no revocation from a *khula* divorce even if only one or two *talak* have been uttered. There is also no revocation possible in Islam after a *fasah* decree. A man whose marriage has been dissolved by *khula* or by *fasah*, which are *talak bain sughra* (irrevocable 'small' *talak*), may, however, marry his wife again, although he may not revoke the divorce. Unlike a *talak bain kubra*,[1] the only necessary condition for a remarriage is his divorced wife's consent. For among the Shafi'is, although a spinster may be given away in marriage by her guardian without her consent, a woman who is not a virgin (although she still needs a guardian for marriage) is emancipated to the extent that she may not be given in marriage without her express consent.

A wife divorced by three *talak* is subject to an *iddah* period, but her husband has no duty to maintain her during this period unless she is pregnant by him. If she is so pregnant he must maintain her until she is delivered, and her *iddah* is extended until delivery. This applies to any pregnant wife, whether she has been divorced by one, two, or three *talak*. A wife divorced by one or two *talak* has the right to be maintained during the usual *iddah* period of three months.

If a woman has gone to considerable expense in order to secure her redemption from a marriage she considers intolerable, and a *khula* divorce is registered, she has at least the consolation that she will not find herself 'returned' to her husband, for there can be no *rojo* after a *khula* divorce. Similarly, if she has gone through the laborious procedure of proving to a kathi or to a religious Court

[1] Cf. p. 88 above.

that she is entitled to the judicial dissolution of her union because her husband is an utter pauper, or impotent, or a leper, or insane, or has a venereal disease, she also knows that the man from whom she has been freed cannot at his whim and without her consent revoke the dissolution, and bind her to him again by registering a *rojo*.

On the other hand, a Muslim husband could (and sometimes did, in Singapore, until the 1960 Amendment to the *Muslims Ordinance, 1957*) register a *rojo* from an 'ordinary' one- or two-*talak* divorce, or from a *ta'alik* divorce, without seeking his wife's approval. In 1957, before the establishment of the Shariah Court, an interesting case occurred. A couple had married in July 1956, and there was a maintenance *ta'alik* in the contract. They had very violent quarrels, and the wife sought a divorce; after numerous attempts at reconciliation by many kinsmen, the couple agreed to submit to the decision of arbitrators and *hakam* were appointed. They decided the couple would be reconciled with a written agreement (but not a *ta'alik*), embodying many clauses, and this was done in May 1957. Two months later the wife had a baby girl. The husband, meanwhile, broke the maintenance *ta'alik* as well as some of the conditions of the written agreement. The wife went to a kathi, who wrote to the husband, giving him three days in which to lodge a defence; when no defence was entered, the kathi registered a *ta'alik* divorce in August 1957.

Within a week, the husband went to the then Chief Kathi of Singapore and registered a *rojo* from this divorce. The Chief Kathi sent a copy of the *rojo* registration entry (i.e. a *surat rojo*, a certificate of revocation of divorce) to the wife, who refused to accept it. The Chief Kathi then wrote to every kathi in Singapore, enclosing a copy of the *rojo* certificate, so that the wife could not remarry (or at least, could not have another marriage registered by a kathi) in Singapore.

Meanwhile the wife had in her possession a copy of the *ta'alik* divorce certificate which she had obtained after she had secured her divorce. After her *iddah* period was over she went to the nearby State of Johore with her divorce certificate in hand, and there she was duly married in February 1958 to another man. When her previous husband and the Singapore Chief Kathi discovered this, they went to Johore, saw the Chief Kathi of that State and explained that the wife had not been free to remarry since her divorce had been lawfully revoked within her *iddah* period. The Johore Chief Kathi annulled the Johore marriage.

The Shariah Court, as we know, was constituted in November 1958, and the case was brought before it in 1959. After many postponements and adjourned hearings, the Court ruled in May 1960 that in Islam a husband does not have to secure his wife's consent before he decides to revoke a divorce. The wife, meanwhile, had had a child by the second union, a boy born in January 1959, and the Court expressed the wish that under the circumstances the husband who had revoked the divorce – and whose revocation was now established to be valid – might consent to release his wife. The husband, in the course of earlier hearings, had stated that if the wife surrendered his daughter to him, he would utter a repudiation; but the Shariah Court decided it could not make an order for the husband to have custody of the baby girl.

The wife lodged an appeal against the Shariah Court decision that the revocation of her *ta'alik* divorce was valid, and eventually she secured a judicial decree of *fasah* which, by order of the Appeal Board, the Shariah Court registered on 2 January 1962.

Apparently it was this case, publicized in 1959 and 1960, which focused attention on the need to amend existing legislation. Section 12 (3) of the *Muslims Ordinance, 1957* stated:

> A *Kathi* shall not register any divorce unless he is satisfied that both the husband and the wife have consented thereto.

The 1960 Amendment to the *Muslims Ordinance, 1957* decreed – among other things – that Section 12 (3) be amended to read:

> A Kathi shall not register any divorce or revocation of divorce unless he is satisfied after inquiry that both the husband and the wife have consented thereto.

It is worth pointing out here, however, that although a Muslim woman's consent to her divorce must be recorded in Singapore by her signing the register of divorces, as well as an application form for divorce, such is not the case *in fact* for a revocation. *The Muslim Marriage and Divorce Rules 1959* specify (rule 4C) that there shall be an entry for the signature of the wife in the registers of revocations. Nevertheless, up to July 1963, the registers of revocations had no such entry: the pre-1960 forms were still in use; and there were no application forms for revocations. I was informed by the Registrar of Muslim Marriages and Divorces, however, that Singapore kathis do ensure that a wife consents to the *rojo*, and that since the 1960 Amendment no woman had lodged a complaint that her divorce had been revoked in Singapore without her consent.

There has been at least one case since 1960, however, when after a Singapore divorce the husband went to a State in the Federation and revoked the divorce without even informing his wife in Singapore. After her *iddah* period was over, she married another man. Only then did she hear from her former husband that he had revoked the divorce outside Singapore, and she came to see the Singapore Chief Kathi in great distress to ask what her status was. The Chief Kathi was obliged to inform her that the revocation was valid in Islam (as this had been established by the case we have just described), and therefore had to be found valid in Singapore. If the revocation was valid, it followed that her second marriage was void. A Singapore kathi cannot register a revocation without the wife's consent, but such a revocation is nevertheless valid in Islam, and the registration of a revocation to which the wife has not consented was valid in several States in the Federation.

The only remedy open to such a wife in Singapore would seem to be a petition for a decree of *fasah* if the husband who revoked the divorce failed to maintain her. However, if he has offered her

Year	*a* *Marriages*	*b* *Divorces*	*c* *Rojo*	*b* as % of *a* *Divorce* %	*c* as % of *b* *Rojo* %
1947	2,784	1,588	157	57·0	9·9
1948	2,605	1,545	222	59·3	14·4
1949	2,516	1,401	144	55·7	10·3
1950	2,506	1,501	144	59·9	9·6
1951	2,699	1,526	174	56·5	11·4
1952	2,658	1,474	165	55·5	11·2
1953	2,445	1,417	168	57·9	11·9
1954	2,457	1,357	168	55·2	12·4
1955	2,472	1,247	164	50·4	13·2
1956	2,414	1,074	168	44·5	15·6
1957	2,303	1,201	183	52·1	15·2
1958	2,332	1,149	156	49·3	13·6
1959	2,116	577	91	27·3	15·8
1960	1,814	574	72	31·6	12·2
1961	1,560	401	47	25·7	11·7
1962	1,483	449	51	30·3	11·4

an unobjectionable home and reasonable maintenance and she has refused to resume cohabitation without just cause, she is unlikely to succeed in her plea for a *fasah* decree in Singapore.

As can be seen from the above table, the percentage of *rojo* from divorces has shown great variations in the last twelve years, as it had done in earlier decades.[1] However, if the situation which obtained in 1961 and 1962 also obtained in earlier years or decades, it may well be that the divorce registration figures do not accurately reflect the number of Singapore couples who consider themselves to have been divorced. For, of all the 51 *rojo* registered in 1962, at least 12 were *rojo* from repudiations which had never been registered. I say 'at least' for there were several other cases where I was unable to trace the registration of the divorce which was officially revoked. In the 12 cases mentioned, the kathi registering the revocation noted against the entry requiring him to give details of the divorce now being revoked: 'The divorce was uttered but not registered.' In 1961 there were 13 such *rojo* from unregistered divorces, out of a total of 47 registered *rojo* for that year; that is, in thirteen cases there was a specific entry that 'the divorce was uttered, but not [or 'not yet, *belum*'] registered'. Usually, the date of the unregistered divorce was given; sometime, it was omitted – perhaps because the parties could not remember it. Whenever the type of divorce was specified, the kathi recorded that it had been a one-*talak* divorce; sometimes the additional (but very necessary) information was recorded as to whether the one-*talak* unregistered divorce had been a first *talak*, or a second *talak*. In some cases, both in 1961 and in 1962, there were no details whatever as to the type of *talak* uttered. The entry simply stated: 'This is a *rojo* from a repudiation (*talak*) uttered, but not registered.'

In 1961, no date was recorded in respect of 7 unregistered divorces. In the other 6 cases, the dates of the unregistered divorce showed that the revocation had been registered within the following lapses of time: 3 days; 6 days; 10 days; 30 days; 38 days; 67 days.

In 1962, out of 12 *rojo* in respect of unregistered divorces, no date was given in only one case. The other 11 *rojo* were registered within the following number of days of the repudiation being uttered: in two cases, the day after it was uttered; in one case within 3 days; in another within 5 days; in yet another within 7

[1] See my *Malay Kinship*, p. 117.

days; in two cases within 11 days; and in one case each within 15, 21, 23, and 39 days.

I discussed the subject of *rojo* from unregistered divorces with Government officials, in view of the fact (which I did not stress) that some of the *rojo* registrations had been effected by Shariah Court kathis. They told me that the aim of the religious authorities was to encourage as many reconciliations and revocations as possible, and that when a couple were eager to resume lawful cohabitation it seemed punitive to require them to pay first the divorce registration fee ($19, which includes $4 for the application form), and then the fee for the registration of the revocation. I refrained from pointing out that by so doing Singapore kathis were aiding and abetting the couple to contravene Section 12 of the 1957 Ordinance which makes registration of every marriage, divorce, and revocation of divorce compulsory.

I then examined the registers of *rojo* for the years 1955 to 1960, studying every registration. In 1955 and in 1956 (there were 164 *rojo* in 1955 and 168 in 1956) every *rojo* was in respect of a registered divorce. In 1957, there were 183 *rojo* registered and in 182 cases the *rojo* was in respect of a registered divorce; in one case the reference to the divorce was left blank, and this may have been an inadvertent omission on the part of the kathi. In 1958 all 156 *rojo* were from registered divorces.

In 1959 there were 91 *rojo*; all but one were from registered divorces. In the one case where the divorce had not been registered, there is a note by the then Chief Kathi who registered the revocation that the divorce, 'according to a letter from the Shariah Court', had taken place a month earlier.

In 1960 there were 72 *rojo*, of which 68 were in respect of registered divorces. In one of the other 4 cases, the kathi effecting the registration noted that the husband had produced a Statutory Declaration as evidence of the divorce which was now being revoked. In another case, the kathi omitted all reference to the divorce – this need not mean that the divorce had not been registered, however, for this particular kathi is often careless about filling in all the entries in registers of marriage, divorce, or revocation; he had not in this case even stamped the entry with his seal. In the other two cases an entry states that the divorce had not been registered.

Not all Singapore kathis show leniency (or disregard for the

Ordinance) in this respect. For example, in 1962 one kathi registered a *rojo* from a divorce registered only on the previous day, and it is likely that he had persuaded the couple in question to register their divorce first, and the next day find the fee necessary to effect the *rojo* registration Another kathi registered a divorce on 1 August 1961, noting that the registration was in respect of a repudiation uttered that day at 6 p.m. On 1 August 1961, i.e. the very same day, he registered a revocation from that divorce. I checked the register of divorces to ensure that there had not been an error, and found that the couple had indeed had a divorce registered on 1 August 1961. In order to be fully satisfied I looked at that kathi's own personal register of divorces and revocations, and again found that the couple had effected the registration of both the divorce and the revocation on the same day, or rather, the same evening.

One may well wonder why a couple who have not gone to register a divorce should decide to register a revocation of this divorce. Surely, they could forget that the fateful words were ever uttered – especially if there had been no witnesses – and quietly resume cohabitation. I was told by reliable informants that such behaviour is not unknown among Singapore Muslims. There is also documentary evidence that it occurs: we saw earlier that a woman successfully petitioned the Shariah Court in 1961 for the registration of a divorce which her husband had uttered before witnesses.[1] There was a similar case before the Court in 1963. For every such case brought to the notice of the Court there may be dozens which are settled quietly between the couple. Islam, of course, does not require registration of either a divorce or a revocation; it is enough for the husband to state that he revokes the repudiation he has uttered.[2] In Singapore, when such a husband comes to register a revocation he is asked to state: 'I return to my wife . . . *binte* . . .', and some kathis record the statement verbatim.

When I enquired of a Singapore kathi why he thought a couple who had not registered a divorce should wish to register a *rojo* from such a divorce, he replied that it was because Singapore Muslims were pious and did not like to live in sin. (Of course, the couple would not sin in Islam if they resumed cohabitation after the husband had uttered a formula of revocation. But some

[1] pp. 116 f. above. [2] *Minhaj et Talibin*, p. 345.

Singapore Muslims believe it is a sin not to register a divorce, and further, many more believe that unless a revocation is also registered cohabitation is tantamount to fornication.) It may well be that it is piety which spurs a Muslim couple to register a revocation from an unregistered divorce. On the other hand, a cynic might comment that a husband, in order to protect himself against the eventuality of his wife later petitioning the Court to register a repudiation, which he now regrets, but which he had uttered before witnesses, persuades her to agree to a reconciliation and promptly takes her to a kathi to register a *rojo* before she changes her mind. Similarly, a wife eager to resume cohabitation (and fearful lest her husband eventually decide to petition the Court to register the divorce he has already uttered before witnesses) may do so. However, since a man can always repeat the words of the repudiation after the *rojo*, whenever he pleases, he stands to lose nothing by registering a *rojo*, except the registration fee.

There are women who agree to a *rojo* when they are dissatisfied with some of the consequences of the divorce. Thus in one case a woman was divorced by mutual consent before a kathi, and then found that her husband had taken away their children. She was in no financial position to sue in the High Court for their custody, and may not have been aware of the existence of the Legal Aid Bureau,[1] so that when the kathi came to tell her that her husband was eager to revoke the divorce, she eventually consented. The couple resumed cohabitation. Having secured possession of her children, the wife took them to her family (where they were jealously guarded) and then petitioned the Court for a divorce. Her plea was bitterly contested by her husband, but eventually a *khula* divorce was registered.

There are also couples who go before a kathi to register a divorce, but because they say they have no money for the divorce registration fee the kathi records the matter in a notebook but does not register the divorce, and therefore he does not give them a divorce certificate, a *surat cherai*, until the fee is paid. This happened when a couple went in December 1959 before a kathi who had married them four years earlier. The kathi tried to dissuade them from divorcing, but the man uttered the repudiation and the kathi made a note of it. The registration fee was not paid, and the

[1] See below, p. 168.

divorce was not registered. Later the couple saw the kathi again and the wife was persuaded to agree to a *rojo*. Again, the husband uttered the formula of *rojo*, but did not pay the registration fee.

The reconciliation was short-lived, and the wife petitioned the Court for a *ta'alik* decree. It was then that the earlier divorce and revocation were mentioned, and the kathi was called as a witness because the wife had alleged that she had been forced into consenting to the *rojo* by the kathi who had deliberately misled her as to her rights. The kathi emphatically denied the allegations, and offered to bring at the next hearing his notebook containing a record of the discussion he had had with her before the *rojo* had been decided. At the date fixed for the next hearing, however, the husband was ill and could not attend. The case was adjourned for three weeks and the couple then stated they were now agreed on the terms of the divorce, which would be by *khula*; the husband uttered a one-*talak khula* formula: 'If you surrender your *nafkah iddah*, worth $90, I will divorce you with one *talak*, which will add up to two *talak*' (*dengan talak satu, menjadi dua talak*). The divorce was thus registered as a second *talak*, because the earlier, unregistered *talak*, had been taken into account.

An interesting point which arises in the context of unregistered divorces is the position of husbands who have uttered a one-*talak* repudiation on three occasions: if they omitted to register one of the repudiations there is no record that the last one is the third and therefore irrevocable *talak*. A kathi will thus register a *rojo* in good faith, and perhaps warn the husband of the danger of a third repudiation. Nevertheless, registration of such a *rojo* would be declared invalid if it were shown that the divorce it revoked was in fact a divorce of a third *talak* although it had been wrongly registered as a second *talak*. A spouse knowingly cohabiting after the union has been dissolved by three *talak* (whether registered or not) would be living in sin. There is no provision in Singapore for punishing such an action.[1]

However, because there was no central index of all Singapore marriages, divorces, or revocations, it was possible for a man to declare (in good or in bad faith) to a kathi that he wished to

[1] In some Malay states, it is a punishable offence. See Ahmad Ibrahim, 'The Status of Women in Family Law in the Federation of Malaya, Singapore and the Borneo Territories', Background Paper B, Prepared for the United Nations Secretariat for the 1962 Seminar on the Status of Women in Family Law held in Tokyo; pp. 166–7.

remarry a divorced wife whom he had previously divorced only twice, when in fact he had divorced her three times and had even registered the divorce on the three occasions. There is no quick way to check the veracity of such a statement.

In August 1962 a man came before the Shariah Court, which had to consider his petition to declare his marriage invalid. These were the facts: he and his wife had married on 24.7.1950; divorced 5.4.1955; *rojo* 8.4.1955; divorced 24.10.1957; remarried 27.1.1958; divorced 20.6.1960; remarried 26.9.1961. The divorce in June 1960 had been the third, and was therefore irrevocable. He stated in Court that he had forgotten about the April 1955 divorce and *rojo*, for these had succeeded one another within a matter of three days, and therefore he had in good faith resumed the union for the fourth (and unlawful) time without the intervention of a *China buta*. When the June 1960 divorce had been registered he had told the kathi that this was a second *talak*, and it was so entered, because he had quite forgotten the April 1955 repudiation.

The Court ruled that the September 1961 marriage was invalid, *tidak sah*. The husband at that date had registered a *mas kahwin* of $22.50 which had been left unpaid. The Court now asked the couple whether they had had intercourse after the solemnization of the invalid marriage; they replied in the affirmative. The President ruled that under the circumstances the wife was entitled to receive the *mas kahwin*. The husband paid it into Court a month later.

It is not unknown for a couple who have gone through the bitterness and expense of a divorce registration obtained after a hearing at the Shariah Court to agree to the divorce being revoked. There was at least one such case in 1962. After ten years of marriage and two children, the wife sought a *ta'alik* decree on the grounds of non-maintenance. The couple had had a serious quarrel precipitated by an argument about one of their children. The child complained about the condition of the clothes he was expected to wear to go to school; the mother rebuked and beat him; her husband was angered at her impatience. She used very strong language to abuse both father and child, and her husband struck her. She swore heatedly that she would never live with him again, and would not let him even touch her. To a question from the Court, she replied that she had not used the name of Allah when she had uttered this oath.

The husband then left her and went to live with his mother. Although he had bought some rice and sugar for the household and given pocket-money to the children, he had not maintained her. The Court found the non-maintenance *ta'alik* proven and registered the divorce. I discovered that the couple had *rojo* when I saw a note in the divorce register to the effect that two months later 'the husband took a copy because he wants to register a *rojo*'. The copy, paid for at the time of the registration of the divorce, is usually given to the wife at the expiry of her *iddah* period if the divorce is revocable.[1] I checked the 1962 *rojo* registrations and found that the couple had indeed formally registered the revocation on the day the husband had taken a copy of the divorce certificate from the Registry.

In some cases the President has attempted to persuade a reluctant husband to utter a repudiation; he has reminded him that the step is not irrevocable, since there is always the possibility of a *rojo*. In 1963 I was present in Court during the hearing of a bitterly contested case; the earlier efforts of a Court kathi to achieve conciliation had been vain. The husband argued that he might have given little or no maintenance over short periods, perhaps for the odd week or month, but never continuously for three months. Moreover, he was now in receipt of a Social Welfare allowance, had a part-time job, and was eager for a reconciliation. There were several children of the marriage.

The wife then alleged that he had been impotent for the eight months preceding their separation, but he hotly denied it. He claimed that although he was in poor health, and suffered from severe myopia which prevented him from pursuing his former occupation of driver, he was the very opposite of impotent. In fact, he declared, his wife had often told him he should take an additional wife for she could not bear his excessive demands. When asked by the Court whether he was willing to submit to a medical examination to determine whether he was impotent, he readily agreed. He added that the kathi who had earlier attempted a conciliation had specifically asked the wife whether her husband had given her *nafkah bathin* (lit. sexual maintenance, as distinct from *nafkah zhahir*, maintenance for food) and she had said that she had no complaints on that score.

The President of the Court sought to persuade the wife to agree

[1] See below, p. 137.

to a last-minute reconciliation, but she refused. The President then tried to persuade the husband to repudiate his wife, pointing out that she felt very bitter and angry, and that if he magnanimously agreed to divorce her, 'she might lose her anger' and later consent to a revocation of the divorce. Islam made special provision for matrimonial disputes such as these, for it allowed a couple to be divorced not once, but twice, and twice to revoke the divorce and resume cohabitation. The *rojo* procedure was, according to Muslim jurists, especially designed to achieve such conciliations. There were, he went on, many cases of husbands who were able to regain their wives by the expedient of granting their wish to be divorced; some of the women, suddenly free, found they were not as happy as they had hoped and eagerly consented to a revocation of the divorce. In this particular case, the husband was not swayed by the argument, and the President adjourned the case in the hope of a reconciliation. At the next hearing, the wife still refused reconciliation, and arbitrators were appointed.

Section 17 of the *Muslims Ordinance, 1957* stated that a Kathi who registers any marriage, divorce, or revocation of divorce

> shall upon application deliver to each party . . . a copy of the entry duly signed and sealed with his seal of office.

It appears that some women, eager to remarry at once, altered the date of the divorce, went to a different kathi, produced the forged divorce certificate, and remarried within the period of their *iddah*, i.e. less than three months after the divorce. The parallel here would be with a person divorced in England who remarries before the decree nisi becomes absolute, except that in the case of Muslims such an act is a sin as well as (in Singapore) an offence against the law of the State.

Accordingly, the 1960 Amendment repealed Section 17 and substituted a section which includes the following:

> Provided that if the divorce is capable of revocation no certificate of divorce shall be issued to the wife until the expiration of the period during which the divorce may lawfully be revoked.

Thus a woman who obtains a *khula* or a *fasah* decree (which are not capable of revocation) may, and does, obtain a divorce certificate as soon as the divorce is registered. Nevertheless she is, of course, still subject (according to Islam and to the law of the State) to an *iddah* period before she may marry another man.

The Registrar of Muslim Marriages and Divorces told me that in Singapore a rule of thumb is applied, and a woman's *iddah* after divorce (unless she is pregnant) is taken to end three calendar months after the recording of the divorce. On the other hand, many Singapore kathis (including the Chief Kathi) fix a period of one hundred days; the same is also true of the clerks in the Registry to whom a woman must apply for a copy of the divorce certificate.[1] A rule of thumb is essential, for women who are well past the menopause are also subject to the *iddah* period after divorce.[2]

The Chief Kathi is further of the opinion that a kathi, before he consents to solemnize or register the marriage of a divorcee, must specifically ask her whether three periods of purity have elapsed since her divorce, for some women have their menses at irregular intervals and it may well be that three months, or even one hundred days, after the divorce a woman is still not free to remarry. It is, of course, possible that a divorcee may lie, but the sin will then be on her head, and the kathi has a duty to warn her – before she replies to his questions – that she must answer truthfully.

In 1957, the year before the Shariah Court was constituted, thirty-three divorcees were married, less than three months after they had been divorced, to men other than their divorced husbands. In some cases the kathi noted that the bride swore that her *iddah* period was over. Twenty-nine of the thirty-three women remarried more than two months after their divorce; of the remaining four, two remarried within one and a half months, one remarried within one month and twenty-four days, and one within twenty-seven days.

Nawawi, in *Minhaj et Talibin*,[3] states that if a woman claims that her *iddah* period is over

> ... on the ground that the three periods of purity required are passed, she has a presumption in her favour provided she takes an oath, and provided also that:
>
> (*a*) A free woman, repudiated during one of her periods of purity, does not allege for the three periods together a shorter time than thirty-two days and two instants; nor, if repudiated during her menstrues, a shorter time than forty-seven days and one instant.
>
> (*b*) A slave, repudiated ...

These rules must be observed both in a case where the alleged expira-

[1] R. J. Wilkinson, *Law*, p. 55 n. mentions a period of 'about 100 days'.

[2] See below, pp. 139 f.

[3] p. 346.

tion is in conformity with a person's ordinary periods, and also where that person usually has shorter or longer periods.

It would appear, therefore, that at least one bride, who remarried within twenty-seven days, may not have been lawfully married according to Shafi'i rules.[1]

In 1957, apart from the thirty-three divorcees just mentioned, four women remarried their divorced husbands within less than three months of their divorce. The remarriage was necessary either because their divorce could not be revoked (being a *fasah* or *khula* divorce), or because they had already gone through three periods of purity, and their *iddah* was over.

In addition, in the course of that year, one divorcee remarried thirty-five days after her divorce, while another remarried within ten days. Both had been divorced after an unconsummated marriage. A woman under such circumstances is not subject to an *iddah* period before she can remarry; when her divorce is registered, a note is made in the divorce certificate to the effect that it is a divorce from an unconsummated marriage (*belum dukhul*, or *belum bersetuboh*). There is also a further statement: 'There is no *iddah*, and no *nafkah iddah*', or else 'There is no *nafkah iddah* because there is no *iddah*', i.e. no *iddah* maintenance is due, because the wife is not subject to an *iddah* period. Such a wife may remarry at once.

In other circumstances the *iddah* period must be observed even if it is absolutely certain that the couple have had no sexual relations for several months before the divorce. This is so, for instance, in the case of a woman who obtains a *fasah* or *ta'alik* decree after having been deserted for several months or years by her husband, who has been living in a different country. Some women appear to be ignorant of the law, and in May 1963 I saw a wife, who had secured a divorce after attempts lasting many months, express her dismay when told she could not remarry for at least another three months. She was then in an advanced stage of pregnancy by her lover and wished the baby to be born in wedlock.

A woman who is well past the menopause is also subject to an *iddah* period. Nawawi[2] states:

[1] Unless she had been divorced before the marriage was consummated; there was no mention of this, however, in the marriage certificate.

[2] *Minhaj et Talibin*, p. 366.

> A free woman who has no menstrues, or has passed the age for them, should observe a retirement of three months, and, if the repudiation took place in the middle of a month, her retirement is not completed until after the appearance of two new moons plus the number of days wanting to complete thirty in the first month; . . .

Some divorced women who are not eligible for *iddah* maintenance are nevertheless subject to an *iddah* period: they are the wives who have been divorced by three *talak*. They may, however, claim that their husbands provide them with shelter during this period.[1] Indeed, in June 1963 a wife – although divorced by three *talak* on account of her admitted adultery – was said by the Shariah Court to be entitled to the rent of the room in which she was to live during her *iddah* period.

To summarize:

(1) After every type of divorce ('ordinary' *talak; khula; ta'alik;* or *fasah*) the divorced wife is subject to an *iddah* period. The only exception is when the marriage has not been consummated.

(2) *Khula* and *fasah* divorces are irrevocable. Likewise, a three-*talak* divorce is irrevocable. The women, nevertheless, are subject to the usual *iddah* period and (except in the case of a wife divorced three times by the same husband) they have a right to maintenance during the period of their *iddah*. In practice, in Singapore, a wife usually surrenders her right to *iddah* maintenance when a *khula* divorce is registered.

ROJO AND POLYGYNY

The 1960 Amendment introduced a restriction on polygyny, making it an offence for a polygynous marriage to be solemnized without the consent of the Chief Kathi. This is contained in a new section, Section 7A. Subsections (2) and (3) of Section 7A read:

> (2) No marriage shall be solemnized under the Ordinance if the man to be wedded is married under the law of Islam to any person other than the other party to the intended marriage, except—
> (*a*) by the Chief *Kathi*; or
> (*b*) with the written consent of the Chief *Kathi* by the *wali* of the woman to be wedded or by a *Kathi* at the request of such *wali*.
>
> (3) Before solemnizing a marriage or giving his written consent to

[1] *Ibid.*, p. 372.

the solemnization of a marriage under subsection (2) of this section the Chief *Kathi* shall satisfy himself after inquiry that there is no lawful obstacle according to the law of Islam to such marriage.

It is clear that the restriction is one relating to the solemnization of a polygynous marriage. However, consider the following case. A man, Ali, is married to Patimah. He divorces her with one *talak*, the first or second (i.e. with a revocable *talak*), which is duly registered. Ali then validly contracts a marriage with another woman, Asmah, a few days after his divorce. He later persuades Patimah, who is ignorant of his remarriage, to consent to a revocation of their divorce. He takes her before any kathi (except, of course, the kathi who solemnized and registered his marriage to Asmah), and registers a revocation of the divorce. In effect, Ali has contracted a polygynous union by revoking the divorce. Yet he does not seem to have committed an offence, for revocation of a divorce does not constitute solemnization of a marriage.

The Singapore Chief Kathi confirmed, in reply to my questions, that there is no praying at a *rojo*, as there usually is when a marriage is solemnized. The only requirement before registering a *rojo* is that the husband utter, or declare that he did utter, words to the effect that he had 'returned', *rojo*, to his wife.[1] Moreover, a *rojo* is not a marriage. Some Singapore Muslims have not been slow in taking advantage of this loophole in the law. Consequently, Singapore kathis have been generally advised to ensure, before consenting to register a *rojo*, that the husband has not meanwhile contracted a marriage with another woman; and that if he has done so, such a husband's *rojo* registration must be referred to the Chief Kathi. Apparently not all Singapore kathis meticulously follow this advice, and since there is no application form for a *rojo* (as there is for a marriage) a man need not make a written declaration that he knows of no impediment to the *rojo*.

In May 1963 there was a loud and angry scene on the premises of the Shariah Court, involving a man who had done precisely what has just been described in the case of the husband referred to as 'Ali'. The two wives and the man had come to see one of the Court kathis, and fought loudly and bitterly while waiting to be interviewed. Eventually there was a scuffle, with each wife pulling at the husband to leave the Court with her; finally the

[1] See above, p. 137.

older wife won the contest. Apparently the man had become seriously involved with a *janda* living in a different district, and had promised to marry her. He secured his wife's agreement to a divorce by mutual consent; then, unknown to her, he married the *janda*. He had two children by the earlier marriage, and later persuaded their mother to agree to a *rojo*, saying he had repented; and the *rojo* was duly registered. Having kept his promise to marry the *janda*, he was, it seems, not eager to live with her. Nevertheless, two months later, in July, he came back to Court to file a petition for divorce in respect of his first wife.

In conclusion it is worth noting that some divorced couples who decide to resume the conjugal tie within the wife's *iddah* period prefer to enter into a fresh contract of marriage, rather than register a revocation. They do so in the full knowledge that the registration fee for a fresh contract ($19 with the application form) is very nearly double that for a revocation ($10). One kathi told me that he regularly meets this type of situation, and that probably such a couple feel they are making a completely fresh start, not just resuming the union which had caused distress or bitterness. A Muslim government official with whom I discussed this matter cynically commented that it was not improbable that some kathis actually encouraged a fresh contract of marriage, since a kathi's personal fee for a marriage was $15, while that for a revocation was only $10.

7

Discussion

THE DECLINE OF THE DIVORCE RATE

There is official satisfaction that the divorce rate has fallen conspicuously in Singapore since the 1957 Ordinance which provided for the establishment of the Shariah Court. (As we know, the Court was constituted at the end of November 1958.) The *Annual Report of the Registry of Muslim Marriages and the Shariah Court 1962* states on its first page:

The new Ordinance provides for several important changes with regard to Muslim marriages and divorces with the aim of enforcing the Law of Islam more carefully and of reducing the number of divorces among the Muslims, in which purpose the Shariah Court has been successful, as shown in the table below:

Year	*Marriages*	*Divorces*	*Revocation of Divorce*
1958	2,332	1,149	156
1959	2,116	577	91
1960	1,814	574	69*
1961	1,560	401	47
1962	1,483	447*	51

[* There were, in fact, 72 revocations registered in 1960, and 449 divorces in 1962. See above, p. 129.]

It is not only the rate of divorce which has exhibited a spectacular decline since 1959. A very important fact, although rarely commented on, is that the absolute numbers of both marriages and divorces registered in Singapore have also conspicuously decreased since that date. The official Registry figures for the decade preceding 1958 are given in the table overleaf.

Several factors probably account for the decrease in the divorce rate since 1959:

(1) Conciliation efforts by officials of the Shariah Court have been successful in many cases; in 1960, 88 couples were reconciled; in 1961, 457; and in 1962, 560.[1]

[1] See Annual Reports of the Shariah Court.

Year	*Marriages*	*Divorces*	*Revocations*
1948	2,605	1,545	222
1949	2,516	1,401	144
1950	2,506	1,501	144
1951	2,699	1,526	174
1952	2,658	1,474	165
1953	2,445	1,417	168
1954	2,457	1,357	168
1955	2,472	1,247	164
1956	2,414	1,074	168
1957	2,303	1,192*	183

[* In fact, there were 1,201 divorces registered in 1957. Errors in numbering caused the total of 1,192 to be given in the official figures.]

(2) Divorces other than by mutual consent require Court proceedings. Consequently, whereas in the old days a man went in a fit of pique, after a conjugal quarrel, to register a divorce, nowadays he can no longer do so alone; and after a breathing spell he may patch up the quarrel with his wife.

(3) It may be that young widows and divorcees are becoming increasingly aware that it is more difficult to entice a married man away from his wife and to make him divorce in order to enter into another union, since a man can no longer register a divorce at his sole wish. Perhaps these women now direct their efforts mainly towards unattached men.

(4) It is said that in the old days some complaisant Singapore kathis lightly granted *ta'alik* or *fasah* decrees, and attracted many Federation women who came to Singapore solely to secure a divorce certificate.

(5) A man's poverty or unemployment sometimes caused his wife to seek and obtain a *ta'alik* or *fasah* decree; nowadays, such poverty can be alleviated by Public Assistance funds. True, the Social Welfare Department antedates the *Muslims Ordinance, 1957*, but it is only in recent years that Muslims have become aware of their right to seek public assistance, and applied for help. (There are no official figures published according to religious or ethnic groups, and I base this statement on the information given me by Public Assistance officials.)

On the other hand, the restriction on polygynous unions has led some men to seek a divorce when they wished to take another wife. Further, the increasing willingness of Muslim wives to apply to the Courts for maintenance from defaulting husbands has led the latter to petition the Shariah Court for divorce. The Annual Report of the Registry for 1962 states:

> . . . several husbands agreed to divorce their wives, from whom they had been separated, in order to avoid paying maintenance to them after the Shariah Magistrate's Court had ordered them to pay such maintenance to their wives . . .

It is impossible to estimate the number of marriages which have ended in practice as well as in Islam (i.e. by the husband uttering a repudiation), but have not been so registered. We know from the revocation records that many divorces do remain unregistered. If a man goes to a kathi to register the repudiation he has uttered, and is told he must either bring his wife and persuade her to sign the divorce register willingly, or else take proceedings in the Shariah Court, it may be that if he fails to secure his wife's agreement he will in fact lodge a petition in Court. However, a third course is possible, and that is to do nothing. If he should want to take another wife at a later stage, and fail to secure the Chief Kathi's consent to marry polygynously, he can be married in one of the Malay States which does not frown on polygyny, or he may declare himself to be unmarried when he signs the Singapore application form for marriage. We know that some men have been prosecuted for making a false declaration, but we do not know how many escape detection or prosecution.

We must now consider the sharp decline in the absolute number of marriages, in a population which has certainly exhibited no decline in the groups of marriageable age. If we take the Census figures for 1947 and 1957 for Malaysians (who are the largest Muslim group in Singapore), we find that in the age group 15–44 years there were 35,369 males and 25,664 females in 1947, whereas in 1957 there were 48,310 males and 41,130 females. There does not appear to have been an exodus of persons in this age group from Singapore, and yet the number of Muslim marriages dropped from 2,605 in 1948 to 2,303 in 1957, and spectacularly to 1,483 in 1962.[1] The following factors have probably been responsible for the decline in the number of marriages:

[1] The total number of Malays and immigrant Indonesians of all ages in 1962 was 246,000 while in 1957 the total had been 197,059. No figures have been available since 1931 for Indian Muslims, but I estimate their number to have been about 31,000 in 1957. See above, p. 8.

(1) In the past, it is said, many women eloped from the Peninsula to get married in Singapore before complaisant kathis who were not very strict about seeking a *wali*'s permission, or about proof that the prospective bride was indeed free to marry; they accepted her word when she asserted that she was a widow or divorcee. We noted earlier that Singapore kathis acted as *wali hakim* in 1957 for 31.4 per cent of all brides; in 1961 (when only the Chief Kathi could act as *wali hakim*) only 13.7 per cent of all brides had a *wali hakim*.[1]

(2) Some Singapore married men who are refused permission to contract a polygynous union now go to a Malay State which does not frown on such unions, and register their marriages in that State.

(3) Since divorces other than by mutual consent are not easily registered in Singapore, and polygyny is severely restricted, a married man who has seriously compromised a woman cannot marry her as quickly as he would have been able to do in the past. We do not know the number of Muslim couples who cohabit outside marriage, but it is probable that such unions have increased since 1958.

(4) Members of the Armed Forces and of the Police must now produce a letter from their superior officer stating that according to official records the prospective bridegroom is not already married, before a Singapore kathi will register the marriage. It is said that in the past many of these men took a wife in every district to which they were posted, and abandoned or repudiated these wives casually.

(5) No kathi is empowered nowadays to register the marriage of a girl who is under fifteen years of age, except with the consent of the Registrar. Such consent is granted, as a rule, only in cases where the prospective bride is already pregnant. Before 1958, there were brides of thirteen and fourteen years; there were also marriage contracts registered of girls who had not yet reached puberty, but consummation was delayed until physical maturity was reached: these were the marriage contracts known as *nikah gantong*.[2] It was not unknown for such marriages to be dissolved before consummation.

(6) Finally, the fact that fewer couples do divorce means that there are fewer adults who may marry again. In 1957, out of

[1] See above, p. 29. [2] See above, p. 99.

2,303 brides, 787 were divorcees, or 34.2 per cent of the total; in 1961, out of 1,560 brides, 410 were divorcees, or 26.3 per cent of the total.

It is often argued in Singapore that the greatest achievement of the 1957 Ordinance has been to restrain men from divorcing their wives as a result of a temporary whim or fit of pique. Much has been written about the plight of the oppressed Muslim wife cast off by a philandering or domineering husband. As far as Singapore is concerned, the available records seem to tell a different story. If we leave aside the cases where divorces were registered by mutual consent, we find that in 1961 there were 61 divorces registered by order of the Shariah Court; 50 of the 61 were at the request of the wife: 28 *ta'alik*, 18 *khula*, 2 *fasah* and 2 *talak*. Thus, only in 11 divorces out of 61 did a husband seek and obtain the registration of a decree; moreover, in several of these cases the wife had deserted the husband and disappeared without trace. In 1962, the Shariah Court ordered the registration of 99 divorces; 78 were at the request of the wife, while 21 were at the request of the husband. Wives obtained 36 *ta'alik* decrees, 20 *khula*, 8 *fasah*, and 14 *talak*; while 1 *khula* divorce and 20 *talak* were registered at the request of the husband. (These figures vary slightly from those published in the 1962 Annual Report of the Registry.)

I said that the records of the Shariah Court *seem* to show that more women are eager to rid themselves of their husbands than vice versa. What the figures do not automatically reveal is that most of the women who obtained *ta'alik* or *fasah* decrees had been neglected or abandoned for months or years. For every wife who decides to take legal action eventually, and who goes through the ordeal of preliminary interviews, Court hearings, and all the expense and discomfort entailed, there must be many who seek no redress from the Shariah Court. They take no official action either because they hope their husband may return, or because they lack the money and/or courage to initiate proceedings, or because they have no suitor or are elderly and stand to gain nothing from an immediate divorce. When a woman does eventually petition for a *ta'alik* or *fasah* decree, she does not necessarily wish to cast a husband off – usually she wishes to have it officially recorded that her husband has cast her off, or has neglected or ill-treated her, and she now seeks to be free to enter in due course into another lawful union.

The majority of divorces are registered 'by mutual consent'. It is impossible to establish on the basis of available data the percentage of (*a*) cases where the husband has persuaded a reluctant wife to agree to be repudiated, (*b*) cases where a wife has deliberately goaded her husband to utter a repudiation and to register it, (*c*) cases where the couple have decided jointly that their union was unsatisfactory and should be terminated, and (*d*) cases where there has been interference from the husband's or from the wife's kin.

However, we can tell from the records that some couples decide to come together again after a repudiation has been uttered or registered, either through the machinery of a revocation or by entering into a fresh contract of marriage. In 1957, there were 1,201 divorces and 183 revocations; in that same year 54 couples married each other again, 10 of them within one year of being divorced, and the remaining 44 from one to thirteen years after being divorced.[1]

In 1961 when there were 401 divorces and 47 revocations, 19 couples married each other again, 8 of them within a year of being divorced and the remaining 11 from one to six years after their divorce. Indeed, as we know, some couples divorce and come together again in marriage more than once; this is made possible by the wise habit Singapore Muslims have of uttering usually only one *talak* at a time when they repudiate their wives.

In 1957, out of 1,201 divorces, 1,109 were registered as one-*talak*, 18 as two-*talak*, and 74 as three-*talak*. In 1961, out of 401 divorces, 386 were registered as one-*talak*, 4 as two-*talak*, and 11 as three-*talak*: thus only 2.7 per cent of all divorces were by triple *talak* in 1961.

After the establishment of the Shariah Court, kathis were generally advised to register a three-*talak* repudiation only in exceptional circumstances. However, in 1957 kathis could freely register triple *talak* divorces, and yet only 74 out of 1,201 divorces were of the triple-*talak* variety, or 6.1 per cent of all divorces. The breakdown for 1957 and 1961 is given in the table opposite.

If to the 74 triple *talak* in 1957 are added the 24 (21+3) *talak* which cumulatively amounted to a triple *talak*, the total is 98 and the percentage of irrevocable divorces 8.2. Thus 91.8 per cent

[1] These 54 remarriages must not be confused with the 52 'renewals of marriage' which took place that same year, and which were mentioned above, pp. 42 f.

of all divorces allowed the couples concerned to resume their unions, or to enter into a fresh contract of marriage.[1]

	1957 *total*	1961 *total*	1961 *kathis*	1961 *Shariah Court*
One *talak*, the first:	992	342	286	56
One *talak*, the second:	96	34	34	—
Two *talak*, at once:	15	3	3	—
Two *talak* at once, added to a previous *talak* (total 3):	3	1	—	1
One *talak*, added to two previous *talak* (total 3):	21	10	9	1
Three *talak* at once:	74	11	8	3
	1,201	401	340	61

In 1957, when 1,201 divorces were registered, 237 couples resumed their unions after being divorced: 183 by husbands revoking the repudiation and 54 by entering into a fresh contract of marriage. In 1961, when 401 divorces were registered, 66 couples came together again: 47 men revoked the repudiation, and 19 couples were remarried.

If we express revocation figures in percentages (i.e. revocations as percentages of divorces in the same year), we have 15.2 per cent in 1957 and 11.7 per cent in 1961, as we saw in the table on p. 129 above. In 1962, the percentage of revocations fell again slightly to 11.4. Moreover, when we bear in mind that in 1961, 13 out of the 47 revocations registered were in respect of unregistered divorces, we arrive at an even lower percentage of revocations. Only 34 revocations were in respect of divorces which had been registered, and there were 401 divorces in 1961; the revised percentage is thus 8.5. In 1962, 12 out of the 51 revocations were of unregistered divorces, and the revised figures for that year are 449 divorces and 39 revocations, or a revocation percentage of 8.7. In 1957 only one revocation out of 183 *may* have been in respect of an unregistered divorce, but there is no evidence that it was so,[2] and the 1951 percentage may safely remain unaltered. In 1956, when every revocation was in respect of a registered divorce, the revocation percentage was 15.6. We thus have for the two years immediately

[1] This is in striking contrast to the situation in Egypt in 1951. William J. Goode in *World Revolution and Family Patterns*, London, 1963, states (p. 161) that in Egypt 'about one fifth of the divorces occurring in 1951 were revocable'; there were 75,000 divorces in that year.

[2] See above, p. 131.

preceding the establishment of the Shariah Court revocation percentages of 15.6 (1956), and 15.2 (1957), while for 1961 and 1962 the revised percentages are, respectively, 8.5 and 8.7.

One is tempted to conclude that the very substantial reduction is due to the effect of the new legislation, and it is not difficult to advance an explanation. Kathis may no longer register unilateral divorces, and men who in the past had gone to secure a divorce certificate to fling at their wives after a quarrel are now told that a kathi may register a divorce only by mutual consent and that both spouses must come before him to sign willingly the divorce register; consequently, the divorces in 1961 and 1962 were probably registered after more serious and lasting disagreements than in 1957, and a smaller percentage of couples became reconciled within three months of divorcing. Furthermore, the 1960 Amendment to the *Muslims Ordinance, 1957* requires a kathi, before he registers a revocation, to satisfy himself that a wife is willing to resume cohabitation.

On the other hand, revocation percentages have fluctuated almost as widely when the law of marriage and divorce was unchanged, in the decade preceding the establishment of the Shariah Court: the table on p. 129 shows that in 1950 the figure was 9.6 per cent while two years earlier, in 1948, it had been 14.4 per cent. In my *Malay Kinship*[1] I commented briefly on the range of variation over the years, and noted that the revocation percentage for 1922 was 4.4, while in 1948 it was 14.4. (It is necessary to note here that I was not able to check systematically every revocation for the years before 1955; consequently it may be that in earlier years there were revocations registered in respect of unregistered divorces.)

It is difficult to predict the trend in years to come for, of course, a change in legislation is not the only factor to be considered though it may appear to be the most obvious factor.

VALIDITY AND REGISTRATION

Islam does not require that a kathi or other religious official solemnize a marriage. However, it has been the practice among Singapore Muslims since the last century that a kathi officiate at a marriage, and that he register the marriage and give (upon payment of the prescribed fee) a copy of the marriage certificate to

[1] p. 117.

the bride or to her guardian. Indeed, in a debate in the Singapore Legislative Assembly on 29 December 1960, the Parliamentary Secretary to the Minister for National Development, a Muslim, declared: 'There are other religions where, when you are in love with each other, no problem arises; it is not an offence. But in Islamic law, the marriage should be solemnized before a priest or *imam* . . .'

This is a belief widely held by Singapore Muslims. However, although the law of Singapore does not require that a kathi or *imam* officiate at a marriage, it does stipulate that registration of a marriage, divorce, or revocation of divorce, be effected within seven days.[1] It is unlawful (Section 18) for any person other than the Registrar or a kathi to keep registers of marriages, divorces, or revocations.

However, as we saw earlier,[2] registration is not proof of validity. Thus, there might easily have arisen a situation among Singapore Muslims of people conducting their matrimonial affairs according to Islam and ignoring the secular requirement of registration. Government is well aware of this, for according to the Minutes of Evidence for 9 April 1960,[3] when the 1960 Amendment to the 1957 Ordinance was being considered by the Select Committee, the State Advocate-General was asked to consider the following situation:

> . . . let us take the case of a husband who has divorced his wife, and then goes to a Kathi. The Kathi refuses to register the divorce on the grounds that the wife has not consented. The Kathi then requests that the matter be referred to the Shariah Court for the divorce to be registered. If the husband still persists in wanting to divorce his wife, and the wife persists in not consenting, then what would be the position?

He replied:

> Sir, that is, in fact, one of my worries in the application of the Muslims Ordinance, because if the Muslims want to wreck the Ordinance, they can do so easily. But, as a matter of fact, Muslims are so law-abiding that they will comply with it.
> *Chairman:* In fact, the Shariah Court has got powers to decree a divorce even if a divorce is not by mutual consent. That is what the Ordinance

[1] Section 12 of the *Muslims Ordinance, 1957*. Section 16 extends the period to three months, with the written consent of the Registrar.

[2] p. 25.

[3] *Report of the Select Committee*, L.A. 14 of 1960.

says. Is that right? And the Muslims have accepted that as a practice? – Yes.

Inche Baharuddin: In that case, Mr. Speaker, Sir, we will then not be really able to prevent divorces? – The answer to that is that the validity of the divorce does not depend on registration. The way in which we can restrict divorces is by the additional powers given to the Court for maintenance.

If it is possible for the State Advocate-General to make suggestions to the effect that the Shariah Court would be in a position to punish those husbands who insist on divorcing their wives, then I think our purpose would be achieved? – That, I would suggest, is a matter of education rather than of law.

As we know, a kathi may register a marriage only after an application form is filled in and signed by the prospective groom and by the bride's *wali*. (If the bride is a Hanafi her *wali* need not sign, but if he does not, she must sign the form herself.) Many application forms by both Shafi'i and Hanafi brides are signed, nevertheless, by all three parties: the groom, the bride, and the latter's *wali*. After the solemnization of the marriage the bride herself (whether she be a Hanafi or a Shafi'i) must sign the marriage register, and so must the groom and the witnesses. A man may have a polygynous marriage registered only after he has obtained the consent of the Chief Kathi. Whoever makes a false declaration is liable to prosecution. Thus, in one case, a woman persuaded a man (whom she later alleged to be her 'adoptive father') to act as her *wali*: her father, who was alive, had refused to give his consent to the proposed match. When the matter was later discovered the case came before a magistrate's court, and a fine was imposed on the culprits. The Shariah Court, in turn, ruled the marriage invalid in Islam, for a woman belonging to the Shafi'i school must be given away only by her *wali* or by a kathi empowered to act as her *wali*.

On the other hand, there have been several cases of a Muslim stating in the application form that he was a 'bachelor' or a divorced man when in fact he was a married man, and entering into a polygynous marriage. When this has come to light, the man has been tried before a magistrate and, on conviction, fined for making a false declaration. In June 1962 a man paid a fine of $100; in 1963 one man paid a $250 fine and another was fined $300. The cases, however, did not come before the Shariah Court, for such a polygynous marriage was deemed to be valid in Islam.

It is generally believed by kathis and Court officials that for every polygynous man thus fined, there are dozens equally guilty who have escaped prosecution.

There is, of course, nothing to stop a Singapore Muslim from going to a State in the Peninsula where there is no restriction on the solemnization and registration of a polygynous union, and being lawfully married there. He does not commit an offence by so doing, and there have been several such cases. The polygynous union is recognized in Singapore as a valid marriage.[1]

On the other hand, it is extremely rare for Muslims to assert they have been married in Singapore according to the law of Islam when the marriage was not registered by a kathi, and to require the validity of such a marriage to be recognized. The only exception I know of concerns a girl who had been married off by her father against her expressed wishes. The marriage was eventually declared valid.

Briefly, these were the facts of the case.[2] An Arab discovered that his daughter was in love with a young Malay whom she wished to marry. He strongly disapproved of the match and forbade the girl to see her suitor. She was nineteen years old, and a very determined young person; she ran away from home, and went to live with her suitor's parents. Her father promptly retaliated by arranging, two days later, to marry her off to a young kinsman. Naturally, she would not consent; but taking full advantage of Shafi'i law which allows the father of a virgin girl to marry her off without her consent (if the groom is not her social inferior) he himself, on 2 September 1958, solemnized the marriage in her absence. He failed, however, in his attempt to secure the registration of the marriage. The Chief Kathi, to whom the matter was referred, had interviewed the young girl who had expressed her very strong objection to the match. He, too, refused to register the marriage. (The *Muslims Ordinance, 1957* had, as we know, caused a great deal of comment in the State and kathis were particularly wary of taking upon themselves responsibility for such a weighty decision.)

After the Shariah Court was constituted the father pleaded that it order the registration of his daughter's marriage. On 4 February

[1] See above, pp. 117 ff.

[2] See 'Syed Abdullah Al-Shatiri v. Shariffa Salmah' in *Malayan Law Journal*, vol. XXV, no. 6, June 1959.

1959 the Court declared the marriage invalid. The father appealed, and the Appeal Board in May 1959 reversed the Court's decision. The Board argued that the girl had testified she was still a virgin at the time her father had solemnized her union to her cousin, and that it was only about a month after her elopement that she had sexual relations with her suitor. (The couple had tried to find a kathi willing to marry them, since the young girl did not consider herself bound in marriage by the ceremony at which her father had officiated, and since the Chief Kathi had refused to register the marriage her father had solemnized. However, no kathi would act as *wali* for the girl to marry her chosen suitor.) The Appeal Board found further that there were no other grounds on which the marriage with her cousin was, in Shafi'i law, invalid: the girl was not at enmity with her father, and the groom he had chosen for her was not her inferior, or otherwise an unsuitable husband in Islam.[1] The Appeal Board quoted at some length the opinions of Shafi'i jurists which were relevant to the case. The groom, however, had appeared aloof throughout the proceedings, and he consented (towards the end of the Appeal hearing) to divorce his bride so that she might marry the man of her choice, much to the anger of the bride's father.

As we know, it is essential that a bride (whether she be a virgin or no) signify her written consent to a marriage before it can be registered. However, there appears to be no obstacle to the father of a virgin Shafi'i girl solemnizing a marriage without her consent to a man who is a suitable husband in Islam, and on the precedent established by the 1959 Appeal case just quoted, securing the recognition of the marriage. I have been told by the Registrar that, in fact, no such applications have been received, although it would be wrong to assume that this is because few Muslims are as autocratic as the Arab father proved to be. There is evidence to show that other girls (Malay and Indian as well as Arab) have been given away in marriage in the last few years against their wishes. This comes to light when a young woman petitions the Shariah Court for a dissolution of her union; or offers no defence when her husband pleads for the registration of a divorce on the grounds of the wife's wilful refusal to consummate the marriage.[2]

[1] See p. 15 above.

[2] The latter cases come before the Court because the husbands seek a return of the marriage expenses; otherwise, if agreement had been reached privately about

It is still the accepted social norm, especially in rural communities, for marriages to be arranged without reference to the bride, and few young girls are bold enough to tell the kathi they are unwilling to sign the marriage register. Moreover, most kathis are elderly men who sincerely believe that the choice of a suitable husband should be left to a girl's parents. Several young women claim the kathi simply ordered them to sign (or, if they were illiterate, affix their right thumbprints to) a form, without explaining what it was they were signing.

In one case before the Shariah Court a young wife (who was then eighteen years old) had filed a petition in January 1962 for a divorce on the grounds that her husband had been her mother's lover, and therefore prohibited to her,[1] and that she had been tricked into marrying him. At the first hearing, in March of that year, she claimed that when festive preparations were taking place at her parents' home, she was told they were in honour of her *khatam Koran*.[2] When, in fact, a marriage ceremony did take place, she was stunned and did not object. She did, however, refuse at first to consummate the marriage; but eventually she yielded to her husband on two occasions.

The hearing was adjourned for the girl's father to give evidence and again adjourned when he failed to appear. Finally, in June 1962, the father gave sworn evidence. He admitted he had told his daughter she was to go through a *khatam Koran* ceremony, when in fact it was to be a wedding ceremony; he knew nothing of allegations that the bridegroom, who had been a lodger in his house over a period of ten years, had been his wife's lover. He, the father, did not think it necessary to consult his daughter about the choice of a husband for her; no other man had sought her hand in marriage; he believed the lodger (aged forty years) was a suitable match, and that the girl would naturally obey her father.

The husband, who had earlier been reluctant to utter a repudiation, now stated he was willing to divorce his wife since 'she does not like me, and also I am thinking of going back to Indonesia. I am willing to pay for the cost of the divorce registration, and also to pay *iddah* maintenance'.

financial compensation the couples would have been divorced quietly before a kathi, by mutual consent.

[1] See above, p. 14, n. 1.

[2] The ceremony to celebrate the fact that a young Muslim has completed the reading of the Koran. See my *Malay Kinship*, p. 107.

Even among educated Muslims, it is still common for parents to arrange their daughters' marriages, and indeed several such brides boasted to me in 1963 that they had been dutiful girls and had not questioned their parents' choice of suitor.

The case of *Syed Abdullah al-Shatiri* v. *Shariffa Salmah* shows how the provisions of the Muslims Ordinance may lead to paradoxical results when Section 19 is invoked. This section, it will be remembered, states that non-registration of a marriage is not proof of non-validity. However, the Ordinance (Section 12) requires every Muslim marriage to be registered. It furthermore requires that the bride sign the marriage register, thus signifying her consent to the match. On the other hand, a marriage which is valid in Islam, although the bride's consent has been most emphatically refused, may be found valid by the Singapore Muslim authorities. (It is an irony of fate that Inche Ahmad Ibrahim – who has been most energetically and boldly campaigning for legislative reform to protect Muslim women from the harsher provisions of traditional marriage and divorce procedure – should have needed, as President of the Appeal Board hearing the case of *Syed Abdullah Al-Shatiri* v. *Shariffa Salmah*, to deliver the judgment finding her forced marriage valid.) A marriage which has been found valid cannot be registered in Singapore when the bride refuses to sign the marriage register. Yet the marriage is valid, and non-registration renders the spouses liable (under Section 58 of the *Muslims Ordinance, 1957*) to a fine not exceeding fifty dollars!

One moral of this case must be truly alarming to Muslim parents. If a chaste girl fears that her father or paternal grandfather may contract her in marriage against her wishes, one certain way to foil the attempt is to hasten to lose her virginity and boast of it to her father (or father's father).[1] Moreover, such loss of virginity must result from sexual intercourse. The Appeal Board in the case under discussion stated:[2] 'The view of the Shafi'i School is, in our view, well summarized in Nawawi's *Minhaj et Talibin*:

> A father can dispose as he pleases of his daughter, without asking her consent, whatever her age may be, provided she is still a virgin. It is however commendable to consult her as to her future husband; and her formal consent to the marriage is necessary if she has already

[1] However, sexual intercourse outside marriage is a serious crime and a sin in Islam.

[2] *Malayan Law Journal*, June 1959, p. 140.

lost her virginity. Where a father disposes of his daughter's hand during her minority, she cannot be delivered to the husband before she attains puberty. In default of the father, the father's father exercises all his powers. Loss of virginity puts an end to the right of disposing of a daughter's hand without her consent; and there is no difference in this respect between a loss caused by lawful cohabitation and one that is the consequence of unlawful intercourse. On the other hand, the right remains intact where the loss takes place without carnal connection, as for example in consequence of a fall upon the ground.'

Few Singapore Muslims know of the distinction between the 'solemnization' of a marriage and its registration. The proof that a marriage has taken place is a *surat nikah*, a marriage certificate, and without it there are not many couples who would consider themselves man and wife. Certainly, for the community at large, a marriage exists only when a kathi solemnizes the union in the presence of witnesses, and makes the appropriate entry in his register.[1]

When we come to consider divorce, we find that the matter is far more complex. First, a husband may utter the divorce formula, saying to his wife in the presence of witnesses, 'I repudiate you with one *talak*', or he may say it to her privately when no witnesses are present; in Muslim law, the woman is divorced. In practice, however, she does not consider herself to be legally divorced until she has a *surat cherai*, a divorce certificate, in her possession. Certainly, no Singapore kathi would nowadays

[1] There are some Muslims in Singapore who do not appear to have ever had in their possession a certificate of their marriage in India or Pakistan. This comes to light when they petition the Court for a divorce; they then have to produce, in lieu of a marriage certificate, a statutory declaration. There are also some cases of Indonesians who claim never to have had a marriage certificate. As we know, in Singapore a marriage certificate is not automatically given to either bride or groom after the solemnization of a union: a fee has to be paid for it, over and above the kathi's fee for registering the marriage. This matter has caused concern among some Muslims: the Select Committee on the Muslims (Amendment) Bill heard a plea, on 16 March 1960, by Inche M. K. Shariff, that Section 17 of the Ordinance be amended to read:

> 'At the conclusion of a marriage ceremony officiated by a Kathi, the marriage certificate must be given to the bridegroom there and then, without further delay.'

He explained: 'The reason for my suggestion is that in February last, in the case of the marriage of my brother, after the marriage ceremony had been performed, an application was made to the Kathi for a copy of the certificate of registration. But the Kathi put it off to the next day, and again to the next day, and up till now the marriage certificate has not been received.' (See L.A. 14 of 1960.) However, Inche Shariff's suggestion was not put into effect.

solemnize her marriage to another man merely on her assertion and that of her witnesses that her husband had repudiated her: a divorcee must produce a copy of the certificate before the kathi will either solemnize or register her marriage to another man.[1] There are contested divorce petitions, in the course of which (as in a case I heard in Court) a woman declares at a hearing: 'Yes, my husband did pronounce the repudiation formula. But I took no notice of it, for when I replied at the time: "Good, so you have repudiated me: now, I await my *surat cherai*", he did nothing about it, and we later patched up our quarrel.' (Many women are not aware that a husband nowadays cannot obtain from a kathi a divorce certificate without his wife's written consent in the presence of the kathi.)

Second, a couple may go together before a kathi to register a divorce by mutual consent, but may not have the minimum amount ($19) required for the registration fee, and an additional dollar for a copy of the certificate.[2] The Kathi may then record the facts of the divorce in his notebook, noting the date and hour of the repudiation, but the divorce will not be registered, and therefore neither party will have a certificate until the cost of the registration has been met. Thus it is that in the Registers of Divorce one may find against the entry 'Date and Hour of Divorce' a date several days or weeks (and sometimes months) preceding that given against the entry 'Date of Registration of Divorce'. (*Mutatis mutandis*, this applies to revocations of divorce.) The delay sometimes occurs when a *ta'alik* divorce has been granted on account of the husband's failure to maintain his wife for three months or longer and neither spouse has been able to produce the registration fee. Since, in any case, a woman divorced by *ta'alik* decree is not given a divorce certificate until the expiry of her *iddah* period, i.e. until about three months after her divorce has been recorded, she may delay payment of the fee (i.e. also delay the actual registration of the divorce) until her *iddah* period has expired. Usually, however, both in the cases of divorce by mutual consent and of divorce recorded in the Shariah Court by the President, the divorce is registered on the same date as it is stated to have been uttered or decreed.

[1] There is one other alternative—a statutory declaration, sworn in the High Court.

[2] The $1 fee is payable to a kathi if the certificate is requested immediately after registration; if it is requested at a later date a $2 fee is payable.

There is no doubt that lack of funds delays, or prevents, the official registration of divorces, and that many marriages have ended in practice as well as in Islam (i.e. the husband has uttered the repudiation formula), but have not been legally registered as dissolved unions. There are also cases of women who apply to the Court for divorce on the grounds that they have been deserted over a period of years by their husbands and left with no maintenance whatever. They declare in Court, in reply to the President's question, 'Why have you waited so long before petitioning for a divorce?', 'Because I had no money!' A woman petitioning for a *ta'alik* or a *fasah* decree must pay the cost of a summons, or advertise in a newspaper if her husband's address is not known, and pay for the transport and other expenses of her witnesses. The total cost, including the registration fee of the divorce, may vary between $35 and $70, or more if there are several hearings and her witnesses live some distance away and require full compensation for their transport and loss of earnings. Before the constitution of the Shariah Court, however, many kathis are said to have been reluctant to register a *ta'alik* decree unless they were paid a handsome advance to cover the cost of such enquiries as they deemed necessary. One woman in Court, on oath, stated that a kathi, whom she named, had asked her for an advance payment of $40, and that she did not then have that amount.

There are instances when a man tells his wife that if she is unbearably unhappy with him, she can go to the Shariah Court to seek a divorce; he refuses, however, to go with her to a kathi and register a mutual agreement divorce. This he may do out of spite, or because he is in fact reluctant to repudiate her and is aware that it takes a great deal of money as well as courage and perseverance for a woman to petition for, and obtain, a divorce. Often a man appears before the Court in response to a summons issued by his wife, and states: 'I am willing to repudiate her if it does not cost me a single cent.' If the wife wants the divorce at all costs, she then agrees to surrender all claims (past, present, and future) upon her husband.

FAMILIARITY WITH THE 'MUSLIMS ORDINANCE, 1957'

It is apparent to an observer regularly attending the hearings of the Shariah Court that the provisions of the new Muslims Ordinance are not clear to many petitioners and respondents. (This is not surprising; one hears from English solicitors that their clients often display astonishment when the principles of English divorce legislation are explained to them.) Many Muslim wives, when they discover that their husbands are powerless to register a divorce before a kathi without their consent, jump to the conclusion that even if a man petitions the Shariah Court he will fail unless he can prove that he has good grounds for the union to be dissolved. The misapprehension starts when a kathi tells a man that he cannot have a divorce certificate to hand over to his wife, because the law has been changed and a divorce certificate can be given only if both husband and wife agree to end the marriage, and that otherwise, the spouse who wishes to dissolve the union must apply to the Shariah Court.

The husband comes to the Court, and is interviewed by one of the Court kathis, who attempts a reconciliation. If the man has already uttered a repudiation, or claims to have done so, the kathi tries to persuade him to revoke it. If the husband has uttered a repudiation for the third time in respect of the wife in question, there can of course be no revocation. Nevertheless, even a Court kathi is not empowered to register such a divorce if the wife will not consent to it, and the husband has to issue a summons. One such puzzled husband (who wished to take another wife) declared in Court: 'The Chief Kathi told me: "In Islam the repudiation you have uttered is valid; but according to the law of the State it is not valid. You must go through the procedure of a petition to the Shariah Court and a formal hearing."' It is likely that the husband had misunderstood the Chief Kathi, who probably told him that the divorce was valid in Islam, but could not be unilaterally registered according to the law of the State. Of course, if polygyny were freely permitted in Singapore, such a husband would not need to divorce his wife.

On the other hand, some men are eager to have their divorces registered not because they wish to take another wife, but because they do not wish to pay maintenance to their estranged wives.[1] It is interesting to observe that although a Muslim husband is not legally bound in Singapore to show cause why he wishes to repudiate his wife, most men do in fact attempt to justify their action by enumerating their wives' alleged failings. Moreover, a woman considers herself grievously injured if her husband seeks

[1] See above, pp. 144 f., and below, pp. 175 f.

a divorce while she is blameless of a conjugal offence. It is therefore not surprising that many women believe the new legislation was enacted in order to deprive husbands of the right to divorce a blameless wife at will.

In May 1963 I was present in Court when a husband pleaded for the registration of a divorce; he claimed to have uttered 'at least twice' a formula of repudiation. The couple had been married for fourteen years and had five children. The husband's case was that during the last year of their marriage there had arisen very serious misunderstandings between his wife and himself, and he had decided to end the union. In answer to his wife's questions, he stated that the misunderstandings had arisen as a result of discussions about property given to the wife by her father; but he was silent when the wife pointed out that she was not personally involved in the quarrels which took place between her husband and her father. She further declared that the real reason he sought a divorce was that he had a mistress whom he now wished to marry, and he did not deny the allegation.

When the wife gave evidence on oath, she admitted that her husband had uttered the formula of repudiation at least twice, and added that no witnesses were present. The President of the Court with great patience explained to her that such a repudiation was effective, '*Awak punya cherai sudah jatoh*' (lit. 'Your divorce has already befallen you'), and added that even if a repudiation was uttered in jest, it was valid – 'although, of course, it is very wrong for a Muslim to make such a declaration in jest'.

The wife enquired: 'But what if I do not consent to the divorce?' The President replied, 'Even if the wife does not consent, the divorce is effective. The only thing is that registration of the divorce is not lightly granted, for the Court must see to it that the divorced wife's rights are safeguarded.' The wife: 'Still, I do not want to be divorced, I disagree'. The President: 'You cannot say this, you cannot. Your divorce is already effective; you have already been repudiated; this hearing is simply held for me to see that you now get what you are entitled to, and to order the registration of the divorce on proper conditions.'

At the beginning of the hearing, the President had attempted to persuade the husband to agree to a reconciliation – i.e. to revoke the repudiations he had uttered – but had failed. The wife had stated that she was not willing to be divorced, because she had done no wrong. The President had then explained to her that a man need not have serious grounds of complaint in order to secure the registration of a divorce, for a Muslim can repudiate his wife even on a slight pretext; only a woman needs to show grave cause in order to secure the dissolution of her marriage. The husband was a police officer, earning $630 per month. After both he and his wife had given evidence, the President again attempted to persuade him to revoke the repudiation, reminding him that he had five young children, and added that when tempers had cooled he might regret the divorce. He said finally: 'I urge you to take your wife back; I cannot force you to do so.' The plea was firmly rejected, with a determined shaking of the head and a statement that a reconciliation was out of the question. The President said, 'Since you insist on registering the divorce, I must now rule on your liabilities. But before I do this, there is the matter of *matta'ah*; this is a consolatory gift which a husband should make to his wife when he repudiates her. There is no fixed amount, but it is only one single payment. What do you offer?'

The husband replied: 'Fifty dollars.' The President suggested: 'Make it one hundred! After all, you earn more than $600 a month.' The husband agreed, and at once produced a wad of notes. When the couple had been interviewed by the Chief Kathi two months earlier, the husband had promised to pay $150 per month maintenance until the Court hearing, in respect of his wife and five children, but had not done so. He now explained that he had agreed to pay this monthly sum only if his wife had been agreeable to a divorce by mutual consent; but the Chief Kathi was called into Court, and produced his record-book in which he had noted that the maintenance agreement was unconditional. The President ruled therefore that the husband was to pay in addition to the consolatory gift:

$300 in respect of past maintenance;

$180 *iddah* maintenance for three months (at the rate of $60 per month);

$22 for registration of the divorce and one copy of the divorce certificate to be given to the wife.

Meanwhile, as soon as it became evident to the wife that the divorce would be registered despite her objection, she collapsed in her chair and wept bitterly but quietly. She had been taken aback by the Court's decision, for until the end of the hearing she had been muttering that she did not wish to be divorced, and that she had been blameless. The hearing lasted from 11.30 a.m. to 1.15 p.m. When the Court rose, the wife's relatives commented on the case, and they too appeared shattered by the outcome, for they had firmly believed that the husband would fail in his plea to have the divorce registered. They were not uneducated; indeed even the older women among them were literate.

This case illustrates various aspects of the application of the new Muslims Ordinance. First, it is clear that knowledge of the law is not widespread. Statements I had heard wives make in Court such as 'My husband promised he would send me a divorce certificate when he left the house', or 'I told my husband to go to a kathi and bring me a divorce certificate if he was unhappy with me!' had led me to cause the following question to be sent in May 1963 to every Singapore kathi: 'Do you find that some men come alone to register a divorce, that is, do not know that you can register a divorce only by mutual consent?' They replied that some husbands still did come to register a unilateral divorce, and that they had to explain to them that the law had been changed. This, of course, shows that there are among some Muslims two diametrically opposed views of the divorce laws: one is the belief that a man has a right to ask a kathi to register a repudiation irrespective of his wife's consent; and the other is the belief (held by the police officer's wife) that a guiltless wife's consent to a repudiation is essential before a divorce can be registered, even by the Shariah Court. Of course, both views are erroneous.

Second, a man who fails to register the repudiation he has uttered is not usually prosecuted, although he is liable to prosecution under Section 58 of the Ordinance. (As we know, some kathis register revocations from unregistered divorces, and those with whom I discussed the matter expressed surprise when I commented that it was an offence not to register a divorce: they had certainly not warned the husbands, let alone threatened to report them; was not the official aim to achieve as many reconciliations as possible, and to curtail the number of divorces?) The President of the Shariah Court, however, when he was trying to persuade the Police officer to revoke the repudiations he had uttered, had told the husband that he had committed a breach of the law by failing to register within seven days the *talak* which he himself claimed to have uttered several months earlier. But the President took no further action, or at least does not seem to have recommended any further action.

Third, if a man contemplating a polygynous marriage in Singapore did not have to submit to a searching enquiry by the Chief Kathi, it is possible that the police officer in the case under discussion, or another husband similarly placed, might have quietly married another wife without troubling to dissolve the first union. This was not infrequent before 1960, and sometimes the man repented, or found the second marriage unsatisfactory, and abandoned or divorced his second wife in order to return to the first woman. Now that a couple have to go through the bitterness and scandal of a contested petition in Court, the chances of their marrying each other again are much slighter. Moreover, since it is well known that polygyny is severely restricted in Singapore, a married man often takes advantage of the fact by begging a woman to become his mistress, since it is very difficult for her to become his wife. In the past a man (whether single or married) did not find it easy to persuade a woman who was not a person of loose morals to engage in an affair with him; for if he loved her, he could marry her; and if he had no money he need not make any marriage payments; he only had to find the marriage registration fee.

MAINTENANCE OF WIFE AND CHILDREN

Until 1961, claims for maintenance of wives and children were made under *The Married Woman and Children (Maintenance) Ordinance*, and *The Maintenance (Facilities for Enforcement) Ordinance, 1959*. The legislation applied to all Singapore residents, irrespective of religion.

The Women's Charter (No. 18 of 1961) was enacted on 30 May 1961 and came into effect on 15 September of that year. It states that it is

> An Ordinance to provide for monogamous marriages and for the solemnization and registration of such marriages; to amend and consolidate the law relating to divorce, the rights and duties of married persons, the maintenance of wives and children and the punishment of offences against women and girls; and to provide for matters incidental thereto.

Most of the present leaders of the various ethnic groups in

Singapore have received a Western education, often in Britain. They are acutely sensitive to the critical (and frequently supercilious) comments of Westerners on the practice of polygyny among Chinese and Muslims. Chinese, Hindu, and Muslim women in the Island openly envy the independence of Western women living among them. Muslim women are particularly sensitive to the shocked incredulity expressed by non-Muslims when they learn that a Muslim may divorce his wife without provocation, by the simple procedure of uttering a formula of repudiation. Reformers in all communities point out that a people's measure of civilization or 'development' may usually be gauged by the status of its women, and that there should be equality between the sexes in the matter of marriage and divorce.

Until 1961 it was generally open to non-Christian Chinese and Indians to conduct their marriages and divorces according to their traditional customs.[1] However, Christian marriage in Singapore (for the resident European and Eurasian population, as well as for those Chinese, Indians, and others who were Christians) has, of course, always been monogamous. So has civil marriage before a Registrar.

The Women's Charter was a brave step designed to give the women of Singapore the rights and privileges of women in most Western countries. It abolished polygyny (but left undisturbed polygynous unions which had been formed before 15 September 1961). It also abolished divorce by mutual consent, which many Chinese and some Hindus had practised. Henceforth, all marriages (whether contracted before or after the coming into force of the Charter) could be dissolved only by order of the court.

But not all Singapore women were to benefit from this legislation. Parts II to VI of the Charter, which deal with monogamous marriages and with the solemnization and registration of marriages, as well as with the rights and duties of the spouses, and Part IX which is entitled 'Divorce'

> . . . shall not apply to any person who is married under, or to any marriage solemnized or registered under, the provisions of the Muslim law or of any written law in Singapore or in the Federation of Malaya providing for the registration of Muslim marriages.[2]

[1] See Maurice Freedman, 'Colonial Law and Chinese Society', *Journal of the Royal Anthropological Institute*, vol. LXXX, 1950 (published 1952).

[2] Section 3 (2) of *The Women's Charter*.

Parts VII and VIII of the Charter, however, entitled respectively 'Maintenance of Wife and Children' and 'Enforcement of Maintenance Orders', apply to all persons resident in Singapore.

In November 1960 the President of the Shariah Court was given authority to sit as a magistrate to hear the pleas of Muslim women suing their husbands for maintenance for themselves and/or their children. On 1 January 1963 all maintenance pleas against Muslim husbands were transferred to the Sixth District Court.

During 1961 a total of 332 maintenance cases were dealt with in the Shariah Magistrate's Court. Table 2 in the *Annual Report of the Registry of Muslim Marriages and the Shariah Court* for 1961 gives the following details:

	Cases
1. Attachment of Earnings Order	2
2. Order to pay	115
3. Postponed *sine die*	1
4. Variation	17
5. Order Rescinded	9
6. Warrant of Arrest	53
7. Discharged on Settlement	73
8. Summons struck out (complainant absent)	52
9. Withdrawn	3
10. Sentenced to imprisonment	5
11. Dismissed	2
Total	332

In 1962 a total of 304 cases were dealt with in the Shariah Magistrate's Court, and Table 3 of the *Annual Report* for 1962 reads:

	Cases
1. Attachment of Earnings Order	12
2. Summons struck out	67
3. Discharged	70
4. Warrant of Arrest issued	47
5. Order Rescinded	9
6. Variation	20
7. Order to pay	74
8. Postponed *sine die*	3
9. Sent to prison	2
Total	304

In May 1963 the Magistrate of the Sixth District Court very

kindly agreed that his Clerk give me details of Muslim maintenance cases dealt with during the first four months of 1963. There were a total of 78 cases: in 57 cases men were ordered to pay maintenance for their children; in 14 cases, the orders were in respect of both wives and children; in 6 cases, the orders were in respect of wives only; while in 1 case there was a variation of an order. In addition to the total of 78 cases dealt with, there were 10 other cases which were still pending.

Singapore Muslims, or at least Singapore Malaysians,[1] have often neglected their responsibility to maintain their estranged wives and their children. It is important here to note that a man recognizes he has a duty to maintain his children, even if he denies he has a duty to maintain a wife he has abandoned or repudiated without her having committed any conjugal offence. However, although a man will freely acknowledge his financial responsibility for his children, he will usually attempt to evade it. In several cases in 1961 and 1962, a man pleaded that he could not pay maintenance to his divorced wife in respect of their children because he owed a large sum of money which he had to repay out of his earnings. When asked how he had incurred such a debt, he replied that it was in order to pay for the expenses of taking another woman in marriage, after his divorce.

I read all the records of maintenance hearings held in the Shariah Magistrate's Court until the end of 1962, and in 1963 I attended several hearings at the Sixth District Court. The men's defence followed a regular pattern, which a callous observer might describe as monotonous: 'I earn barely enough to support myself'; 'I have many debts'; 'I have another wife and children, and surely my first duty is to them'; 'I promise to pay all I can as soon as I can earn more money'.

When the magistrate insisted that the man pay maintenance in respect of his children to their mother, the man's next move was sometimes a threat to seek the custody of the children. Many mothers, rather than risk losing their children (which, moreover, frequently meant that the latter would be brought up by a stepmother), abruptly surrendered their claims upon the father. Although in the majority of cases such threats were not in fact carried out, there have nevertheless been some successful instances of a man obtaining custody of his children. This a father can do

[1] See my *Malay Kinship*, pp. 125–6.

in two ways: either by pleading before the High Court (which can be expensive and time-consuming), or (and this is far more common) enticing the child or children away. The police will not normally interfere if one parent has gained possession of his or her children by fair means or foul, so long as no court order has been contravened.

From 1959 to 1962 there were nine decided cases in which Muslim parents fought in the High Court of Singapore for custody of their children; in three cases the mother was legally aided, while in one case the father was aided. (Provisions for legal aid were introduced in 1958 in Singapore, with the establishment of the Legal Aid Bureau.) The nine cases were decided as follows:

1959: 2 cases, in both of which the father was successful;
1960: 2 cases, in both of which the mother succeeded;
1961: 3 cases, in two of which the mother was granted custody, while the father succeeded in one case;
1962: 2 cases, in both of which the father succeeded.

As for 1963, up to the end of June 1963 there were two cases involving Muslim parents, in both of which the mother sought custody. The cases were still proceeding when I left Singapore.

In 1961, an interesting case involving the issues of custody and maintenance came before the Shariah Magistrate's Court. A woman sued her divorced husband for arrears of maintenance in respect of their two children. In 1949 a court order had granted the mother custody of the children until January 1954, and directed that the father during that period pay for their maintenance; in January 1954, the children had to be returned to him. In defending his divorced wife's action for recovery of arrears of maintenance since January 1954, the man claimed that when he went to take his children at the beginning of 1954, their mother struck a bargain with him: she offered to be financially responsible for them if he allowed her to retain their custody. He had agreed, but now she was suing him for arrears of maintenance. The wife denied her husband's allegation, saying she had entered into no such bargain. The man was unable to produce evidence in his favour, such as a written agreement between his wife and himself, or witnesses to the bargain, and the Court ordered him to pay the arrears due.

Although many men attempt to evade their financial responsi-

bility for their young children by offering to take them away from their mother, some are reluctant to make such an offer in case their bluff is called. Others seek a reduction of the monthly sum awarded by the Court to the children's mother by alleging other kinship commitments. Thus one man in May 1962 pleaded that he had to remit money to his mother in India. His divorced Malay wife commented: 'I put it to you that it is more important to support your children here than to support your mother in India.'
Husband: 'According to the custom in India a good son should support the mother first. Then the wife and then the children.'
Wife: 'Your mother is looked after by her two sons-in-law in India.'
Husband: 'According to the usual custom in India the son should support the mother and not the son-in-law.'[1]
The Court varied the maintenance order: it allowed the man to pay $5 less per month.

Singapore courts naturally do not have to take into account 'the custom in India' when deciding issues of maintenance. It is worth noting here that all Schools of Islam agree that a man is absolutely bound to maintain his minor children, whether or not they be in his custody.[2] N. B. E. Baillie, in *A Digest of Moohummadan Law on the Subjects to which it is Usually Applied by the British Courts of Justice in India, Compiled and Translated from Authorities in the Original Arabic*[3] states in vol. 1 (which is concerned with 'The Doctrines of the Hanifeea Code of Jurisprudence . . .'):

> When a mother is poor, her son is bound to maintain her, though he be in straitened circumstances himself, and she not infirm. When a son is able to maintain only one of his parents, the mother has the better right; and if he have both parents and a minor son, and is able to maintain only one of them, the son has the preferable right. . . .
>
> The maintenance of a mere relative is not incumbent on any poor person; contrary to the maintenance of a wife and child, for whom poor and rich are equally liable.[4]

Some men find themselves faced with maintenance orders in respect of children of several wives. One man before the Court in

[1] The Court record of maintenance proceedings in the building of the Shariah Court was kept in English.
[2] Vesey-Fitzgerald, *op. cit.*, p. 96.
[3] 2 vols., vol. 1 second edition, London, 1875; vol. 2, London, 1869.
[4] pp. 466 f.

1962 had divorced three wives and was responsible for the maintenance of one child by the first wife, two by the second, and three by the third. He had remarried, and since his present wife had borne him no children, they had legally adopted a child. He was contesting the plea by the third wife to increase the monthly sum he paid for their three sons, who now needed school clothes, bus fares, and textbooks.

Some men contest their wives' pleas for maintenance on the ground that they repudiated them several months earlier, although the divorce was not registered because the wives refused to sign the divorce register. There were at least two such cases, one in 1961 and one in 1962. Both wives were granted maintenance after the husbands had failed to produce witnesses willing to swear that they had heard the *talak* uttered.

Although maintenance summonses had ceased to be issued by the Shariah Magistrate's Court in 1963, nevertheless there were hearings in that Court in the spring and summer of 1963 resulting from maintenance summonses which had been issued in 1962. As I said earlier, during that period I also attended maintenance hearings in the Sixth District Court. In theory, both Courts were applying the provisions of *The Women's Charter*; but it was perhaps inevitable for orders made in the Shariah Court building to be influenced sometimes by Muslim principles. Thus there was one case where a woman was refused maintenance on the ground that she had been a recalcitrant wife, that she stood guilty of *nushuz*,[1] because she refused to share her bedroom with her husband. She had ten children by him, and she feared a further pregnancy.

On the other hand, when in other (earlier) cases the Shariah Court magistrate had granted a wife maintenance although in Islam she could be said to be recalcitrant and therefore not entitled to maintenance, there had been protests by several Muslim leaders that the law of Islam was being defied in the very precincts of the Shariah Court. This may have been one of the reasons which led to the transfer of all maintenance pleas to the building of the Magistrates' Court more than a mile away. The magistrates dealing with Muslim maintenance cases from January to July 1963 were Chinese or non-Muslim Indians. They were not familiar with the detailed principles of Islam which were, strictly

[1] See above, p. 23.

speaking, irrelevant since they had to enforce only the provisions of *The Women's Charter*. During the hearings I attended, in no case did the Court entertain a husband's defence that his wife was not entitled to maintenance because she had been disobedient or recalcitrant.

Conclusion

The crucial problem facing Muslim reformers in Singapore is the emotion the diehards can stimulate by simply warning, 'Islam is being attacked', or 'They want to make Islam modern'. Precisely because most Singapore Muslims have received an extremely sketchy religious education, appeal to the texts and quiet discussions on a rational basis are rare. Moreover, the handful of determined Muslim men and women who seek to introduce further legislation to protect the status of a Muslim wife must fight the conservatism of the bulk of Muslim *women* in the State. When one of them, possessed of great perseverance and endurance, organized protest meetings and stood up to speak on a platform, the audience (largely composed of women) reacted with mixed feelings, and some women were heard to mutter: 'Why does she want to exhibit herself like this? She is a woman, and she ought to behave with more modesty. What does she want to do, become a kathi herself?'

Appeals to the texts of the Koran, to the passages where the Prophet enjoins men to treat their wives with kindness and mercy, and to the famous verse concerning polygyny '. . . But if ye fear ye shall not act with equity towards so many, marry one only . . .' generally fail to generate enthusiasm. Reformers cite the example of an independent Muslim country (such as Tunisia) which has introduced legislation to ban polygyny, and urge that Singapore should follow suit, but they face a solid wall of pious resistance from many kathis and from Malay, Arab, and Indian leaders.

Singapore is not, of course, a Muslim state. The Legislative Assembly has a minority of Muslim members, and most Assemblymen are understandably reluctant to antagonize the bulk of the Muslim electorate. Singapore Muslims are not always strict in their observance of the five daily prayers and in adhering to the fast during the entire month of Ramadan. On the other hand, they do pay more than lip service to what they consider to be sacred Muslim precepts, and if religious teachers assure them that polygyny is the inalienable right of a man, they readily believe it to be so. Women who have not been abandoned by their husbands, and those who have no co-wife, generally think that most of their less fortunate sisters have only themselves to blame for the plight in which they find themselves: they must have been bad housekeepers, or flighty, or irascible, or impertinent. They recognize that occasionally an absolutely guiltless woman is deserted, or neglected, or left without maintenance for herself and her children; but they argue that such a situation must be accepted as one of the inevitable perils of conjugal life, and that a woman should be resigned to it as she must be to illness or any other misfortune. It becomes such a woman to show dignity and courage, and to earn her living by taking in laundry if she is totally unskilled, or making and hawking snacks; or, which is more genteel, dressmaking. When I was living in a working-class area in town in 1950, one of my neighbours explained to me that when her husband deserted her and their four young children and married another woman in the same district, she borrowed money from a usurer, bought a sewing machine, and stitched away from morning until night to repay the principal and the interest on the loan. Eventually she acquired enough capital to buy some lengths of cloth and make children's garments for sale in the periods when she did not have enough dressmaking orders. In 1963, I heard similar comments from women in the same position, although they could be assured of a small allowance from Public Assistance funds if they were out of work and had young children to support.

The earnest reformers, especially those who are totally opposed to polygyny, resent the argument that the abolition of polygyny may create more problems than it would solve, and may indeed cause more hardship. Present legislation in Singapore makes no provision for a Muslim to pay maintenance to his divorced wife. Whereas prior to the restrictions on polygyny now in force in Singapore, a Muslim did not always divorce his wife when he wished to marry another woman, nowadays he usually has to secure a divorce from his existing wife in order to enter into another union. The former wife is then left without maintenance (apart from the three months of her *iddah* period). In earlier years it was not uncommon for a man in such a position to marry either openly or surreptitiously, and to continue living with his earlier wife. Sometimes, he tired of the newer spouse and divorced her (especially if she had borne him no children), and returned permanently to the older woman. These short-lived polygynous unions were treated by patient and wise Muslim wives very much as some Western women in earlier decades treated the sporadic infidelities of their husbands: as long as there was no open scandal, they bided their time. Moreover, Singapore Muslim wives often console themselves with the belief that a man may be enticed away by magic, which can by counteracted by appropriate measures; and if the latter fail, it is still no slur on their charm or general behaviour if their husbands have been attracted by younger, or more attractive, or more scheming women. It is the accepted norm of their society that men may have their fling, and some wives are happier in a temporary separation, or in sharing their husband with a co-wife, than in the utter rejection of a divorce. This is of course especially true of older women, who have very little hope of remarriage.

Polygyny is not the only field where there is an attempt to impose Western ideals on a society which considers itself bound to the sacred principles of Muslim family law. There has been a great deal of concern in recent years in Singapore over the practice of young girls eloping to marry the men of their choice, when such men were unacceptable to the girls' fathers as sons-in-law. As we know, until the *Muslims Ordinance, 1957* came into effect, any Singapore kathi could act as guardian for marriage (*wali*) to a female who swore that she had no *wali* available, or that her *wali* unreasonably refused his consent. If the kathi suspected the couple might engage in illicit relations, he believed it to be his duty to arrange and register a marriage contract in which he acted as the girl's *wali*, her *wali hakim*. In 1949 and 1950 I lived very close to a Singapore kathi's house, and witnessed many such incidents.

One such case before the Shariah Court in 1963 created a great deal of publicity. In February 1962 a Singapore Indian girl who had reached puberty (but was not quite fourteen years of age) had eloped with a young Indian to Negri Sembilan, a Malay State, where a kathi married them. The young man was first prosecuted in Singapore for kidnapping the girl, was found not guilty, and on appeal by the State was found guilty only of a technical offence and not punished. The girl had testified that she had exerted a great deal of pressure on the young man to force him to take her away, and that she had threatened suicide if he would not do as she wished.

In April, June, and July 1963 I attended hearings in the Shariah Court of a petition brought by the girl's father to have the marriage annulled. She had, meanwhile, given birth to a child and was living in the Muslim Women's Welfare Home. I discussed the case with some of the most active leaders in the movement for Muslim legislative reform, and pointed out that Hanafi law allowed a girl who had reached puberty to give herself in marriage. (The lawyer for the father had argued that eighteen years is the minimum age of independence for a Hanafi female to enter into a contract of marriage, but the argument had been rejected by the Court.) I was told bluntly that even if this were so, it was inconceivable that any fourteen-year old should be allowed to run away from home and get married; such a situation ran contrary to all general principles of morality, and even if there were no grounds on which the marriage could be annulled, some safeguards had to be found in order to prevent other girls from follow- such a disastrous example; the accepted Muslim legal texts on the matter had to be re-interpreted. This attitude was shared by Muslims who adhered to old traditions and who opposed reforms in the realms of polygyny and divorce. Therefore, the conclusion one must reach is that where young girls are concerned, both camps are united in the belief that parental authority must be strengthened by initiating legal reforms, even if this is at the cost of running counter to traditional principles of Muslim law. (In this case the marriage contract was rescinded. The father's objection to the husband on the grounds of the latter's inferior social status was declared valid; the Court noted that the Hanafi school attaches great importance to the matter of equivalent status (*kufu*) and found the husband inferior in regard to occupation, property, character, and religious observance.)

Legislators in Singapore have had a difficult task when they have attempted to apply at least some of the provisions of *The Women's Charter* to Muslims. On the face of it, it seems that by making Muslim men liable to observe the maintenance regulations they are protecting Muslim women. The Charter in so far as it applies to Muslims does not provide for maintenance in respect of divorced wives; but a non-Muslim is unlikely to succeed in a divorce petition against a wife who is guiltless of any conjugal offence, and if such a woman obtains a maintenance order, she is reasonably secure. Section 81 of the Charter states:

> Subject to the provisions contained in this Part of this Ordinance, the court shall in all suits and proceedings hereunder act and give relief on principles which in the opinion of the court are, as nearly as may be, conformable to the principles on which the High Court of Justice in England acts and gives relief in matrimonial proceedings.

On the other hand, as we know, a Singapore Muslim man seems to have an undisputed right to secure the registration of a repudiation he has uttered, and he does not have to show cause why he wishes the union dissolved. True, the Shariah Court may delay such registration, but only for a matter of weeks or at most of months. Consequently many Muslim women, who have imperfectly understood the new legislation, have sued their husbands for maintenance and have been shocked to learn that the men can, and do, retaliate by repudiating them. After the expiry of the *iddah* period they have no right to maintenance and little hope that their husbands would wish to remarry them; if they are middle-aged or elderly, this is a bitter blow, and I have heard several of them rue the day on which they sued for maintenance. In some cases, wives who took no official action, but waited patiently, regained their husbands.

In 1963, writing in the Singapore periodical *Seed* (vol. 3, no. 1) in a personal capacity, Inche Ahmad Ibrahim (State Advocate-General, Singapore) said, in an article entitled 'Malays Harmed by "Special Rights"':

> The Women's Charter, 1961, permits divorce on grounds which are substantially common to the husband and to the wife. It is only the Muslims in Singapore who claim that the Muslim husband should have an unrestricted right of repudiating his wife. Is this freedom really beneficial to the Muslims? Is it to the interest of the Muslim community that a husband should be able to abandon his wife and children for no fault of the wife and to leave the wife without support after the three months of *eddah*? Again in most other Muslim countries the right of the Muslim husband has been restricted and it is only bigoted fanaticism and a lack of social consciousness which leads the Muslim men in Singapore to claim their exclusive rights in this matter.

The President of the Shariah Court is faced with a desperately complex task. First, he must try to make decisions which are in accordance with the letter as well as the spirit of Islam, for his Court is nothing if not a religious court; and the Shafi'i School which he generally follows is very strict on the matter of the wife's obedience. Second, he must make rulings which take into account the traditional practices of the people who come before him, for if he imposed restrictions which were utterly at variance with such practices (for instance, if he severely limited a married woman's freedom of movement to only such errands as were previously sanctioned by her husband), his orders might be deliberately flouted. Clearly, he does take into account local custom; as we saw earlier,[1] he told one husband that whenever his wife asks permission to visit her parents, he must grant it ('If she wants to visit her parents, she may do so'), implying that the wife's formal request was merely a courtesy on her part, and that she had the right to pay such visits. Third, the President tries to follow the spirit of the legislators who introduced the 1957 Ordinance and the 1960 Amendment, and who sought to reduce the rate of divorce and to safeguard the financial interests of a divorced woman. He must exhort his staff to achieve as many reconciliations as possible, and he himself attempts even at a divorce hearing to bring the couple together again; according to the Annual Reports of the Court, he thus effected five reconciliations in 1961 and four in 1962.

On the whole, the President has been successful in his difficult task. He has, whenever possible, cited religious authority or moral precept when he has persuaded a reluctant husband to set his wife free, or when he has granted a woman a judicial decree of divorce. In one case in 1963, he pointed out that although the Prophet Muhammad had stated that divorce is abhorred, he had also stated that oppression of the weak and defenceless is abhorred, and that when it was clear that a wife was oppressed by the continuance of a marriage it was the duty of the Court to attempt to find a remedy. In most such cases he has referred the issue to arbitrators, a contingency for which there is authority in the Koran itself, in the Chapter on Women (iv, 39):

> And if ye fear a breach between the *husband and wife*, send a judge out of his family, and a judge out of her family; if they shall desire a reconcilation, GOD will cause them to agree . . .[2]

[1] Cf. p. 76 above.

[2] Sale's translation.

Although the President is entitled under the Ordinance to make orders for consolatory gifts and for *iddah* maintenance, he has generally persuaded the husband that it is a man's religious duty to make such payments, and he has often asked that the husband himself suggest a suitable amount as a gift, and sometimes succeeded in extracting a little more money than the sum originally offered. At the end of a hearing a husband is more often persuaded than compelled to follow the Court's guidance.

There has been some criticism of the fact that the President does not take full advantage of the powers the Court has under Section 36A of the Muslims Ordinance (a Section introduced in the 1960 Amendment to the Ordinance) to 'make such orders as it thinks fit with respect to . . . the payment of a consolatory gift or *matta'ah* to the wife'. In his article, 'Muslim Marriage and Divorce in Singapore', Inche Ahmad Ibrahim states:

> The payment of a consolatory gift on divorce or *mata'ah* is enjoined in the Holy Quran and according to the Shafi'i School of Law the payment of *mata'ah* is incumbent in the case of every divorced woman, except a woman whose *maskahwin* has been stipulated and who is divorced before consummation of the marriage. The Shariah Court may therefore in a proper case order the payment of *mata'ah* to compensate the wife where she has unreasonably been repudiated by her husband but unfortunately the practice in Singapore has been to award very small sums for *mata'ah*, for example a sum of ten dollars.

He adds that in Syria a kathi may order a husband to pay, in certain circumstances, up to one year's maintenance to a wife divorced without reasonable cause.

The officials who have to interpret and apply the *Muslims Ordinance, 1957* are bound to antagonize either the reformers or the conservatives. In 1961 and 1962 the Chief Kathi usually allowed the registration of a polygynous union only after he had sought the views of the applicant's present wife and had satisfied himself that she did not object to a co-wife. When this fact became widely known, many influential Singapore Muslims voiced their condemnation of the practice, arguing that it was an intolerable interference and it seems that they succeeded in abolishing it. *The Straits Times* of 11 July 1963 reported that at a political meeting in Singapore, when a former Singapore Chief Kathi raised the matter, the chairman of the meeting 'said that his investigations showed that the Court was no longer practising the rule'. When I discussed this issue with members of the anti-polygyny movement, they admitted sadly that they had suffered a set-back.[1]

There is one extremely important aspect of the movement for legislative reform among Singapore Muslims: the impetus so far has come exclusively from lay leaders. Religious officials have at best been passive, and at the other extreme openly critical. By religious officials I mean kathis, and *imam* or mosque employees, for I am aware that there are several young teachers in religious schools for children who are eager to see more drastic legislation to protect Muslim women. As we know, Singapore has no *mufti*, that is, it has no learned theologian and jurist who may give an authoritative answer (*fatwa*) on a specific point of law.[2] In some Muslim countries, *mufti* have been instrumental in promoting reform, while in others they have come out sharply on the side of the traditionalists.

Most Singapore Muslims have not been brought up to believe that divorce is inherently evil, but rather that broken marriages are common and often inevitable. Many deplore the high rate of divorce, especially when they are made aware that by comparison with some other Muslim countries the Singapore rate is still very high, but on the whole they are resigned to the situation. Marriage among Singapore Muslims has not been the cornerstone of family life, and the children of a divorced couple are not the object of pity and concern they so often are in Western countries.[3] A marriage is a contract between the spouses and can be, and often is, dissolved without reference to the children of the union. In the brief summary of the results of the *1962 Seminar on the Status of*

[1] The Colony of Singapore Annual Report for 1953 stated (p. 15):

> 'There has been a movement amongst Malay women against polygamy. Islam permits a Muslim to marry up to four wives at a time provided certain conditions are fulfilled. In practice monogamy is usual.'

This passage appeared again in the Annual Reports for 1954, 1955, and 1956. The Annual Report for 1957 omits the first sentence; the relevant passage reads (p. 35):

> 'Although Islam permits a Muslim to marry up to four wives at a time provided certain conditions are fulfilled, in practice monogamy is usual.'

The Annual Reports of the Registry of Muslim Marriages state that the Chief Kathi solemnized 2 polygynous unions in 1961 and 4 in 1962.

[2] See above, pp. 12 f., 78.

[3] See my *Malay Kinship*, pp. 139–40.

Women in Family Law (Tokyo), the following statement was made:[1]

> Stress was laid on a recent development in the law of some countries whereby a court would not make a final order for divorce unless satisfied that the best possible arrangements had been made to protect the interests of the children, and it was felt that this development could be usefully followed by other countries. In particular, one participant considered that moslem (*sic*) courts paid insufficient attention to the interests of the children.

In Singapore, as we know, the Shariah Court does not make orders as to the custody of the young children of couples involved in matrimonial disputes: the parents are referred to the High Court, if they fail to reach agreement.

So far as the present divorce reform in Singapore goes, it restricts unilateral divorce by requiring process of law to ensure its registration; and it also seeks to ensure that a guiltless wife who is repudiated is given a minimum amount of money to tide her over the first three months after the divorce. But there is no attempt to limit divorce by mutual consent, only to ensure that the consent is in fact mutual, and that a wife is not coerced into signing the application form for divorce and the divorce register. Indeed, once a Court kathi is satisfied that a couple cannot be reconciled, he attempts to persuade them to agree to an 'amicable' divorce (*cherai dengan baik*) rather than to go through the procedure of a Court hearing. A kathi's attitude may be summarized thus: divorce is abhorred in Islam, but if it must take place then let it be done with the minimum of rancour.

As for unilateral divorce, it is impossible to tell on the evidence available how many husbands who have uttered a formula of repudiation have failed to register the divorce either because they were unable to secure their wife's agreement, or because they did not have the minimum amount of $19 to pay for the application form and the registration. But of course such a repudiation is valid in Islam, and in cases where a wife has produced witnesses who have testified that they heard the repudiation uttered, she has secured from the Shariah Court the registration of the divorce.

The crucial factor in the present legislative reform is that the

[1] United Nations, New York, 1962 ST/TAO/HR/14, p. 25, para. 112.

success of the 1957 Muslims Ordinance is almost exclusively dependent upon the popular belief that registration of a marriage or of a divorce is the proof of its validity. However, if the knowledge that lack of registration does not affect the validity of a change in marital status should spread, and Muslims should decide to take advantage of the relevant Section in the Muslims Ordinance, chaos might result. So far, however, there appear to be no serious grounds for worry on that account. As we saw earlier, even a Muslim member of the Legislative Assembly was under the impression that 'in Islamic law, the marriage should be solemnized before a priest or *imam*', when in fact this is not so.

Most couples carefully guard the copy of the marriage certificate which the officiating kathi gives them after the ceremony. I have never seen these certificates framed or otherwise exhibited in a Muslim home, but there is no doubt that they are usually preserved. Petitioning spouses in the Shariah Court produce their marriage certificates often yellowed with age and frayed at the folds and edges. Where divorce certificates are concerned, as a rule a woman will be fully convinced that she is divorced and (after her *iddah* period) free to remarry only if she has in her possession a certificate of divorce issued by a kathi or by the Shariah Court. Indeed, as we know, a kathi will not normally agree to officiate at the marriage of a divorcee unless he sees such a certificate.

The Shariah Court was constituted in November 1958, and the years 1959 to 1963 witnessed a dramatic decline in the divorce rate. The marriage contracts of child brides are no longer registered; a man may no longer ask a kathi to register his divorce or the revocation of his divorce without his wife's consent; a bride must sign the marriage register; only the Chief Kathi may allow the registration of a polygynous union, and only he may act as a bride's guardian to give her away in marriage if she has no guardian or if her guardian unreasonably withholds his consent; members of the Armed Forces and of the Police must produce official evidence that they are not already married before a Singapore kathi will register their marriage; men who have taken away their wife's jewelry or other personal possessions to sell or pawn, and then sought to register a repudiation, have been ordered to repay their debt before registration was granted. Perhaps the most notable contribution of Shariah Court officials has been in the realm of conciliation: 457 couples were reconciled in 1961, and 560 in 1962.

These are very real achievements. However, the restrictions may be successfully ignored by determined Singaporeans who can afford to travel to some Malay States which have no comparable legislation. When I left Singapore, Malaysia was about to come into existence. (In September 1963, the Federation of Malaya, Singapore, Sarawak, and North Borneo (Sabah) formed themselves into the new Malaysia.[1]) Muslim reformers thought the time was ripe for unified and stricter legislation in the realm of marriage and divorce, but the more realistic among them were fully aware that such a victory would not be easily won: some of the Malay States have staunchly conservative Muslim groups which are vocal and well organized.

[1] Singapore left the Federation of Malaysia in August 1965.

POSTSCRIPT

Inche Ahmad Ibrahim, State Advocate-General, Singapore, read a copy of the page proofs; I am deeply grateful to him for various suggestions and elucidations. He also kindly provided me with additional data on developments in Singapore up to September 1965. The most significant of these are:

I. The divorce rate has been further reduced in 1963 and 1964. (See p. 143.)

	Marriages	*Divorces*	*Revocations*
1963	1690	430	59
1964	1698	324	30

II. In the case referred to at pp. 12, 16, 174, the man was eventually allowed to marry the girl again, and the marriage was duly registered. See Note 'Enticement of Minor and the Validity of her Marriage Under Muslim Law' by Mrs M. Siraj, *Malaya Law Review*, vol. 5, no. 2, December 1963, pp. 392–7.

III. The reciprocal arrangements between Singapore and the States of the Malay Peninsula referred to at pp. 32 f., 182, are working more satisfactorily. It is no longer so easy, for determined Singaporeans who can afford to travel to some Malay State, to marry or get a divorce in the Peninsula.

IV. In the case mentioned on pp. 93–4, the husband came to the Shariah Court in August 1963 to say that he was now eager to register a divorce, because he wanted to contract another marriage. The wife was asked to come to the Court for an interview with the President, who also requested the husband to be present. She came with her stepfather, and said that she would agree to the divorce on two conditions:

1. Her husband must give her the birth certificate of their two children.
2. He must also return to her the dresses which she had left in the conjugal home.

He agreed to comply with the first condition, but refused the second, on the grounds that he had disposed of the dresses. The wife refused to sign the register for a mutual agreement divorce unless the dresses were returned, and left the Court building. The husband remained in Court, and told the President that he was determined to repudiate his wife. The President, in view of the fact that the wife had obstinately refused to pay the $50 redemption money ordered by the Court in the course of an earlier hearing, agreed to register the repudiation. The registration took place that same day, on 23 August 1963.

V. Pp. 152 f. A Muslim convicted of making a false declaration in an application form for marriage is now dealt with much more severely. In 1964 the State Advocate-General personally argued an appeal against a sentence of one day's imprisonment and a fine of $150 imposed in the District Court on a man who had pleaded guilty to making a false declaration. The High Court allowed the appeal. The case, *Public Prosecutor v. Zaini*, is reported in the *Malayan Law Journal*, vol. XXX, 1964, pp. 221 f. The sentence was increased to six months' imprisonment.

Che Ahmad informs me that since *P.P. v. Zaini*, prison sentences have been imposed for false declarations by Muslims who sought to contract and register a polygynous marriage without the consent of the Chief Kathi; moreover, the registration of the second marriage has in all such cases been cancelled by the Registrar.

VI. Mrs M. Siraj, Muslim Woman Social Worker, who had been transferred to the Department of Social Welfare in 1962, returned to the Shariah Court in September 1965. (See p. 22 n.)

13 *October* 1965 J.D.

LIST OF WORKS CITED

AHMAD IBRAHIM, 'The Status of Women in Family Law in the Federation of Malaya, Singapore and the Borneo Territories', Background Paper B, Prepared for the United Nations Secretariat for the 1962 Seminar on the Status of Women in Family Law held in Tokyo.

—— 'Muslim Marriage and Divorce in Singapore', *The Malayan Law Journal*, vol. XXVIII, February 1962.

—— 'Malays Harmed by "Special Rights"', *Seed*, vol. 3, no. 1, 1963, Singapore.

AMEER ALI, *The Personal Law of the Mahommedans (According to all the Schools)*, London, 1880.

ANDERSON, J. N. D., *Islamic Law in the Modern World*, London, 1959.

BAILLIE, N. E. B., *A Digest of Moohummadan Law on the Subjects to which it is Usually Applied by the British Courts of Justice in India*, 2 vols.: vol. 1, second edition, London, 1875; vol. 2, London, 1869.

BRADDELL, R., *The Laws of the Straits Settlements. A Commentary*, 2 vols., Singapore, 1931.

DJAMOUR, J., *Malay Kinship and Marriage in Singapore*, London School of Economics Monographs on Social Anthropology, no. 21, London, 1959.

FREEDMAN, M., 'Colonial Law and Chinese Society', *Journal of the Royal Anthropological Institute*, vol. LXXX, 1950 (published 1952).

GIBB, H. A. R., and KRAMERS, J. H., *Shorter Encyclopaedia of Islam*, Leiden and London, 1953.

Ibn Khallikan's Biographical Dictionary, M. G. de Slane, trans., 4 vols., Paris, 1842, 1843, 1868, 1871.

JONES, R., review of J. Djamour, *Malay Kinship . . .*, *Oceania*, vol. XXXIII, no. 4, June 1963.

KARIM, A. K. NAZMUL, 'Changing Patterns of an East Pakistan Family', in Ward, B. E. (ed.) *Women in the New Asia, The changing roles of men and women in South and South-East Asia*, Paris, 1963.

LANE, E. W., *Modern Egyptians*, London, 1890.

NAWAWI, *Minhaj et Talibin*, translated by E. C. Howard from the French ed. of L. W. C. Van Den Berg, London, 1914.

RONART, S. and N., *Concise Encyclopaedia of Arabic Civilization*, Amsterdam, 1959.

SALE, G., *The Koran, Translated from the Original Arabic*, London, n.d.

SETHI, R. B., *Muslim Marriage and Dissolution*, second edition, Allahabad, 1961.

SIRAJ, M., 'The Shariah Court of Singapore and its control of the Divorce Rate', *Malaya Law Review*, vol. v, no. 1, July 1963.

TAYLOR, E. N., 'Malay Family Law', *Journal of the Royal Asiatic Society, Malayan Branch*, vol. XV, Part 1, 1937.

—— 'Mohammedan Divorce by Khula', *Journal of the Royal Asiatic Society, Malayan Branch*, vol. XXI, Part 2, 1948.

UNESCO, *1962 Seminar on the Status of Women in Family Law* (Tokyo), United Nations, New York, 1962 ST/TAO/HR/14.

VESEY-FITZGERALD, S., *Muhammadan Law, An Abridgement According to its Various Schools*, London, 1931.

WILKINSON, R. J., *Law, Part I, An Introductory Sketch*, in *Papers on Malay Subjects*, Kuala Lumpur, 1908.

WINSTEDT, R. O., *The Malays, A Cultural History*, London, 1950.

Official Publications

Colony of Singapore Annual Reports.

State of Singapore Annual Reports.

Census Reports for 1931, 1947, and 1957.

Annual Reports of the Registry of Muslim Marriages and the Shariah Court for 1960, 1961, and 1962.

Report from the Select Committee on the Muslims Bill, L.A. 5 of 1957.

Report of the Select Committee on the Muslims (Amendment) Bill, L.A. 14 of 1960.

The Mahomedan Marriage Ordinance, 1880.

The Laws of the Colony of Singapore (8 vols., prepared by Davies, E. J., Butterfield, C. H., and Simpson, A. H.), Singapore, 1955.

The *Muslims Ordinance, 1957*, no. 25 of 1957.

The Muslim Marriage and Divorce Rules, 1959.

The Married Women and Children (Maintenance) Ordinance.

The Maintenance (Facilities for Enforcement) Ordinance, 1959, no. 63 of 1959.

The Muslims (Amendment) Ordinance, 1960, no. 40 of 1960.

The Women's Charter, 1961, no. 18 of 1961.

Chief Statistician, Singapore, *Monthly Digest of Statistics.*

State of Pahang, *Administration of the Law of the Religion of Islam Enactment, 1965.*

Index

London School of Economics Monographs on Social Anthropology series
Series Editor: Charles Stafford

With over 70 volumes published since 1949, including classic work by Gell, Barth, Leach and Firth, the LSE Monographs now form one of the most prestigious series in the discipline of Anthropology. Presenting scholarly work from all branches of Social Anthropology the series continues to build on its history with both theoretical and ethnographic studies of the contemporary world.

74. Between China and Europe
Person, Culture and Emotion in Macao
Joao de Pina-Cabral

73. The Earth Shakers of Madagascar
An Anthropological Study of Authority, Fertility and Creation
Oliver Woolley

72. Chinese Sociologics
An Anthropological Account of Alienation and Social Reproduction
P. Steven Sangren

71. The Performance of Gender
An Anthropology of Everyday Life in a South Indian Fishing Village
Cecilia Busby

70. Arguments with Ethnography
Comparative Approaches to History, Politics and Religion
Ioan M. Lewis

69. Those Who Play with Fire
Gender, Fertility and Transformation in East and Southern Africa
Henrietta L. Moore, Todd Sanders and Bwire Kaare

68. Conceiving Persons
Ethnographies of Procreation, Fertility and Growth
Edited by Peter Z. Loizos and P. Heady

67. The Art of Anthropology
Essays and Diagrams
Alfred Gell (Edited by Eric Hirsch)

66. Leadership and Change in the Western Pacific
Edited by Richard Feinberg and Karen Ann Watson-Gegeo

65. Hierarchy and Egalitarianism
Castle, Class and Power in Sinhalese Peasant Society
Tamara Gunasekera

64. The Harambee Movement in Kenya
Self-help, Development and Education among the Kamba of Kitui District
Martin J. D. Hill

63. Society and Politics in India
Essays in a Comparative Perspective
Andre Beteille

62. The Power of Love
The Moral Use of Knowledge amongst the Amuesha of Central Peru
Fernando Santos-Granero

61. Making Sense of Hierarchy
Cognition as Social Process in Fiji
Christina Toren

60. The Social Practice of Symbolization
An Anthropological Analysis
Ivo Strecker

59. Gods on Earth
The Management of Religious Experience and Identity in a North Indian Pilgrimage Centre
Peter van der Veer

58. Ritual, History and Power
Selected Papers in Anthropology
Maurice Bloch

57. Sacrifice and Sharing in the Philippine Highlands
Religion and Society among the Buid of Mindoro
Thomas P. Gibson

56. Communication, Social Structure and Development in Rural Malaysia
A Study of Kampung Kuala Bera
William D. Wilder

55. Forest Traders
A Socio-Economic Study of the Hill Pandaram
Brian Morris

54. Ma'Betisék Concepts of Living Things
Wazir-Jahan Karim

53. White Nile Arabs
Political Leadership and Economic Change
Abbas Ahmed Mohamed

52. Knowledge of Illness in Sepik Society
A Study of the Gnau, New Guinea
Gilbert Lewis

51. Metamorphosis of the Cassowaries
Umeda Society, Language and Ritual
Alfred Gell

50. Choice and Change
Edited by John Davis

49. Beyond the Village
Local Politics in Madang, Papua New Guinea
Louise Morauta

48. Land and Family in Pisticci
J. Davis

47. West Indian Migration
The Montserrat Case
Stuart B. Philpott

46. Uncertainties in Peasant Farming
A Colombian Case
Sutti Ortiz

45. Pioneers in the Tropics
The Political Organization of Japanese in an Immigrant Community in Brazil
Philip Staniford

44. Political Systems of Highland Burma
A Study of Kachin Social Structure
E. R. Leach

43. Tribal Innovators
Tswana Chiefs and Social Change 1795–1940
Isaac Schapera

42. The Political Structure of the Chinese Community in Cambodia
W. E. Willmott

41. Report on the Iban
Derek Freeman

40. Time and Social Structure and Other Essays
Meyer Fortes

39. Take Out Hunger
Two Case Studies of Rural Development in Basutoland
Sandra Wallman

38. Anthropology and Social Change
Lucy Mair

37. Kinship and Marriage among the Anlo Ewe
G. K. Nukunya

36. Christianity and the Shona
Marshall Murphree

35. The Keresan Bridge
A Problem in Pueblo Ethnology
Robin Fox

34. Kinship and Social Organisation
W. H. R. Rivers

33. Chinese Lineage and Society
Fukien and Kwantung
Maurice Freedman

32. Kinship and Economic Organization in Rural Japan
Chie Nakane

31. The Muslim Matrimonial Court in Singapore
Judith Djamour

30. Saints and Fireworks
Religion and Politics in Rural Malta
Jeremy Boissevain

29. Malay Peasant Society in Jelebu
M. G. Swift

28. Essays on Social Organization and Values
Raymond Firth

27. A New Maori Migration
Rural and Urban Relations in Northern New Zealand
Joan Metge

26. Kinship and Marriage in a New Guinea Village
H. Ian Hogbin

25. Conflict and Solidarity in a Guianese Plantation
Chandra Jayawardena

24. Legal Institutions in Manchu China
A Sociological Analysis
Sybille van der Sprenkel

23. Marsh Dwellers of the Euphrates Delta
S. M. Salim

22. Rethinking Anthropology
E. R. Leach

21. Malay Kinship and Marriage in Singapore
Judith Djamour

20. Social Status and Power in Java
L. H. Palmier

19. Political Leadership among Swat Pathans
Fredrik Barth

18. Lineage Organization in South-Eastern China
Maurice Freedman

17. Indigenous Political Systems of Western Malaya
J. M. Gullick

16. Studies in Applied Anthropology
Lucy Mair
Replaced by Volume No. 38

15. Two Studies of Kinship in London
Raymond Firth

14. Chinese Spirit-Medium Cults in Singapore
Alan J. A. Elliott

13. Changing Lapps
Gutorm Gjessing

12. The Chinese of Sarawak
A Study of Social Structure
Ju-K'ang Tien

11. The Ethnic Composition of Tswana Tribes
Isaac Schapera

10. Akokoaso
A Survey of a Gold Coast Village
W. H. Beckett

9. Tribal Legislation among the Tswana of the Bechuanaland Protectorate
Isaac Schapera
Replaced by Volume No.43

8. A Demographic Study of an Egyptian Province (Sharquiya)
A. M. Ammar

7. Housekeeping among Malay Peasants
Rosemary Firth

6. Land Tenure of an Ibo Village in South-Eastern Nigeria
M. M. Green

5. Marriage and the Family among the Yakö in South-Eastern Nigeria
Darryl Forde

4. The Political System of the Anuak of the Anglo-Egyptian Sudan
E. E. Evans-Pritchard

3. Social and Economic Organization of the Rowanduz Kurds
Edmund Leach

1 & 2. The Work of the Gods in Tikopia
Raymond Firth

For Product Safety Concerns and Information please contact our EU representative GPSR@taylorandfrancis.com
Taylor & Francis Verlag GmbH, Kaufingerstraße 24, 80331 München, Germany

www.ingramcontent.com/pod-product-compliance
Lightning Source LLC
LaVergne TN
LVHW020626300926
849161LV00004B/625